T0323281

Selling Hope, Selling Risk

Selling Hope, Selling Risk

Corporations, Wall Street, and the Dilemmas of Investor Protection

Donald C. Langevoort

OXFORD
UNIVERSITY PRESS

OXFORD
UNIVERSITY PRESS

Oxford University Press is a department of the University of Oxford. It furthers
the University's objective of excellence in research, scholarship, and education
by publishing worldwide. Oxford is a registered trade mark of Oxford University
Press in the UK and certain other countries.

Published in the United States of America by Oxford University Press
198 Madison Avenue, New York, NY 10016, United States of America.

© Oxford University Press 2016

Cataloging-in-Publication data is on file at the Library of Congress
ISBN 978-0-19-022566-7

3 5 7 9 8 6 4 2
Printed by Sheridan, USA

For Joni

Contents

Acknowledgments

No one can write a book like this without drawing from the work of others, both consciously and implicitly. Thus no set of endnotes or bibliography is ever adequate, either to give credit for what has become part of the scholarly discourse or for treatments of ideas that are deeper and go beyond what a short book like this can discuss. While trying to keep notes to a minimum, I have made a special effort to cite recent work, hoping that interested readers can find in these sources current and more detailed citation trails and pointers to related books and articles.

I have spent my professional lifetime largely thinking about the challenges of securities regulation, my interest in the subject first lit in law school by Louis Loss, who became a mentor. A few years later I spent time at the Securities and Exchange Commission, where I worked with an extraordinarily talented group of people from whom I learned much that inspired my scholarly career: Bob Pozen, Ralph Ferrara, Alan Rosenblat, Paul Gonson, Jake Stillman, Elisse Walter, Linda Feinberg, Dan Goelzer, John Huber, Steve Lamb, Marty Lybecker, and Eric Roiter, in particular. One of the commissioners then, Irv Pollack, became one of my heroes, and still is. That was long ago, but they all deserve a belated thank you. Once I moved to academia, the number of colleagues who helped and influenced my work grew steadily; Joel Seligman, Jim Cox, and Jack Coffee deserve special thanks, from the beginning to today. The names of many others to whom I owe intellectual debts are scattered throughout the bibliography, though I realize that is inadequate credit for their inspiration and insight. I hope I've at least paid it forward.

My gratitude also to those who agreed to review chapters and offer comments, either anonymously or at my request. As to the latter: Bob Thompson, Hillary Sale, Claire Hill, Joan Heminway, and Usha Rodrigues. Bob also gets credit as my coauthor on a recent series of law review articles about contemporary securities regulation, ideas from which have made their way into the book. Four of my research assistants at Georgetown—Josh Lewis, Anna Sandor, Meredith Wood, and Josh Coombes—worked on the book and were terrifically helpful, too. And my wife, Joni, was a big help with the bibliography.

Introduction

In the United States, and increasingly throughout the developed world, a strikingly large portion of the population invests. Most adult Americans are actively exposed to the risks and rewards of the financial markets through direct investments in stocks and bonds, or indirect holdings in mutual funds and pension plans. Many are passive investors, while others speculate aggressively, trading in newly issued stock, options, commodities, alternative investments, and the like. The financial media offers real-time coverage of the markets, and the Internet creates seductive access to real-time trading opportunities.

This so-called democratization of finance has powerful social consequences. Investors face choices that are both tantalizing and anxiety-inducing, and a massive, powerful industry—colloquially known as Wall Street—has grown to satisfy the demand. Some of their decisions will be bad ones, for reasons ranging from simple bad luck to pump-and-dump sales practices of the "Wolf of Wall Street" variety. Investing is a smart thing to do, necessary for long-term financial security. But it comes with risk, which is internalized in many different ways throughout society. Research shows that the incidence of hospital admissions, especially for stress-related conditions, increases on days the stock market falls.[1] The rate of crime by *non*investors apparently rises when the stock market goes up, presumably out of resentment or envy.[2]

That simmering risk sets in motion a complicated political dynamic. Losing wealth, or even just the fear of losing, leads to angst, anger, and blame. When widespread enough among the population, this generates a strong political demand for both protection and corrective justice. Ever since the financial misery occasioned by the onset of the Great Depression there has been a federal regulatory agency tasked with delivering both, the US Securities and Exchange Commission (SEC). But the extraordinary money made by both Wall Street and businesses that issue securities creates a powerful resistance to regulation that can severely and cleverly undermine it. The story of how Wall Street turned subprime mortgage lending into a global money machine by deflecting threats of regulatory intrusion is now familiar enough, and the world is still suffering the consequences of the meltdown that followed.

That leaves those who invest in a quandary. Are we protected, or is the system rigged? Shortly after Bernard Madoff's Ponzi scheme was exposed—and while we were still in the painful stages of the global financial crisis—famous author Michael Lewis and big-time hedge fund manager David Einhorn wrote an op-ed piece in the

New York Times saying that those in the know realize that the SEC is corrupted by the desire to "keep sweet the Wall Street elite," so that the its message to the public of investor protection is itself a deceit.

This book explores the complicated world of investor protection—what investors get from the regulatory system, what they don't, and why. The efficacy of our system of securities regulation is compromised. To attribute this just to special-interest politics, however, misses deeper storylines. Listen to the many voices of those who influence regulatory outcomes—big investors, lobbyists, politicians, journalists, business people, regulators—and one hears different, discordant ways of talking about investor protection. These discourses are not easily sorted into the legitimate and illegitimate. Consider this, for example: investors collectively lost many billions of dollars investing in high-tech stocks in the 1990s before the big popping of the bubble that happened in 2000–2001. At least some of this can probably be attributed to Wall Street's overhyping. There was a visibly harsh political reaction, led by New York's then attorney general, Eliot Spitzer, with the SEC following close behind. We can persuasively tell a breakdown-of-investor-protection story here. But more than one person has observed that those same overenthusiastic investments in the 1990s funded the creative energy—and creative destruction—that produced the Internet as we now know it. Even if we can attribute the bubble mainly to Wall Street–fueled opportunism, it's possible that the social good offset the investor harm suffered.

That same "greater good" argument is with us currently. In 2012, Congress—with backing from the Obama administration—passed the JOBS Act (a heavy-handed acronym for Jumpstart Our Business Startups). The JOBS Act removes regulatory requirements that were part of the investor protection apparatus built by Congress and the SEC. For example, there can now be much more aggressive marketing of so-called private placements, largely unregulated offerings made to people wealthy enough to be deemed able to "fend for themselves." But who is it, precisely, who doesn't need regulatory protection? That is not, as we shall see, an easy question to answer, but the law does so quite bluntly: have a large enough net worth and you're on your own. That "millionaire" may well include your mother or grandmother, the money (rolled over from a life insurance policy or retirement plan, perhaps) the main source of income for the rest of her life. We are also at the dawn of an entirely new deregulated form of capital-raising, "crowdfunding." The JOBS Act says that putting more risk on these investors is worth it to enable small-business entrepreneurship and job creation.

Nor is the business community the only contrarian voice. Those inclined toward "Occupy Wall Street" hate the culture of risk-taking and the inequality of wealth generated by the financial services industry. But they are not entirely sympathetic to an overprivileged investor class, either. The ideological and political strings tug in many different directions. Often enough, we find nagging doubts about our economic future when we pull on these strings, making us wonder whether we're just guessing about regulatory policy with industrial-era assumptions that no longer work.

Investing is a choice; people can do many different things with their money. If people choose not to invest (or invest less), the capital markets—and the financial community—suffer. Given the inevitability and repeated salient examples of opportunism, the level of investment should vary based on how confident investors feel that they will not be exploited when parting with their hard-earned money. The standard economic justification for investor protection regulation is that some public commitment to fight marketplace abuses is necessary to offset fear of exploitation and instill investor confidence. Regulation at this base-line level can be cost-efficient and justifiable even to the most ardent free-marketeer, promoting the conservative trilogy (now baked into the law) of "efficiency, competition and capital formation." But where that sweet spot is, no one knows. Economists, by and large, think we have too much—or at least too much of the wrong kind—of securities regulation.

As you read on, I want you to put yourself in the role of a securities regulator, perhaps the SEC chair. Here is the mental image with which to begin: There are more than a hundred million investor households in the United States, all making difficult financial choices. There are tens of thousands of businesses and entrepreneurs seeking capital from investors. There are competing stock exchanges and electronic trading platforms facilitating the secondary trading of hundreds of millions of shares every day, and thousands of large institutional investors like mutual funds, hedge funds, pension funds that now dominate these financial markets, with massive conflicts of interest. Legions of brokers and investment advisers engage in a never-ending effort to get deeply into their clients' wallets. Much of this takes place globally, often outside the reach of any one domestic regulator. Imagine that you were asked to make this wide-open territory "safe" for investors, many of whom seem habitually disinclined toward prudence, and also to promote robust capital formation. How would you do it? How much in the way of resources would you insist on as a condition for taking the job and doing it well? How would you know whether you are succeeding or failing, or being used? What does investor protection even mean?

This book is my effort to respond to that question, an academic's contribution on the assumption that a wise regulator needs to bring more to the task than just a Machiavellian savvy for the political lay of the land. In the last couple of decades, there has been a burst of research that has advanced our understanding of how our capital markets work. Much of this is quite orthodox, in the traditions of rational choice, efficient markets, and a public choice theory of regulation that assumes that the strongest lobbyists usually win. But a particularly striking scholarly turn has been behavioral. Psychologists, sociologists, neuroscientists, political scientists, and new-age economists are turning out theories and empirical observations (in the laboratory and in field studies) that enrich but complicate otherwise simple-seeming predictions about how people perceive, think, and act in economic settings.

Some of this new learning is about whether, how, and when investors behave in ways driven more by emotion—hope and fear, in particular—than careful calculation. A written disclosure document means little to a motivated buyer. Skilled salespeople are adept at pushing buttons that suppress careful deliberation. The financial media and the Internet make beliefs particularly contagious. Bernie Madoff's Ponzi scheme defies comprehension in a world of rational choice. But are these traits cause for more intrusive regulation, or should those who display such weakness of mind be damned to the consequences, with hope that they and others will learn from the painful experience? Here again we encounter conflicting ideologies as to who is to blame and what, if anything, can or should be done.

An even more intriguing strand of this research studies the behavior of what I'll call the sell side—those, who in some way or another, seek to influence the behavior of investors in the pursuit of their own self-interest. These include traders, brokers, investment bankers, analysts, even corporate executives. In the orthodox view, these are savvy, sly types who have learned the dark arts of deceit, taking advantage of naive (or maybe even the not so naive) investors when opportunities arise. Most economists still make the simplifying assumption that *everyone* in the financial world is a guileful opportunist.

That paints far too dark a picture. Good behavior exists plentifully in the world of finance, for many different reasons: conscience, social norms about fair play, institutional constraints, and the reputational penalties that come from being caught cheating. Trust is valuable, and worth cultivating. But trust is also vulnerable; there can be immense profit in cheating through clever opportunism.

Many institutional structures exist to deter and constrain those tempted to cheat in the financial markets, including the complex body of laws relating to investor protection (securities regulation). Ideally, those laws should send a message to would-be cheaters of the reasonable likelihood of detection and punishment. But for reasons that will take most of the book to explain, much of what we call wrongdoing in the financial markets comes from a far larger set of people who see themselves—and are seen by others who know them—as normal, decent, responsible, maybe even exemplary human beings. They've gained their status and power precisely because they are viewed as such. The new wave of research, however, suggests that success and the rise to power can be enabled by beliefs, biases, traits, and dispositions that allow people to pursue preferred outcomes (including self-interest) while maintaining a strong reputation and self-image. Many of these biases relate to overconfidence, a term I'll be using loosely to capture a larger cluster of tendencies having to do with optimism, power, control, competitive arousal, and the like. Those are disproportionately male traits, naturally drawing our attention to pervasive gender discrimination and the virtues of diversity.

For those adept at self-deception, the law's command of good behavior is filtered and distorted. Such people are convinced, at the time, that what they are doing is right, or they don't see an issue at all. There is no perception of significant risk, much less guilt, at least until they are in deep muck. And precisely because of the links to the positive (focus, intensity, need for achievement), too heavy an effort to deter has adverse consequences even if it could break through the thick self-protective coating in executive minds and corporate cultures. Our society applauds success and risk-taking in the financial markets, even when selling and swindling start to blur. As a result, public-regarding norms of good behavior get diluted very quickly.

That's the regulatory frustration, and the challenge. It takes a clear, confident voice—making real threats—to break through the protective filters. But the regulatory voice today is neither clear nor confident. This is partly pure politics, in an ever more efficient political marketplace. But it is also due to our inability to agree about the tensions between capital formation and paternalism, or what investor confidence means when confidence is socially constructed. And in a world of immense private economic power—and Wall Street and corporate America surely have that—regulation becomes an outlet for demanding at least minimal adherence to values that legitimize (or at least appear to legitimize) that raw muscle. Some academics call this "social license," others the demands of "publicness."[3] Conservative critics of regulation hate such talk, but those who ignore such public expectations—whether politicians, regulators, or business people—do so at their peril. In between these two opposing forces, the SEC has become disoriented; investor protection as we thought we knew it gets crunched.

It would take many lengthy, dense books to explore all of securities regulation in light of this contemporary, somewhat postmodern take on economic and political behavior. This is only one relatively short book. I will thus be selective in choosing what to cover, picking topics that illustrate the clash of politics, economics, and human nature in an engaging way, and avoid technical legal detail. Our focus will be on fraud and disclosure, the core of investor protection, not the technical detail of market structure, financial stability, and the like. As global a capital marketplace as we have, we'll focus mainly on American investor protection, because this country has a unique economic history and political ecology. There are many lessons here for international securities regulation, but I will have to leave the explicit comparative and international law explorations to others.[4] The book is meant for a general audience, though I hope both legal academics and social scientists will find it provocative even if they already know some or much of the background detail.

Chapter 1 is introductory, exploring the "who, what, and why" of investor protection. It introduces the extraordinary range of contemporary interdisciplinary thinking about economic behavior that might help us understand the clash between investor protection and capital formation, and the resulting regulatory dynamics. Chapter 2 is about corporate fraud, exploring its motivation in particular, and how it is supposedly deterred by both public enforcement and private lawsuits. Chapter 3 explores insider trading, the edge conferred by privileged access to information. Chapter 4 takes on the disclosure system that has evolved to inform investors, prevent fraud, and perform an ever-increasing list of societal tasks, and the so-called gatekeepers enlisted to support the system. Chapter 5 turns to Internet fraud, Ponzi schemes, initial public offerings, private placements, the new world of crowdfunding, and investing in mutual funds—various settings where some sort of salesmanship is particularly potent. Chapter 6 uses the global financial crisis as an object lesson, a behavioral look at the securities industry in particular. The conclusion turns all this insight back on the process of regulation itself (particularly the SEC as lawmaker), a sober look at investor protection when long-held assumptions become matters of deep doubt.

To me, the frustrations of regulation evoke an image from rural contests from earlier days where pigs would be coated with a thick layer of grease and locals would try to catch them, looking foolish in front of large crowds as the slippery beasts escaped time and time again. This image strikes me as particularly apt for Wall Street and the task of investor protection. Regulation has a persistent greased pig problem, in that the impulses that drive aggressive financial behavior are very hard to get hold of, and you can look very bad trying to do so. As to who the pigs are, the reader gets to decide.

1

Myths and Skepticism

For most of the last century, securities regulation led a charmed life. The dramatic creation of the federal securities laws—and of the Securities and Exchange Commission (SEC)—in the early 1930s was the work of some of the famous legal masters of the New Deal: Felix Frankfurter, James Landis, Benjamin Cohen, all working under the magnetic influence of Louis Brandeis. The regulatory scope soon expanded beyond its initial focus on corporate financing and stock exchange trading to the substantive regulation of public utilities, broker-dealers, and investment pools. These were great political battles. That so much was achieved against the powerful "moneyed interests" on Wall Street was because of sustained pain and resentment in the aftermath of the stock market crash of 1929 and the onset of the Great Depression, and strong political will from Franklin Roosevelt's White House.

This New Deal history has been thoroughly explored by others,[1] and my book offers nothing to add to the historical record. Looking back, we realize today that some of the public resentment was fueled by entrepreneurial politicians eager to seize a political advantage—the famous Pecora legislative hearings in particular, which exposed abuses on Wall Street in ways that were not always fair or accurate. The Roosevelt administration compromised repeatedly as the decade wore on (to the disappointment of its most fervent believers in bringing those moneyed interests to submission) in the face of sustained industry lobbying. Nonetheless, a creation myth was in place that later on made US-style securities regulation into an inspirational legal story about the triumph of the public interest against establishment greed and arrogance.

After a period of relative quiescence brought on by World War II and its aftermath, the American financial markets flourished. Securities ownership spread among individuals and households to a level unmatched throughout the world, creating a "retail" investment culture that grew steadily even in the face of occasional recessions, setbacks, and scandals. By the mid-1960s, there was a vibrant triumphalism to the regulatory enterprise—drawing liberally on the creation myth, lawyers, judges, and legal academics agreed among themselves that securities regulation deserved a substantial portion of the credit for that financial marketplace success. Regulation had supposedly rescued Wall Street from its demise and brought it legitimacy. American securities regulation thus became a model for the world of finance to admire and emulate to the extent that other countries wanted deep and liquid capital markets, too.

That was quite an expectation to live up to. Again, the economic reality was always more complicated, but such was the tone in both public discourse and the legal scholarship of the time. Veterans of the New Deal were still powerful in Washington, and the SEC had key political supporters in Congress committed to the regulatory mission. The judiciary seemed convinced as well; this was a period of not only strong respect for the SEC, but of self-generated liberalism in the courts, which read the laws and regulations expansively, not restrictively.

Today, that all seems distant. To be sure, there is still a legacy—the SEC trumpets this history in its aspiration to be "the investors' champion," and some still draw on the creation myth. But in both public and academic discourse, securities regulation is a much more tarnished enterprise, especially in the aftermath of the recent global financial crisis and a series of embarrassing scandals that it was seemingly unable to prevent.

That tarnish comes with dramatically different explanations. From the left comes a story of regulatory capture. Through a variety of subtle and not-so-subtle ways, Wall Street and the business community have enough sway over the SEC so that crucial portions of regulation are muted and insincere. On the right, there is the now-conventional story of bureaucratic overreach and slack, the consequence of habitually intrusive government regulation. We have much more securities regulation than we need for a robust capital market, and the mission of investor protection is too often just code for habits of paternalism that sap entrepreneurship, innovation, and job creation. Critics point to a persistent loss of capital market activity to other locations with more efficient (i.e., less) regulation, the United Kingdom and Hong Kong in particular, but with China, India, Brazil, and others also poised to out-compete an increasingly hobbled Wall Street.

This is the political battlefield, interesting enough in itself. The clash of discourse is also the starting point for any serious exploration of the state of contemporary securities regulation. Objectively, how would we know whether we have too much, too little, the wrong kind, or—implausibly, perhaps—exactly the right kind of regulation, and why? These are crucial questions to scholars, but should be to general readers as well. After all, if securities regulation is about inspiring investor confidence, investors (indeed all members of the public) should think more carefully about whether confidence is warranted, and what more (or less) should be done.

Until the mid-1960s, there was little serious academic interest in the "whether and why" questions. The value of securities regulation was largely taken for granted, as was the SEC's expertise in crafting the law. But about that time a critical academic voice emerged, skeptical of the orthodoxy, using the tools of financial economics to cast doubt on even the most fundamental tenets of the creation myth. Economic journals published studies suggesting that the adoption of the Securities Act of 1933 may have hurt capital-raising more than helped, while dampening competition.[2] A law professor, Henry Manne, took on the role of legal gadfly and challenged many of the cherished beliefs and institutions (like the prohibition against insider trading) that were seen as fundamental investor protection mechanisms. Key to this critical view was faith in markets' ability to police for abuse without heavy-handed legal intervention. Experience shows that private ordering works, if far from perfectly, via reputational checks and balances, and intermediaries who understand the importance of (and make money from) clearing away abuse so as to minimize the costs associated with investor mistrust.

Subsequent chapters will follow all this in more detail; suffice it for now to say that criticism of securities regulation grounded in the tools of financial economics is standard today among both finance and legal scholars. The skepticism also delivers a political message, drawn from public choice theory: the regulation we see is often not meant to serve the public interest, but rather is molded to the preferences of organized and well-financed interest groups. While one might think such powerful groups would simply oppose (and thus defeat) any kind of burdensome regulation, public choice theory notes that it may be smarter for powerful firms to submit regulatory burdens so long as they harm their competitors and potential entrants even more. All the more so when those burdens appease an angry public who might otherwise demand more from its politicians.

In sum, critics came to doubt the intrinsic quality of the messages being sent in the name of investor protection. Their academic lens was neoclassical economic theory, which makes certain assumptions in order to gain traction—most notably, that economic actors are rational, selfish "utility maximizers." There is a long intellectual history behind this assumption, and much controversy, but it enabled economics to build and test a wide range of behavioral predictions. In the area of investment and finance, the plausibility of this assumption is enhanced because of the considerable money to be made, the repeat-play nature of the interactions (which facilitates learning from experience), opportunities to exploit the mistakes of others, and the relative transparency of the settings in which securities are bought and sold. All this *seems* so compelling that it's tempting to take the rational actor model for granted in how we approach securities regulation.

What follows, however, is the case for a more capacious view of human nature. This is not because rationality and opportunism aren't potent features in economic activity—they surely are, and any serious inquiry in securities regulation should begin with those assumptions. But there are many places where those assumptions are unrealistic. In the past two decades, behavioral research has exploded in volume and visibility, offering a rich set of possible additions and alternatives to the conventional orthodoxy.

The richness and diversity of this new research pose problems, too, because so much of it is tentative or mightily contested. One can easily pick and choose among the findings to support preferred conclusions, ignoring that the evidence is often mixed and the methodologies subject to severe limitations. Careful social scientists rightly warn lawyers and regulators against taking their rigorously controlled empirical findings as anything more than slow progress toward a distant goal of understanding the human condition.

From an academic standpoint, that's fair enough. Researchers surely don't have human behavior figured out. But we have a body of securities law that is currently under stress, and we cannot wait for conclusive scientific understanding of the workings of the investment marketplace in formulating the law. Congress and the SEC are making controversial judgments today, in the face of woefully incomplete knowledge. Academics have to respond, using the best inferences available, even though the risks of doing so are obvious. That comes most often in the form of a "what if?" Initiatives that are based on no plausible theory of behavior can be tagged as such; those that have a plausible theory can be evaluated by asking what if a different theory turns out to be a better explanation. Securities regulation has not asked enough "what if" questions about its preferred legal strategies, instead settling much too easily on convenient or habitual assumptions. In what follows, we'll draw from many different research studies in the social sciences without meaning to suggest that they are conclusive, uncontested, or clear in their legal implications. They are offered to expand the conversation about the effort it takes for successful investor protection, and the considerable costs and frustrations of so doing. The payoff for the reader is twofold: understanding the nature and limits of investor protection better, and understanding investing better, including our own imperfect (and thus exploitable) choices. The rest of this chapter offers a set of conceptual building-blocks for this journey, getting ready for the legal issues that follow.

THE HUMAN DIMENSION OF INVESTING

The famous physicist Richard Feynman is often quoted as asking us to imagine how much harder physics would be if neutrons had feelings.[3] In many ways—intriguingly so—neoclassical economics treats financial activity as a form of physics, a highly mathematical field of inquiry entirely without feelings.

By contrast, the move to develop a more robust, realistic theory of human behavior in economic settings is referred to as behavioral economics (and as applied to legal problems, behavioral law and economics). Human beings have limited cognitive capacity, and live in a world filled with information. We can't give due attention to everything, and so the brain—via the process of evolution—has learned automatic short-cuts to optimize performance. These work well enough most of the time, but will sometimes lead to errors. Ideally, our brains should toggle back and forth between heuristics and more careful deliberation as circumstances dictate, but this dual-process sorting is not always reliable in a noisy, fast-paced environment.[4] This is the cognitive heuristics perspective, often identified with the pioneering work of Daniel Kahneman and Amos Tversky, which has prompted a massive amount of follow-up research. Here is just a sampling of some key findings about investor behavior (we'll elaborate as needed later on).[5]

Attention. The Kahneman-Tversky research program stressed the limits of human attention. As Kahneman puts it, automatic mental processing tends toward "what you see is all there is."[6] Particularly salient information is overweighted, and salient coincidences perceived as trends without sufficient attention to the possibility of randomness. People anchor on early evidence to which their attention is directed, and then fail to adjust appropriately in light of disconfirming evidence, sticking too much to first impressions. On the other hand—and this research is filled with heuristics that seem at odds with one another—people sometimes overweight the most recent evidence that comes to mind. Thus, investors chase trends, which can lead to momentum in stock prices, followed by a reversal. News that grabs attention crowds out other information, leading to overreaction to some news, underreaction to other. Slow, gradual change is perceived poorly, meaning that investors often persist in a course of behavior (holding a stock, for example) longer than is warranted. There is a strong bias toward the status quo—the more choices an investor has, and fearing regret, the more likely he or she will do nothing.

Framing. Put simply, losses loom larger in our thinking than gains. Via "mental accounting" we often segment our endowments and reference points into artificial categories. Together, these two tendencies mean that we will be more cautious and risk averse when thinking about a chance of gaining something we don't have, but more risk-preferring in order to avoid a loss. Of course, the framing can be artificial, or induced. (A famous Kahneman-Tversky experiment found a difference in risk attitudes depending on whether a medical intervention was described as saving lives or avoiding deaths.)[7] Loss aversion may have something to do with why investors are more likely to sell stocks that have risen in value and hold on to those that have lost money (the "disposition effect"), though this effect seems to reverse itself if the investor can blame someone else for bad choices.[8] Closely related is the endowment effect, which finds—curiously—that the price that someone would be willing to pay to buy an asset is lower than what the same person would be willing to sell it for.

Hyperbolic discounting. There is a tendency toward impatience, valuing the immediate over the future in ways unexplained by either risk aversion or the time value of money. Hence, mutual funds might waive a fee up front, which an investor might grab even though later fees mean a much higher cost in the long run.

Emotions. As this research evolved, there was an important turn toward a recognition of how important the emotions are in judgment and decision-making—self-esteem, anxiety, desire, disgust, and the like. These "hot" influences brought the heuristics and biases perspective closer to earlier lines of research in cognitive and social psychology. Attitudes toward financial risk seem particularly driven by emotion. Once emotions produce a particular investment preference, subsequent information is evaluated to maintain the emotion, even if illusory.[9] Anger seems to lead to greater risk-taking; anxiety to more paralysis; and sadness to impatient financial decisions.[10] Today, much of this research focuses on neuroscience and genetics, with observations that what leads people to invest in equities, find active investment management desirable, and open lines of credit all have a strong biological component.

Overconfidence. In many circumstances, people (especially younger men) overestimate the accuracy of their knowledge and their ability to control external forces via skill. While this may simply be a cognitive bias, it also connects to an older line of research in psychology wherein people form inflated self-perceptions—egotistical inference—as a means of managing anxiety and maintaining self-esteem. Overconfidence is often invoked to explain why retail investors trade as frequently as they do even though (because of trading costs) they lose money on average.[11] It can also lead to underdiversification and other poor allocation strategies.

Motivated inference. People have a tendency to see what they want to see, as well as what they expect to see. Hope and fear can influence judgments so that what seems right is highly conditional, not necessarily shared by more objective observers. This line, too, connects back to classic work in psychology on cognitive dissonance and the self-serving attribution bias, the manipulability of our cherished beliefs in order to preserve self-esteem and mute anxiety.

Social contagion. A particularly important set of findings—connecting to the fields of social psychology and sociology—emphasizes how susceptible economic actors are to social influence.[12] Investment ideas are contagious, for example, spreading more quickly locally or though network connections rather than randomly. For example, mutual fund managers in the same city have more similar portfolios compared to those elsewhere, even controlling for home bias investments.[13] Some contagion seems entirely sensible in a world of uncertainty ("rational herding"), while it can also be infected by bias. If conversations tend to emphasize the speakers' successes but suppress failures, for instance, word of mouth can be misleading ("persuasion bias"). A particularly interesting study of the contagion of wishful thinking in financial markets connects these social forces back to motivated inference.[14]

There is laboratory and field evidence that all of the above are important phenomena, affecting *some* investors *some* of the time. But for all the advances over the last decades, no general theory of human behavior has emerged with the simplicity and elegance of the rational actor. The behavioral cacophony plays into the hands of orthodox economists, most of who readily concede that there are many human beings who are far from rational utility-maximizers. In competitive marketplace settings, however, survivors should be those who have good sense; those who are not endowed with that fitness become economic trivia—shark bait. Such Darwinism seems a bit distasteful, to be sure, but there is an important point here that has to be taken seriously. We can't just assume foolishness to justify regulatory intervention.

Another contemporary research perspective also deserves our attention, even if it has the aim of further destabilizing what we think we know about securities markets and regulation. Sociologists and cultural anthropologists have long opposed the methodological individualism that is explicit in both economics and cognitive psychology, saying that we have to look to social forces to best understand human behavior.[15] Individuals are highly constrained by norms and cultural beliefs that limit both awareness and opportunity, including in economic settings.[16] Money and investing are social constructs, and economic behavior is best explored through the lens of social interactions and institutions: mimetics, network theory, and the like. Sociology stresses uncertainty and ambiguity, how little human beings—even the most accomplished CEOs—are capable of actually knowing, and the socially constructed beliefs that fill that epistemological void. Efficiency can be performative—cultural accounts emerge as to what is efficient, which become a self-fulfilling prophecy via social conformity to the expectation.

Classical economists' heads practically explode at this idea. They are often harsh critics of sociological methods, probably right in asking how we can observe so much apparently rational behavior in the world if everything we know deconstructs into culture, myth, ceremony, and politics. As with all siege-like intellectual battles, however, there is much disciplinary intermarrying going on. Many economic sociologists and anthropologists take the criticism seriously and soften the antifunctionalist assumptions as they delve into deep, sustained observations of people and institutions involved in complex economic activity. Ezra Zuckerman of MIT, for example, has developed an intriguing account of market efficiency where stock prices are socially constructed yet somewhat constrained by indicators of fundamental value.

The critical perspective makes a crucial point that we should keep in mind. What we believe about finance is in excess of what we are capable of knowing, and it is easy for lawyers and regulators (and academics who crave a seat at the table) to limit their imagination to agreed-upon categories and familiar sets of questions. Any inquiry into a subject like securities regulation risks that to the extent that it draws from existing categories, labels, and first principles. The human element in the world of investing and finance necessarily means we are always taking too much for granted.

INVESTOR DIVERSITY

Investor protection struggles with the many different kinds of investors in the marketplace. Through the first part of the last century, individual investors dominated. These included many ordinary folk, generally referred to as retail investors. The disclosure philosophy of securities regulation developed out of concern that small investors needed substantial help.

One of the great disruptions of the last century was a marked increase in the percentage of investment activity that is institutional, that is, professionally managed. Today, institutions predominate in the ownership of shares of publicly traded companies (70%–80% if not more), and in most debt markets. That is partly because of the complexity and challenge of investing—ordinary people reluctant to invest on their own for fear of being shark bait. It is also about the ways we encourage retirement savings, which strongly favor institutional accounts. Although traditional pension funds still exist (and they are exceedingly important as investors, especially in the public sector), the typical investor's tax-advantaged retirement savings are in a 401(k) plan or IRA that involves a menu of choices among managed mutual fund portfolios. The US mutual fund industry alone manages more than $15 trillion in investor money.

As a result of institutionalization, we have a more richly populated continuum of investors to whom securities regulation attends. There are still plenty of ordinary investors who invest directly in individual stocks and bonds, some of whom are quite naive and unsophisticated. Other retail investors are more experienced and knowledgeable, though this does not necessarily translate into good decision-making (for example, day traders—a fairly well-studied underperforming class of investors).

As to professionally managed investment, we see diversity as well. Some institutions have captive beneficiaries with no choice as to where their money goes, for example funds managing retirement money for public employees like teachers and firefighters. (These were noteworthy victims of the sale of complicated securitized instruments and derivatives in the lead-up to the financial crisis, as we'll see in chapter 6.) Toward the other end are the supersophisticated, particularly hedge funds and other private investments for the wealthy, with immense pressure to deliver supranormal returns. There is a wide variety of strategies for trying to generate such performance, including activist investing (taking positions in companies and then trying to alter their strategies using shareholder rights tactics to produce a higher stock price) and old-fashioned fundamental research that sometimes edges into the sleazy world of insider trading.

The conundrum this creates for securities regulation is apparent. There are so many different kinds of investors, with such different interests and needs, that any given strategy will have diffuse effects at best. Disclosure aimed at the average investor, for instance, may be costly and wasteful from the perspective of the portfolio manager. Where institutions dominate and individuals can free ride on the prices they set, less regulation would seem necessary. Indeed, many people think that had institutionalization dominated in the 1930s the way it does today, the securities statutes of that period would have been far less intrusive, making their contemporary legacy one of overreach with respect to trading in the stock of public companies.[17]

There is a major complication here, however. Institutions are investors, to be sure, and dominate the public markets. But they seek their money from other investors, who may include other institutions but often devolve to a highly individual or household-oriented investor base. As a result, especially among mutual funds and hedge funds, securities regulation has two contrasting points of involvement. These portfolios are investors, and may (or may not) need investor protection. They are also issuers of securities, and so *their* investors may need protection. Take the actively managed mutual fund. The fund may be faithfully seeking out the best investment opportunities for its shareholders, in which case it needs some— but not all that much—regulatory help. But research suggests a wide variety of behaviors by mutual fund managers, such as herding (mimicking what others are doing), trend-chasing (following market momentum in what is bought or sold), and window-dressing (trading at the end of a reporting period just to improve the appearance of what has to be reported to its investors). Investors may be wasting billions of dollars every year simply in bad choices about who should manage their money.

We will dig much more deeply into this, but the puzzle is getting harder. What is the right regulatory stance to take with respect to institutional investors who derive considerable (and not always well earned) profit from their relationship with their own retail investors? Will the effect be simply to drive money toward other financial products and relationships (like those offered by banks and insurance companies) that may be *worse* for the retail investor? If active management declines in favor of more mindless index investing, what will be the effects on market efficiency? Are retail investors actually deriving value in the form of peace of mind or some visceral entertainment from such managed accounts that makes them not so clearly the deadweight social loss that academics so stridently claim? Given the political power of the money management industry, it takes an abundance of courage—and good answers to each of these questions—to even start this fight.

WHY REGULATE?

To some, the question of why regulate may seem so obvious that it is largely rhetorical; to others, it is born of the deep, skeptical belief that we often (usually?) regulate without solid reason for doing so. That difference is reflected in two ways of answering—are we talking about why we should regulate (a normative question), or why we actually do so (a descriptive question)?

The Imaginary World of No Regulation

Imagine a world with no securities regulation at all. What would that do to our economy? That is a fair question because in the United States there was no body of federal securities regulation until 1933, and the piecemeal state securities regulation that preceded started spreading under the name of "blue sky law" only a couple of decades earlier. Yet a culture of investing emerged anyway. We must be cautious here because much of securities regulation is an effort to deter dishonest practices in capital raising and securities trading, and dishonest practices have long been unlawful under a variety of state and federal laws of more general applicability, like criminal mail and wire fraud statutes and the common law of deceit. There have also been highly specific laws to control speculation dating back to the earliest days of our history—even earlier in Great Britain and elsewhere in Europe—as responses to the social dislocation and anger that follows the bursting of any investment bubble, which has been happening for centuries.[18] But it is certainly possible to think about a financial world with nothing of the regulatory apparatus we have come to assume.

Investing makes no rational sense unless there is some reason to expect future returns (dividends and capital appreciation) that justify the price, and so the act of investing is necessarily one of speculation—what do I know about the enterprise or the financial instrument that allows me to predict a stream of earnings that justifies the risk? That requires information about the company, its business, its past performance, its management, and much else, not easily obtainable by those on the outside. But those inside the business have a conflict of interest to the extent that either they want to raise capital from investors or sell their own holdings. They will be tempted to inflate the business and its prospects beyond their worth.

In theory, honest enterprises will have a hard time raising capital unless investors have a good way of distinguishing them from the "lemons"—that is, opportunistic sellers. If we can't trust what such companies say, we discount what everyone says and put less money at risk, or none at all (what economists call an adverse selection problem). Companies that are truly valuable suffer because they can't get investors to accept a fair price for the securities. The investment marketplace unravels. That is troubling to the honest entrepreneurs, of course, but also to society at large. Because entrepreneurship creates value in the form of innovation, jobs, tax revenues, spending, and the like, we all suffer from that trust deficit.

Even without law, market forces will emerge to help overcome this version of the lemons problem. If a firm or its managers have been around for a while and developed a reputation for trustworthiness, there are grounds—though hardly conclusive—for predicting that it is not a lemon. Firms with good reputations can vouch for others, thus becoming "reputational intermediaries." As we will see later on, initial public offerings are almost entirely underwritten by investment banking firms who are repeat players, going back time and time again to their customers with new deals that they are recommending. If those recommendations are bad, presumably the clients will not stick around for long. Today, the law-and-economics literature is filled with private marketplace "bonding" solutions—contractual or extralegal mechanisms designed to overcome the rational investor's reluctance to invest. Stock exchanges, for example, set listing standards insisting on good corporate behavior as a condition for trading decades before either the federal or state securities laws were adopted. Under the right conditions, cultural forces (social norms) may also deter cheating. Economist Luigi Guiso and colleagues have developed impressive empirical evidence that the level of social trust in a society (something that varies considerably around the world) correlates well with the emergence of robust capital markets.

But these are all imperfect solutions, leaving open opportunities for exploitation. A strict legal prohibition on investment fraud—punishing lemons who lie—is a way of helping overcome this problem, and thus at the heart of all strategies of investor protection. The honest enterprise can describe itself as such so long as credible reasons can be given; the dishonest cannot lawfully mimic it.

Human Behavior and the Lemons Problem

But let's ask how likely it is that investors behave as the lemons theory predicts—the human nature question. In a set of experiments, a team of economists created a setting in which "sellers" of financial assets were free to talk up their products to a group of "buyers" who knew only that quality varied among sellers. Where there was no antifraud prohibition, theory predicted that buyers would pay little or nothing—the salesmanship was just cheap talk. What they found, however, was a surprisingly high level of reliance on the cheap talk—in other words, gullibility. Buyers are frequently taken in by the salesmanship and bid too much. This was so even though in the experiments, subjects switched roles so as to be buyers after being sellers, and vice versa. Remarkably, sellers who were the most dishonest in their sales pitches were *more* gullible when assuming the roles of buyers. The researchers then repeated the same experiment with a penalty for lying (but not for mere "puffery," that is, sales talk considered too loose or general to be fraudulent). This helped considerably, though not enough to match the theory's prediction—there was still too little skepticism of the seller's blandishments. Of course we have to be cautious in drawing inferences about real-world behavior from laboratory experiments—maybe gullibility gets washed away by painful learning from experience. Still, the authors take their results as supporting the case for more vigorous securities regulation than economic theory alone predicts.[19]

The possibility of sustained gullibility takes us to a fork in the road in thinking about the reasons for securities regulation. If all we care about is capital formation, a certain amount of investor gullibility might be a good thing for society. Investors will instinctively offer too much, meaning that the cost of capital goes down. Enterprises thrive, jobs follow—not necessarily a bad transfer of wealth. And this is not entirely facetious, either. Recall the idea that we should be thankful that so many retail investors invested with reckless abandon in dot-com stocks in the mid to late 1990s. Amid all the creative destruction when the bubble formed and then popped, the Internet was born and began maturing, with the United States well in the lead in global technology innovation. To be sure, too much exuberance has the effect of misallocating economic resources from the sound and sensible to the exciting and hot, and there is always the risk that investors will finally sense they are being taken advantage of and become the lemon avoiders that economic theory predicts. But you can see the point: a moderate excess of investor confidence can enhance capital formation. If so, we might want to tolerate some degree of sell-side opportunism, that is, the sort that heightens that desire. The law should take a light touch.

On the other hand—taking us down the other fork in the road—a considerable number of people see investor protection not as a means to the end of capital formation, but as an end in itself. Most of our collective wealth is tied up in the financial system; people are hurt by rent-seeking (i.e., opportunistic) practices in the financial markets that are enabled, not deterred, by marketplace institutions. These advocates want protection from abusive behavior, especially when part of a vulnerable class (of which senior citizens today head the list). In this view, the SEC and the other institutions of securities regulation should be righteous champions of the vulnerable, demanding an ethic of greater care from those who promote trading in securities. To the extent that biases interfere with good choices, regulation should firmly penalize their exploitation.

Publicness

This fault line is hardly unique to securities regulation; it describes the ideological divide between those who prefer governmental policies that lean against the exploitation of private economic power and those who prefer a wide swath of private economic liberty. The divide about protecting people from their own frailties is itself deeply rooted in human psychology. Philip Tetlock has an interesting study showing that excuses based on cognitive biases are less likely to be accepted by corporate managers when those managers have a conservative (authoritarian) political orientation than when they're liberal (fairness-based).[20] In turn, political orientation is itself driven by differing cognitive styles. This makes the politics of securities regulation something more than just the balance between capital formation and investor protection, because a political wins or losses for either side count toward a much larger battle about the role of government. A victory for "investors" against the financial establishment has political currency even among noninvestors who feel threatened by elite economic power. Winning a regulation-free zone has high value for defenders of economic freedom well beyond the specifics of the issue. What this means, unfortunately, is that current issues in securities regulation can become as much about symbolic or expressive politics as about the specifics of *either* capital formation or investor protection. Add that to the self-interested lobbying money influencing these debates and we see how regulatory issues easily become disconnected from the underlying merits, and the business of lawmaking paralyzed.

This is the impulse that we'll call "publicness." It relates to cultural legitimacy, a concept familiar in sociology. A capitalist system confers on corporate managers and owners immense private economic and political power. Their decisions have effects not just on investors but on a variety of constituencies, including the public. In a democracy, such power instinctively requires some level of accountability. Indeed, we see around the world calls for greater public voice, transparency, and accountability in nongovernmental settings where power lies, not just corporations. Failures to respect "social license" can have considerable adverse consequences, and a natural question is whether the public should expect ex ante that private economic decisions be made with attention to these inchoate public values.

In the corporate setting, the main externality issues relate to risk-taking. There can be immense private gains (and social ones, to be sure) from successful risk-taking. Failures are privately painful, but because shareholders and managers are not personally liable for the full social costs of a disaster, more of the burden falls on other stakeholders. Employees lose jobs, retirees' pensions are at risk, suppliers, customers, and local communities suffer, and so on. When the firm is too big to fail, taxpayers foot the bailout bill. There is a palpable tendency to want restraints on the aggressiveness with which private economic power is exercised, because we are all potential victims of excess.

In such settings, the public-private divide blurs. Hillary Sale offers an interesting illustration, involving J.P. Morgan Chase. A trader there (exhibiting a classic form of cognitive bias) took what was initially a risk-reducing position and gradually transformed it into a massive bet—all in the face of what was supposed to be state-of-the-art supervision and compliance. When $6.2 billion in losses by "the London Whale" surfaced, Morgan executives downplayed the incident, essentially saying that it was just an internal business matter of which it was the only victim. But just after the financial crisis and all its bailouts, claiming that the risk-taking and defective controls were just a tempest in a teapot and none of the public's business wasn't wise. The negative press and congressional and regulatory reactions were severe; Morgan ultimately paid more than a billion dollars in penalties to go with its $6.2 billion investment losses. The point is that any institution possessing a large footprint in our economy must accept that in today's world, heightened accountability is a given, and not confined by the preferences of its "owners."

Perhaps the most politically contested question today in securities regulation is how much, if at all, publicness should share with investor protection, efficiency, and capital formation as a discrete regulatory goal. We'll see specific manifestations of this controversy in chapter 5 as we look at the subtle regulatory accretions in terms of transparency (social disclosure), accountability (internal controls and liability risks), and outsider voice (boards of directors independent of those in control) designed to make managers less secure in the exercise of the private benefits of incumbency. Without getting ahead of ourselves here, the problem is a cost-benefit one. Are there real benefits from such interventions, or is this just an emotional expression of frustration, a way of getting even in the aftermath of an excess of risk? There are no solid metrics, and so success is a subjective—and hence political—judgment. And what are the costs of such expressive intervention, in terms of dampening entrepreneurial innovation or just adding to the added out-of-pocket costs of being a public company, costs borne by investors as well as managers? To true believers in private economic freedom, the threat is that any form of intrusion into the corporate boardroom or executive suite, no matter how inefficient, can be grounded in publicness. Hence the conservative move to make investor protection the sole legitimate aim of securities regulation, and to define investor protection entirely in terms of efficiency and capital formation. I have a great deal of ambivalence about the consequences of embracing publicness within the regulatory mission, for reasons we'll explore, but have no doubt of its political force.

The intellectual and political battle over publicness is a reminder that questions relating to why we should regulate do not exhaust the possibilities for why regulation actually occurs. As public choice theory predicts, much securities regulation (like regulation in general) is promoted by economic actors because it will hurt their competitors but not them, or hurt them less. Firms that get lots of revenue from facilitating certain kinds of investments will strongly but quietly try to kill deregulation that improves the set of options for both sellers and buyers and cut off that revenue stream. That is often unhealthy rent-seeking, the economists' word for exploitation of power. And of course some lawmaking is just political theater, to play on public anger or angst, or to bolster a story of blame for some crisis or scandal when the government itself was partly the culprit. We'll soon see examples of all of these.

DISCLOSURE

Securities regulation's instinctive answer to the problem of sales pressure is full disclosure. Tell the investor the truth—the whole truth—about the investment and let him or her decide whether it is worthwhile or not. That was the animating idea behind the first federal investor protection law, the Securities Act of 1933, soon extended more broadly. The drafting of the Securities Act was heavily influenced by Felix Frankfurter, then a Harvard Law professor and soon to become a Supreme Court justice. Looking back at the speculative frenzy of stock-buying in the 1920s, Frankfurter was dismayed at the large portion of household savings (55%, he said) that went into publicly marketed securities, attributing it to "the subtle and mesmerizing arts of modern salesmanship."[21]

But does disclosure work, especially when up against skilled salesmanship? One of the first critics of the Securities Act was another law professor and soon-to-be Supreme Court justice (after a year and a half as chairman of the SEC in the late 1930s), William O. Douglas. Douglas was a proponent of stronger regulation—maybe even the de facto federalization of the world of investment banking as part of the New Deal—and made a point that many have repeated since: investors smart enough to protect themselves ask the right questions and don't need mandated disclosure; those foolish enough to be susceptible to salesmanship won't know what to do with the disclosure, especially if it comes delivered in bulky, turgid legalese.

Whether Douglas's criticism was fair is debatable—we are only at the beginning of our story. But his doubts about the ability of disclosure to improve the investment decisions of the naive investor ring true, which takes us back to human nature. The contemporary social science literature is fairly critical of disclosure as a solution, for good reason—it fails in its intended purpose under many conditions, particularly in the face of adept salesmanship.[22]

One thing is quite clear: financial illiteracy and ignorance is widespread.[23] A study done on investor susceptibility to fraud gave a fairly simple test in order to see whether investors recognize danger signs; asking, for instance, whether a pitch claiming more than a 100% annual return would incline you toward a purchase as opposed to making you want to run the other way, which you should do. Surprising numbers said yes.[24] Comprehension of financial basics like the effects of compound interest is disturbingly low, and, sadly, many investors overestimate their own sophistication. Even when we look at well-educated, fairly affluent populations, serious investment mistakes are common. This is not to give up entirely on disclosure—it is useful to some investors even in face-to-face encounters, and disclosure can have healthy indirect effects in informing others (including the sellers' competitors) who might intervene on the investors' behalf.[25] But the risk with relying too heavily on disclosure is that we may just be inviting the industry to a rent-seeking party.

Disclosure's effects are not limited to providing useful information. Louis Brandeis famously said that the sunlight of disclosure is also a disinfectant, meaning that people behave better simply knowing that they are being watched. But the behavioral consequences of disclosure are actually more mixed. For example, disclosure of conflicts of interest may not help as much as we would expect, and can actually make the situation worse. Those who receive the warnings don't become sufficiently more cautious. More perniciously, those who make the disclosures may feel freer to be selfish because of the warning (a form of self-serving inference). Worse yet, some who receive such disclosure may feel "insinuation anxiety" to signal that they still trust their person with the conflict, and so may become even more willing to follow the advice, not less.[26]

EFFICIENT MARKETS

For quite a while, a common argument against the importance of investor biases is that well-functioning markets can cleanse them. Market efficiency is a measure of the degree to which market prices impound new information relevant to the value of the stock quickly and without bias. Say, for example, that Apple discloses some information about the sales of one of its key products that traders in the market had not anticipated. If the market for Apple stock is highly efficient (and it probably is), the price of Apple stock will fully adjust to that new information quickly, in a manner of hours at most, perhaps minutes or fractions of a second. After that adjustment, there are no profit opportunities anymore from having learned that news apart from simple luck. This idea is the primary reason for why most investors shouldn't spend money trying to beat the market—the wise crowd works so quickly that profit opportunities disappear. It's also a reason why it might not matter if particular investors are emotional or mindless—the prices they trade at are disciplined by the mechanisms of efficiency, and presumptively fair.

From this simple description, you might already be able to detect some soft spots in claims of strong market efficiency. First, how does this adjustment occur? At the risk of oversimplifying a bit, imagine that a company's stock price is holding steady at around $50 when the company releases information about slower-than-expected sales of an important product. Imagine also that you're a smart investor who follows the company, and this news causes you to think that the company's future stream of earnings is less than what you had expected, so that in your opinion the stock is now worth only $47. If you can sell the stock at 50 or anywhere close, you could buy it back at its new value (you assume) at 47 and make a profit. But now imagine that there are 10 (or 10,000) other smart investors doing the same thing as you. If everyone agrees with you and pushes the sell button quickly enough, the stock price will drop immediately and the ability to sell at anywhere near 50 disappears.

But doesn't that prove too much—why would anyone do fundamental value research if there is no money to be made? Good question, which suggests that markets will never be *perfectly* efficient. There has to be enough money to be made to make it worthwhile to do the kind of trading that drives the markets toward efficiency. Keep in mind, moreover, that valuing a security is ultimately an exercise in predicting the future (estimating the company's future earnings, discounted to present value and adjusted for risk). Surely there is the potential for disagreement as to what news means for a company's stock, and some traders will have more skill at this than others.

That is probably right, but identifying skilled investors (i.e., those who can beat the market on a sustained basis) has been remarkably hard to do. There may be a few exceptions: Warren Buffett is a favorite example.[27] We will see the implications of this misperception later in the book, when we turn to how investors behave in the world of mutual funds. The best short answer is this: assuming that you were one of a small number of truly skilled investors, you probably wouldn't make yourself known too widely. You'd attract money on a private and confidential basis, and demand an extraordinary level of compensation for managing that money. And it would be harder and harder to live up to expectations, especially as other smart money notices your success and tries to copy your trading. Welcome to the world of hedge funds. To the extent there are truly skilled investors—as opposed to the very lucky—they are keeping most of the rents for themselves, and probably not sleeping all that well at night. The less skilled (but lucky enough for an attractive track record of past performance) will seek out money with the pretense of being another Buffett or the latest hedge fund equivalent, but rarely deliver as hoped.

So what is the debate about market efficiency? Strong claims of market efficiency emerged in the 1970s based on observations of very quick adjustment of prices to significant news and the difficulty that mutual fund managers and others had in beating the market on any sustained basis. But there was also evidence of less efficiency (or inefficiency, if that is the semantic preference): dramatic anomalies like sudden stock market crashes, as well as more subtle observations.

One major impediment to a high level of market efficiency soon became evident. The key to price adjustment is arbitrage—investors quickly buying or selling in reaction to new news, profiting from differences between market price and perceived value. That works well on the upside. Any trader can buy as much as she wants on good news. But for bad news you are limited (putting aside the options and futures market for a moment) to selling *if* you happen to own the stock or engaging in short selling—selling stock you don't own, by borrowing it for as long as it takes, you hope, for the price to drop. There are both regulatory and practical limits on short selling. In other words, we might not be able to depend on arbitrage as much as we'd want to keep prices from rising. Bad news might therefore travel more slowly than good news.

Research has also bolstered other intuitions about imperfect markets. Obviously, the more heavily traded and widely followed the stock, the higher the speed of adjustment. The more public and unambiguous the news, the quicker the price responds. This was all consistent with a vision of market efficiency the emphasized that acquiring and acting on information is costly, and that these costs vary depending on both the company in question and the accessibility of the information. In a world of very high efficiency, a report in the *New York Times* about a company's prospects should have no price impact if that news was disclosed earlier, even if it was buried in some technical filing. But the evidence is that it does.[28] What the market does or does not pay attention to matters.

Here is where research on human nature comes into play, and the field of behavioral finance.[29] If investors are prone to heuristics, biases, mood swings, and the like, shouldn't market prices naturally reflect such sentiment? Market volatility (for individual stocks, industries, and as a whole) seems to suggest something more than cold, hard information processing. Beginning in the early 1980s and picking up steam ever since, researchers have examined market prices for evidence of departures from rationality that indicate mass psychology at work. There are now hundreds of examples offered as such—one of the most famous, drawn from the tech stock boom of the late 1990s, was that a company's stock price could be expected to rise simply because the company added ".com" to its name, without any other change in the business.[30] Another highly publicized result is that sunshine—good weather—positively affects stock prices.[31] There are now many books available on the financial economics of market psychology—the best known, perhaps, by Robert Shiller, alone and together with George Akerlof, both winners of the Nobel Prize. They remind of us Keynes's insight that stock markets are human institutions where money is made by predicting how others will behave, not necessarily in discovering the truth. Economic sociologists have put forward a related argument in which much of what we observe as market efficiency is little more than self-fulfilling prophecy—performative behavior where people come to believe something and buy or sell in the markets, with the resulting impact "proof" of the accuracy of their beliefs.[32]

A recent study by financial economists Brad Cornell of Caltech and Aswath Damodaran of New York University illustrates. The stock price of Tesla increased 700% between March 2013 and February 2014, roughly a one-year period. Yet even though Tesla was an innovator in electric cars, its business model operates in a fairly mature and well-understood setting. For that kind of price increase to be based on rational valuation methods, a whole lot of new positive news would have to have entered the market during that period of time. So the two researchers did what they could to find fundamental reasons that would affect Tesla's discounted cash flow (the standard valuation model). They simply couldn't, and estimated that there was a 150% difference between market and fundamental value. But then why didn't the smart money sell, or sell short? Short-sale constraints could be part of it, but there is also the risk that a sentiment-driven bubble will persist for a lengthy period of time, making it too risky and expensive to bet on a near-term decline. Indeed, the behavioral finance literature posits that sometimes smart traders will *buy* overvalued stock if it might drive further upward momentum, so long as they are confident that they can bail out before the bubble pops. Other institutions cater to investor biases, and thus may strengthen them.

This debate is far from over.[33] Much of what we observe might be understandable without reference to mass psychology when we remember how costly information is to acquire and act upon, and how speculative and risky the act of investing really is, even for the most informed trader. Shiller shared his 2013 Nobel Prize with Eugene Fama, one of the fathers of market efficiency research. You can find plenty of discussions of "rational bubbles," particularly given the limits on arbitrage that everyone acknowledges. Efficiency proponents stress that beating the market still proves an elusive skill, suggesting that there is considerable wisdom to be found in market prices.

We will be coming back to this debate many times. For now, a few observations. First, speed of adjustment (what is often called "informational efficiency") is not the same as saying that the market is "right" ("fundamental efficiency"). The latter can never be conclusively demonstrated scientifically, because there is no agreed-upon value for a stock against which to measure departures. Fundamental efficiency is an inference that some draw based on the belief that the mechanisms of informational efficiency *should*, in a world populated by enough rational actors, move prices in the direction of intrinsic value. But the two images of efficiency don't always have to be in synch. Fischer Black, an esteemed financial economist, once suggested defining an efficient market as one in which price fluctuates within a factor of two of intrinsic value, leaving considerable room for volatility.[34]

Second, the market is constantly learning, even if it makes mistakes. MIT's Andrew Lo, who has contributed much on the behavioral side, calls this an "adaptive market hypothesis"—powerful forces on the smart money side do exploit, expose, and gradually eliminate frictions and inefficiencies. But because the economy changes so much through innovation and creative destruction, new pricing challenges keep emerging— we're neither smart nor knowledgeable enough to get ahead of the curve, so that a pattern of trial and error persists. We're seeing that in the rapid spread of social media, which alters the patterns by which information spreads: tweets get messages out to more people, allowing for greater issuer control over the message, though right now retweets seem to *increase* informational asymmetry the noise as investors less familiar with the company join the quick trading.[35]

Third, although the debate over market efficiency often puts retail investors on the dumb side and professionally managed institutions on the smart side, the truth is more muddied. We've seen that some institutions do not contribute much—mutual funds, for example, often seem to follow the herd more than add analytical value. And retail investors are not always useless noise traders.[36]

Finally, the connection between market efficiency and investor protection is complicated. Even highly efficient markets can be deceived—there will always be secrets hidden from the markets. So regulation has a role to play in any event. On the other hand, to the extent that animal spirits and market mood swings come to influence prices, it seems doubtful that disclosure or other interventions will do much to counter them. These are strong social forces, not easily moved by regulatory edict.

And that brings us back to politics. Proefficiency rhetoric has been adopted with vigor by those opposed to regulation, whether out of ideology or self-interest. When we get to our chapter on the recent global financial crisis, we'll see how an inflated vision of market efficiency was used to deflect the regulation of the derivatives marketplace, leaving that market woefully undermonitored. Two leading legal scholars on market efficiency, Ron Gilson and Reinier Kraakman, say that the academic research was "hijacked" by those who wanted no nuance or ambiguity that would allow regulators a foot in the door.[37] Predictably, those favoring more regulation responded in kind by attacking market efficiency and its proponents as if efficiency and deregulation were evil twins. Both extremes may be dangerous, both intellectually and politically.

ALGORITHMS

In our stress on human frailty in the world of investing, we need to acknowledge how technology-driven so much of trading has become. Somewhere around half of all equity market trades are executed by computers, without human intervention. Michael Lewis's best-selling book *Flash Boys* gave voice to the fear that this degree of mechanized intrusion into the markets operates as high-speed exploitation.

We'll skip a deep discussion of the most common kind of high-frequency trading—investing in computer systems, often "co-located" nearby exchanges and data providers, that give high-frequency traders microsecond advantages in the display, cancellation, or execution of orders so that they can effectively step ahead of orders coming from others and pick off a penny or so of value. That's not much, but if done millions of times a day it adds up, and obviously those millions of pennies are coming from someone else's pocket. In 2010 there was a well-publicized "flash crash" where an erroneous order caused brief chaos in the trading of a number of securities because of how the algorithms reacted. All this sounds ominous, especially when coupled with stories about dark pools of off-exchange trading. But those who have looked seriously at the issue find a mix of benefits (better liquidity) and risks associated with high-frequency trading that suggests that, while better policing, control, and transparency than we have right now are surely warranted, this kind of algorithmic trading is a mixed blessing that probably shouldn't provoke an excess of fear or loathing.[38]

The most interesting algorithms relate to a stock's fundamental value. Humans can react to news in seconds, perhaps, but more likely minutes or hours. Today, however, computers can be programmed to use news feeds that do quick counts of whether the words or numbers signal good or bad news, responding with orders in microseconds that are then unwound at a profit as soon as the market price catches up. There is a wide array of data sources that can be gamed like this—we'll see how this relates to insider trading in chapter 3. A false social media story about an attack on the White House caused a very brief but massive stock-price sell-off because those feeds were being processed by high-frequency traders. In that sense, the social and the algorithmic interact, not always with accuracy.[39] Computers also play a big role in data analytics of the sort that support fundamental analysis and longer-term investment decisions. Smart money is increasingly a blend of human and artificial intelligence.

What the average investor should take from all this is muddled. The shiny displays and data feeds that brokers and the financial media make available to retail investors may seem empowering, but they are hopelessly short of what professionals have at their disposal. Day trading is a losing proposition for most,[40] which reinforces the lesson that ordinary investors shouldn't try (and certainly not spend lots of money) to outguess the market. The smart money inevitably has an edge, and most people are not smart money. Yet the stock market remains a deeply human institution even with all these technological interventions, and its allure—and illusion of predictability if you're clever enough—is powerfully tempting. As a result, envy and resentment directed at those who stand in the way is a constant political risk, or opportunity, in how securities law gets crafted.

There is another important point here. From a societal standpoint, the co-location of computer facilities just to get a microsecond trading edge is a waste. Numerous economists have described the arms race of computerized trading as drawing resources away from more productive activity, something generalizable to much of what Wall Street seems to do. Indeed, the cost of the technology is dwarfed by the amount of human capital (at distortedly high salaries, attracting many of the best and brightest) that is invested in financial activity, some portion of which is rent-seeking.[41] In theory, that might be a good reason for regulation to dampen the enthusiasm for high-frequency trading and aggressive product innovation. The problem is that we don't know quite how to intervene without running the risk of adversely affecting that unknowable portion of the activity that does enhance capital formation and market efficiency. The political and emotional sentiments discussed earlier no doubt influence how willing anyone is to take that risk. In the face of such ambiguity, the status quo is very powerful.

(OVER)CONFIDENCE

In investor behavior, one of the most noted biases is overconfidence—the belief that one's knowledge or abilities are better than objective evidence indicates. This is a common explanation for why there is so much trading. It's also an exploitable bias, especially in the face of positive but illusory feedback.

But overconfidence is hardly limited to the buy-side, and one of the most robust lines of research in contemporary behavioral economics involves overconfidence on the sell-side: among corporate executives, investment bankers, traders, and the like. A famous story illustrates how positive illusions can be success-enhancing, even (especially) among leaders.[42] A group of soldiers got lost in the Alps. The struggled and became dejected until one of the officers found a map, which led them to push on through a sequence of mountain passages until they finally encountered safety. They later discovered that the map was of the Pyrenees, not the Alps, and thus had nothing to do with the route they took to survival. In other words, the men were better off acting confidently under a false impression than in the despair of uncertainty, where they probably would have just frozen to death.

This idea has sprouted in all sorts of intellectual domains, including investor and managerial behavior, and is central to much of what follows in this book. In a recent essay in the scientific journal *Nature*, the authors show how overconfidence can be favored as an evolutionary trait when the payoffs from contesting for greater resources in the face of massive uncertainty are large. They conclude such contests are common in the modern world, notably those generated by "novel or complex technologies (such as the Internet bubble or modern financial instruments)."[43] There is a similar evolutionary story behind a closely related bias, overoptimism.[44] A robust literature in psychology extolls the virtues of positive illusions, including an inflated sense of self-confidence and control. Overconfidence and overoptimism are associated with behaviors like drive, persistence, and ambition. You don't give up because you believe you'll succeed, and sometimes (if simply as a matter of luck) you do. This motivational theme is a long-standing one in sociology, too, on the origins of belief systems.

As we've just seen, confidence inspires and motivates even when it is unrealistic, because it has the capacity to become self-fulfilling. Robust confidence is thus a leadership trait—subordinates and stakeholders respond better to those who communicate a strong sense of control. Overconfidence enhances status within a group, with surprisingly little reputational penalty even when revealed.[45] An important connection here is to risk-taking: overconfident people (and organizations where the confidence is broadly shared) take more risks, believing the risks to be smaller than they really are, and innovate more aggressively.[46] This in turn intrigues economists, who understand the correlation between risk and return. Over a large number of iterations, lucky risk-preferrers will do better than the risk neutral or the risk averse. An economic model of how executives succeed in promotion tournaments demonstrates that there will almost always be those who get more than their fair share of luck when they've taken on risk.[47]

The point is not that all successful executives are overconfident. Rather, it's that overconfidence can thrive under the right conditions—boom times, especially. Of course, that's not how it's perceived in the moment, either by the risk-taker or observers. Psychologists call this an attribution bias—the human tendency to ascribe outcomes to character or other traits rather than situational forces like luck. As a result, the tournament shifts. Early round "winners" are anointed as gifted and talented, and get more resources and support as they move on, putting the odds even more in their favor. With that, confidence grows (and becomes less of an illusion as a result). When setbacks do occur, they are likely to be attributed to bad luck and thus rationalized away, leaving the confidence, persistence, and healthy appetite for risk undisturbed. To the survivors comes power. There is a large amount of work by business scholars on both the prevalence and consequences of managerial overconfidence and overoptimism, both for the additional risk-taking and innovation that they bring and for the darker side wherein a charismatic CEO hired by a lazy board of directors finally meets his or her comeuppance, at significant harm to shareholders.

DECEPTION, SELF-DECEPTION, AND HONESTY

Overconfidence reflects genuine belief, which takes us to another striking evolutionary insight. The sociobiologist Robert Trivers writes that deception is a survival trait in a world of aggression and scarce resources. Accordingly, we have developed a capacity to spot liars by their "tips and tells." But it is a very imperfect capacity, and frustrated entirely if the speaker believes that what is said is true. So, to Trivers, the ability to deceive is most potent in those who have first deceived themselves. Recent experimental evidence supports this potency in the business setting among those who have "drunk the Kool-Aid."[48] Believers really are more persuasive to others.

Would we want to change this, to induce more realism? It actually seems possible to alter the brain chemistry by transcranial magnetic stimulation to reduce natural optimism in favor of more cautious perception.[49] Of course, we're not at the point in society where that would be conceivable; even if it were, one can imagine the company being worse off for its investors with an induced level of doubt. That's another greased-pig problem—trying to get hold of the risky behavior means you're also affecting intensity, focus, and motivation, highly prized in the human resources playbook. There is a Janus-faced coupling between sought-after characteristics in the business world like energy, self-confidence, the need for achievement and independence, and their evil twin pairings: aggressiveness, narcissism, ruthlessness, and irresponsibility.[50]

Self-deception and adaptive biases have an obvious relevance to truth-telling, and hence directly to investor protection. Another of the important findings in the behavioral research is motivated inference, the tendency to see what you want to see. People often interpret information in a self-serving way; indeed, the inclination to internalize a view of what is right and good that coincidentally serves your best interest is, sadly, foundational to the field of behavioral ethics.[51] Psychologists note how frequently people exploit "moral wiggle-room,"[52] that is, the willingness to go as far as the unconscious rationalization of self-interest will take them, yet stopping before the point at which they would be forced to perceive themselves as corrupt.

The world of business and finance is filled with ambiguity that invites self-serving inference. It's not hard to see how the likely survivor of a corporate promotion tournament would be especially adept at doing what it takes to succeed within a cognitive framework that allows him or her to espouse and display with genuine fervor the organizationally prized virtues of cooperation, loyalty, and selflessness. There are many implications of this to consider, and so this idea of adaptive deception and self-deception will be with us throughout this book. For now, keep in mind how much these Janus-like cognitive risk-factors are often success-producing and thus valued within competitive organizations. They will not be thwarted easily.

From all this, the picture seems fairly dark with respect to human ethicality, all the more so in competitive settings. In fact, there is a great deal of honesty and trustworthiness in our society, on which the success of our capital markets depends. One of the striking insights from research in behavioral ethics is that there is more good behavior that the economists' model of rational opportunism predicts, even if there is less than in a perfect world. Evolutionary theory shows that conscience and prosociality are survivorship traits, too.

The behavioral insight to keep in mind is this. Honesty is valued; most of us genuinely want to think of ourselves as such. So long as ethical choices have enough clarity, *most* people—in finance and elsewhere—will do the right thing. But the cognitive makeup of most people also leaves room for the kind of self-deception we've just described when there is enough ambiguity to trigger some sort of ethical fading. It's entirely possible that competition rewards plasticity, so that we'll see a clustering of such traits among the winners in fields like business and finance. The regulatory challenge is twofold. First, attack the habitual opportunists who have somehow escaped the market's own search for the unreliable. Second—and just as hard—confront the larger set of people who don't see themselves as cheaters, but are hypocritically adept at promoting their own success anyway. Neither will be easy to accomplish.

REGULATORY BOUNDARIES

The final two introductory ideas are legal ones, not immediately related to human nature but important building blocks nonetheless for understanding securities regulation. Investing is about putting your money in the hands of others, with an expectation of pecuniary gain. The core investments in our financial marketplace—stocks, bonds, options—fit neatly enough into this definition, but the category is more capacious. As a legal matter, securities regulation has struggled for years with the question of what is a security, with line drawing that seems fairly arbitrary. Buy a plot of land in Florida on which orange trees grow and it's a real estate transaction outside the scope of the securities laws, even if you're mainly hoping to make a killing if the surrounding land is commercially developed. But if you and others buy the same plot of land with an agreement to manage your property and a promise of a check in the mail to reflect the income from harvesting the oranges, then it becomes a security.[53] More and more, investments are complex bundles of other investments, with debt and derivative features baked in.

Regulators like the SEC seem to act by fiat, demanding adherence, and those who favor stronger regulation often assume that the ability to control risky behavior is just a matter of political will. But securities regulation is hampered by arbitrary jurisdictional lines. Sometimes Congress wants (for rational or political reasons) to assign responsibility elsewhere than the SEC. Commodities futures, for example, go to a separate regulatory agency (the Commodities Futures Trading Commission) even though commodities futures are part of many investors' portfolios and many financial futures have stocks and bonds as their reference points. People have said for years that there is no good reason to separate securities and commodities regulation, and that the separation invites regulatory arbitrage—industry participants deliberately structuring products to play one agency off against the other as a way of thwarting strong regulation. (Congress created a much bigger problem when it decided in 2000 to place a certain category of investment, the "over-the-counter derivative," out of the reach of *both* the SEC and the CFTC.) Since the financial crisis, there have been efforts to reduce these arbitrage opportunities, but Congress did not have the stomach to consolidate, and so many opportunities persist. Other awkward line-drawing comes with respect to bank instruments and insurance products, where once again we have highly politicized questions of who is the "best" regulator.[54]

The lines may not make much sense, but the consequence is dramatic. If the SEC, for example, were to impose regulation "burdening" a particular kind of financial product, lawyers may well be able to restructure the product in substantively trivial ways to make it something that legally is not a security (or at least so they might argue). If such strategic recategorization simply results in the product moving to a different regulator, the SEC has accomplished little or nothing in terms of investor protection. The other regulator and its supporters in Congress gain turf, perhaps seeing the advantage in being more industry friendly. Sometimes, as we will see, such regulatory arbitrage happens even among products within one agency's jurisdiction—designing a product to have features resembling others that the agency regulates—as a way of daring the regulator to extend the burdens to that entire category. That extension will be time-consuming and politically costly given the opposition it will trigger from others who would now face those burdens. When the SEC has sought to push hard on its jurisdictional boundaries to cover more territory in an effort to diminish the ability to escape, the courts have more than once struck down the effort in lawsuits brought by those making money as a result of the arbitrary line-drawing.

From the regulator's perspective, this endless financial engineering is another of the many ways in which regulation resembles chasing a greased pig. And even if somehow the United States were able to reduce these kinds of arbitrage opportunities, it might still face the possibility that market activity might migrate to other countries around the world that might provide more friendly regulation: global arbitrage.[55] This worry, of course, assumes the wisdom of the regulation. Someone who thinks that overregulation is a problem—that regulators need to be constrained—finds a virtue in regulatory arbitrage. Much of the legal scholarship in securities regulation since the turn toward criticism in the late 1970s and early 1980s is built on promoting regulatory competition (and thus regulatory constraint) as the route to efficient regulation, both nationally and globally. The goal is *increased* choice in what regulatory treatment ensues, on the assumption that efficient markets will discipline too much opportunism.[56]

Because that sort of regulatory competition led to the kinds of behaviors that generated the global financial crisis, it has gone a bit out of favor. But so long as the pathologies of regulation persist—along with the ideological distaste for the regulatory state that is part of so much public discourse—the search for some limits on bureaucratic autonomy goes on. The diversity of financial products, the constant innovation, the arbitrary legal lines, and the opportunities for clever architectural design have to be taken as a given without more fundamental reform than has yet proved politically possible.

THE FEDERAL GOVERNMENT AND THE STATES

The relationship between the states and the federal government in investor protection is complicated. State securities law ("blue sky laws") predated the federal securities laws by a couple of decades. While there is limited preemption of state securities law in the regulatory arena, by and large the ability of state regulators to police misconduct in their own jurisdictions is still well accepted. This gives state regulators from New York (Wall Street), Massachusetts (a cluster of major mutual funds, like Fidelity), and other large states a base from which to compete with the SEC. For roughly the last decade, New York's attorneys general—Eliot Spitzer, initially—outran the SEC on a series of scandals and caused considerable embarrassment at the federal level. New York has an especially open-ended statute, the Martin Act, creating unusual leverage for an ambitious prosecutor because those with criminal convictions face considerable restraints on their ability to do business in the financial field. The equilibrium of political power will often be different in New York than in Washington.[57]

A separate line of tension is between federal securities law and state corporate law. Corporations are artificial persons created by the states, not the federal government. There is nothing inevitable about that, but it is unmistakably part of our legal history. As a result, the law of corporate governance has historically been state based, which includes defining the authority of the corporate board of directors, the nature and limits of shareholder power, fiduciary responsibilities of officers, directors, and controlling shareholders, and the like. The idea that shareholders elect corporate directors, for example, is a matter of state law, not federal law. Delaware is by far the leading state of incorporation for large public companies. When the securities laws were drafted in the 1930s, some in the Roosevelt administration wanted to federalize corporate law, but the initiative failed.[58] That plus a consistent disinclination to revisit federal chartering has been read as implicit congressional acceptance of state primacy, with the implication that the federal government (and the SEC in particular) should respect a line of separation that leaves much of corporate governance to Delaware's expert judiciary and legislative processes.

The appeal of corporate law federalism is based on choice-of-law competition.[59] In theory, one might argue that states will compete with each other to attract corporations (and the franchise tax revenue they pay) by devising corporate law that finds an optimal balance between managerial autonomy and shareholder rights, something known as the "race to the top" hypothesis. Delaware's primacy would thus be well earned, and deserving of respect. But as Mark Roe has pointed out in his extensive writings on all this, evidence of actual competition for incorporations is sparse. Any competition ended long ago, and Delaware won.[60] It now has insurmountable advantages in terms of the richness and depth of its case law, and the expertise that comes from such hegemony, if that is what selectors of state of incorporation want.

So there is a distinctly political story here. Roe notes that Delaware's victory came in part because it has a moderate political environment lacking strong public pressure groups like labor unions, progressive political movements, and so on. So it can concentrate on finding a stable equilibrium on the main fault lines of corporate law, without the populist distractions that would predictably pop up in California or New York. It need not be optimal, just balanced enough so that shareholders do not get overly upset, which might affect the firm's cost of capital.

If this is right, the political nature of Delaware's primacy becomes clear: it is a way of deflecting political pressures that might threaten an attractive equilibrium in terms of the private economic power shared by managers and investors. So Delaware's real competition is the federal government, to the extent that shareholder or stakeholder interests think they might get a better deal in Washington, from Congress or the SEC. At least when scandals occur, such opportunities may surface; we will see some examples. One of the great political battles at the federal level today is the effort to limit the focus of securities regulation so it mimics Delaware and simply seeks an efficient solution to the conflicts of interest between managers and shareholders, nothing else. But because securities law is so clearly also about the externalities—the spillovers, positive and negative—of fair and efficient capital markets, that political effort is little more than a distrust of giving voice to other interests. As the demands of publicness grow, that effort to limit interests at play in federal lawmaking is doomed.

Looking at corporate law federalism in these terms offers another important insight. Although the Delaware law on fiduciary responsibility is indeed deep and rich, it's hard to see precisely how it works with respect to the core interest of protecting shareholders from managerial disloyalty. Loyalty breaches are redressed typically by the awkward shareholders' derivative suit (a lawsuit brought by a shareholder on behalf of the corporation), which depends on the shareholder's lawyer knowing enough about the cheating to bring the action in the first place. That is a problem with respect to well-hidden or disguised forms of self-dealing. The more likely possibility—which state primacists are loath to dwell on—is that federal securities law is already carrying much of the weight here. It is federal law, though extensive disclosure requirements, that is likely to bring conflicts of interest to investors' attention.

The SEC enforcement apparatus has the capacity to enforce disclosure violations more powerfully than any derivative suit (including the threat of a criminal prosecution beyond any civil action).

With respect to the public corporation, state corporate law and the federal securities laws are symbiotic. The federal securities laws are already deeply into corporate governance and fiduciary responsibility. Corporate disclosure is in many ways designed to make corporate governance work.[61] A claim that there is some sacred corporate law space belonging solely to the states, to which the federal government must defer, is pure politics.

2

Making Sense of Corporate Fraud

Sometimes when a company's stock price has been soaring high, word comes out that its business or financial condition is not what the company represented to investors. As the truth is revealed, the stock price crashes. Investors are furious with the sudden loss of what could be billions of dollars in the collective market value of their investments. Enron and WorldCom, widely admired and respected companies that suddenly collapsed in the aftermath of accounting scandals in 2001–2, are both still etched in the financial and regulatory mindset. Such spectacular flameouts are rare, but less dramatic revelations that a company had not been honest with the market about some financial or operational development are not. There were 212 identified financial reporting frauds during that same time period, less dramatic but severely troubling in the aggregate.[1]

It is easy to draw a cartoon caricature of corporate fraud: greedy executives lying to innocent, trusting investors. As we'll see, it is far more complicated. Even characterizing investors' "loss" from fraud is too simple. The high stock price was an illusion, never really reflecting the true value of the company. You can't really lose what you never had. And for every "suckered" buyer of the company's stock during the time of the fraud, there was a lucky seller, the vast majority of who were entirely innocent. Still, investors feel violated, and many truly were. There are also serious negative externalities from fraud, beyond the impact on investors. Companies with inflated indicators value issue stock, incur debt, and acquire other companies more easily than they should. In highly regulated industries, deception affects regulatory choices because regulators are blind to the true financial conditions in the industry. Empirical studies of the WorldCom scandal identified billions of dollars in distortions in the market— adversely affecting its major competitors, and causing telecom regulators to alter their policies.[2] After the fraud is revealed, the pain is felt not only by managers and shareholders, but employees, retirees, suppliers, customers, and local communities.[3]

Congress passed the Securities Exchange Act in 1934 to protect the integrity of stock prices from manipulation, fraud, and other kinds of abuse. The main solution is disclosure—quarterly (and to some extent continuous) financial reporting and narrative self-depiction by all public companies, bolstered by a set of procedures designed to make those disclosures more likely to be accurate. That disclosure, and corporate honesty generally, is policed by the SEC. Most people would probably say that fighting corporate fraud is the SEC's main job.

Researchers have no direct measure of how much securities fraud there is in our markets. We can count SEC actions, criminal investigations, and investor class actions, but those numbers are both overinclusive (cases charging fraud but not necessarily proving it) and underinclusive (because some frauds are successfully concealed or simply ignored by both public and private enforcers). Besides, fraud is cyclical—motives and opportunity ebb and flow. Financial fraud peaks in the later stages of boom markets, when both investor enthusiasm and investor expectations are frothy, and revealed when the downturn comes.[4]

To make an educated—but disturbing—guess, three well-known financial economists drew inferences from changes in company behavior after the Enron-related demise of the accounting firm of Arthur Andersen (i.e., that other companies forced to find a new auditor would change their ways, believing that their new auditor would be tougher) to posit that the likelihood of a public company engaging in some form of financial reporting fraud in a given year at 14.5%.[5] The average corporate fraud, they suggest, results in a 22% loss in enterprise value when uncovered. Separately, a survey of CFOs reports a consensus that as much as 20% of all companies may be deliberately managing earnings to hide the truth.[6] These are crude estimates, to be sure, but sobering if the reality is anywhere even close.[7] Even if spectacular frauds are rare, the truth may be that fraud is more common a commodity than it should be.

Of course, even those estimates indicate that fraud is less common than honesty (or at least compliance with the law), and that perspective is worth keeping in mind. Most people, in business or otherwise, intend to be honest, and social norms usually nudge them to behave. (These norms vary but surely have some force—it's noteworthy, for example, that companies located in more religious geographic regions engage in less questionable accounting practices than those located elsewhere.)[8] A variety of institutional structures exist to reduce fraud risk, of which law is just a part.[9] Some combination of conscience, norms, and structure works most of the time.

In an entirely rational world, we might wonder why there is an appreciable risk of corporate fraud at all. True, the probability of detection and sanction is substantially less than 100%, and the payoffs to a successful fraud considerable, especially to executives with big stock option packages. On the other hand, the consequences to both firms and managers when caught cooking the books are considerable.[10] There are the possibilities of SEC sanctions for individuals, maybe even criminal prosecution. There are also adverse career effects (most companies don't want to touch an executive with a tarnished legal record, and even those who avoid sanction can have a reputational taint). For executives who, like most, have large stock and options holdings, the loss of wealth from the discovery of fraud by itself can be massive. Companies themselves face sizable fines and other penalties. They usually have to pay considerable legal fees and other costs in the process, which themselves can run into the tens of millions of dollars. And there is a credibility hit—a drop in stock price just to reflect the fact that investors and other stakeholders have lost confidence in what management says. Future financing gets harder until the company rebuilds its reputation.

Plus, large-scale fraud is hard to pull off. Big companies are complex organizations with many sets of eyes, any one of which, despite pressures to the contrary, could become a whistle-blower. They also have directors, lawyers, and accountants who may be positioned to see what is going on, who thus also have to be deceived or brought into the conspiracy. The market isn't that easy to fool, either, once we assume some degree of market efficiency. Short sellers in particular are anxiously looking to spot dishonest companies with pumped-up stock prices, and more than willing to bring the investigatory glare of media and regulatory attention in an effort to torpedo the stock's price.

So, one would think the clear-thinking managers (especially ones already well-off) would hesitate to gamble on fraud just to make themselves richer than they already are. To work, a rational greed-based account has to assume a high enough probability of success and low enough probability of detection to outweigh all of this. Perhaps, but maybe you're starting to see why a different kind of motivational story might explain better why we see the amount of deception that we do.

WHAT MOTIVATES CORPORATE FRAUD?

As we've just seen, the common portrait of corporate fraud involves senior executives of a company with already lavish compensation packages who "cook the books" simply in order to pump up the value of their stock holdings and incentive compensation packages, and position themselves to demand even more from a gullible or sycophantic board of directors. In fact, there is plenty of research to support this story: companies whose executives have more than average stock-based compensation (and thus more reason to distort the price upward) are more likely to commit fraud.[11] But again, we come back to the palpable riskiness of that gamble, suggesting that it might not be quite as simple as that.

Cognitive Distortions and Slippery Slopes

Try this instead.[12] Imagine a company where the top executives are highly focused, driven, and convinced of their special skills as managers. In other words, they're both overconfident and overly optimistic. (Recent survey evidence indicates that financial managers believe that excessive optimism is *very* common among their peers.)[13] Much corporate publicity—even accounting and financial reporting—involves estimates of what the future will bring. Because the managers are optimistic, those estimates will be favorably high, genuinely so.[14] Let's also assume that the company has had some past success that leads the market to trust management's judgment, so that the market price accepts management's optimism without skepticism.

But reality bites, and now management privately discovers that performance is falling short. Still overconfident, management's tendency is to interpret this as temporary bad luck, surely not likely to repeat. So they deny it—given the company's prospects, revealing the shortfall would actually mislead those inclined to think the worst. Yet the next quarter is disappointing again. Managers deflect the truth once more, maybe in a greater amount, still sure things will turn around and reverse the temporary shortfalls, consigning them to oblivion.

What if the situation doesn't improve, however? By this time, the genuine optimism may finally be fading (though this happens in people and organizations far more slowly than you'd think in the face of positive illusions). When the optimism does disappear, and reality sets in, management faces a number of disturbing possibilities. First, the company is in trouble, facing a serious threat to its credibility if not its survival. Second, the company (and management) may be said to have lied all along (here is where internal emails like "We're all going to jail" tend to pop up).

It is human, and organizational, nature in these circumstances to deny the facts. As John Darley of Princeton points out, social identity is at stake. You're already in deep, and the only chance for survival is to double down and buy time with further (maybe now fairly deliberate) deception. At this late stage, even if you realize the deceit, the cover-up doesn't seem all that wrong. The institution and its stakeholders—innocent fellow executives and employees, customers, suppliers—are under threat if the deception is revealed.[15] They deserve a chance at survival. Fooling a soulless financial market can seem the lesser evil, loyalty the greater good. Psychology research shows that people are more willing to cheat when the benefit will go to a family member or colleague rather than only to themselves. The more leaders believe in group goals, the more they think of themselves as justified in taking unethical actions on behalf of the group.[16] There is also research indicating that the process of trying to meet frustratingly high performance goals leads to depletion of ethicality, making it more likely the actor eventually gives in to dishonesty.[17]

Researchers Catherine Schrand and Sarah Zechman found precisely this optimism-commitment pattern when they studied SEC enforcement actions brought against companies and their executives for false financial reporting. Using interesting metrics that we'll talk about more shortly, they assessed a sample of companies that became subject to SEC enforcement actions for indications of managerial overconfidence, compared to nonviolators. They then looked at how the misreporting evolved from the time from which indications of abnormal accounting began and the culmination of the scheme. What they found is a classic slippery slope—wrongdoing, as we've just suggested, that starts small and innocently and then builds. Strikingly, that trip down the slippery slope correlates positively with evidence of managerial overconfidence at the outset. This is itself an interesting amalgam of psychological tendencies. Simply in terms of perception, our minds are conservative, construing new information with a bias toward consistency with the past. Rather than interpreting some new information as evidence of change, we instead prefer to reconcile it with prior beliefs and perceptions. Even without any motivation, we notice change poorly and catch on slowly, but this is all the more so when we've made some kind of commitment that would be threatened by disconfirming facts (the basis for cognitive dissonance). A follow-up study shows that the transitional stage in the rationalization of financial misreporting is easier when managers imagine earnings management by others in a more corrupt form, which makes what they are doing categorically different and acceptable by comparison.[18]

This conception of slippery slope fraud involves delayed reaction, making it different from those deceptions that involve deliberateness from the very beginning. Even those are often rationalized, of course, but in the moral sense that "normalizes" the behavior through justifications and excuses, often genuinely believed. But the perpetrators know all along that what they are doing is deceptive, even if they've justified it to themselves. By contrast, what we've described is a process that begins with some period of time during which there is no perception of wrongfulness that needs rationalization, which only later turns into awareness that something is amiss. Precisely because of the now-deep commitment, the cognitive pressure to justify deception at this point is stronger than it would be at the outset, and self-serving inference goes to work in a way more akin—though far from conscious awareness—to what we normally think of as rationalization. The third stage comes late in the process: the realization that one's rationalizations were just that. Many people accused of fraud stay stuck in a prior stage, however, not letting go of the blind spots or the rationalizations. This process is even more potent for supervisory executives not directly involved in the perpetration of the fraud, for whom awareness will come more slowly, if ever.

Scandals and Loss Aversion

The Enron debacle, which surely did evolve into deliberate deceit, fits nicely within this alternative account of how fraud starts. Enron essentially transformed itself from an energy company into an energy banker (or dealer). Management was convinced of the brilliance and originality of this shift, creating a new paradigm for the energy marketplace (and eventually other markets like Internet broadband, etc.).[19] The complex, derivatives-like transactions that it was doing had to be reported using accounting principles that management seemed to consider (with some justification) unsuited for the new world. From the beginning, the exercise of accounting judgment was self-serving, but accepted as reflecting the enterprise's true (i.e., forward-looking) value. With the help of complicit bankers and accountants, the accounting gradually became more aggressive and rule-bending, all with the same "fair value" rationalization. For a time, the inflated revenues and earnings made Enron's stock price soar.

To an extent, that stock price became an end in itself, a celebration of wealth and greed (the company had a large ticker with its stock price in its main lobby for all to see). But meeting inflated expectations was actually crucial for Enron's survival. Enron was a heavy borrower in the debt markets, which required a high credit rating based on balance sheet and income statement metrics. As is common, certain of its credit instruments provided for default were the rating to be downgraded. And its own stock was collateral for other financial arrangements. As the financial structure became more elaborate, in other words, Enron *had* to report good financials and maintain a high stock price. Enron's insiders were trapped by their own illusions.

One of the fundamental claims in the heuristics and biases literature is prospect theory—the idea that our propensity to take risk is affected by how the risky choice is framed. Put simply, we accept more risk to avoid a loss than to pursue a gain. Enron got to the point where acknowledging the truth would have been devastating to the company and all its future prospects. Survival required denial.[20] And we can say this about other frauds as well. One researcher has collected a series of fraud studies that illustrate the psychology of increasing risk-taking in the face of fear of loss—fifty-eight episodes with combined losses of $126 billion.[21] (That included J.P. Morgan's stunning "London Whale" fiasco, discussed earlier, which cost the firm massively in economic costs and legal payouts for a series of trades that turned hedging upside down.) A surprisingly large number of the notorious corporate frauds in the last two decades have involved companies in hypercompetitive markets, often technology based, where lagging can be fatal in terms of attracting key resources (customers, employees, capital). When lagging behind isn't an acceptable option and the information environment is sufficiently noisy, corporate managers are primed for a distorted assessment of risk.

CONFIDENCE, RISK-TAKING, AND THE PATHWAYS TO POWER

Strong Beliefs and Distorted Perceptions

We've now built an explanation for corporate fraud that stresses overconfidence at the onset of the slippery slope, an optimism-commitment whipsaw. We saw in chapter 1 that overconfidence is an adaptive bias, which may be favored in corporate promotion tournaments.[22] The effects are largely unconscious, at least in the early stages, so that the diminished perception of risk early on is genuine. Warning bells that should ring don't.

Research on both the causes and effects of managerial overconfidence and overoptimism is extensive. A recent study asked corporate managers to make a prediction with an 80% confidence level, but the results fell within their predictions only 36% of the time.[23] There are connections between measures of executive overconfidence to such outcomes as product innovation, merger and acquisition activity, corporate financing, strategic learning (as to the latter, overconfident executives are poorer at learning from experience because they are less likely to acknowledge their own mistakes),[24] and fraud.[25] How do researchers identify overconfident and overoptimistic executives, since most don't willingly submit to intrusive psychological testing? The most common measurement involves the number of unexercised executive stock options, which represents a rather concentrated bet on the future of the company. When conditions are otherwise the same as among a number of companies, those bets are a useful (though hardly conclusive) way of judging how self-confident the senior managers are.

Testosterone and Risky Behavior

Overconfidence is not a stand-alone trait, however, but part of a larger cluster encompassing sensation-seeking, a desire for competitive dominance, and an appetite for risk. (Narcissism, also commonplace among business leaders, has similar correlations and implications for financial misreporting.)[26] Those tendencies are familiar enough in a historically male-dominated business world, leading many researchers to suspect a link to testosterone. Greater-than-normal testosterone levels can be observed indirectly by a number of means. One is facial width relative to facial height, another has to do with finger size ratios (both of which relate back to fetal growth and physiological change at puberty). The former allows researchers to use pictures of CEOs as a proxy for testosterone level. The high incidence of high testosterone among executives is in synch with norms in the business world that prize toughness over fairness.[27] Researchers have found evidence of a positive association of high testosterone with financial misreporting, insider trading, and being a named subject in an SEC enforcement action.[28] The authors of this study determined that this result was not simply due to overconfidence but to the bigger cluster of hormonal traits. Relatedly, another team of researchers discovered a link between financial misreporting and risky off-the-job behavior as measured by minor legal infractions like reckless driving.[29] Hopefully, you see the connection here to issues of gender and diversity, to which will come back explicitly later in the book.

Interestingly, testosterone also relates to moral judgment. There is evidence that elevated levels connect to a more utilitarian kind of ethical reasoning, that means justify the ends.[30] Fitting that with self-serving inference—seeing the ends and means in a biased fashion—suggests a greater risk of both the slippery slope and the big lie that accompanies the cover-up. This entire cluster of traits can be adaptive in the pathways to corporate power, the crucibles where up-and-coming executives are tested in competition with their peers. Winners are not likely to be sociopaths—too much cooperation and loyalty is needed inside firms for that kind of person to thrive for long. But some degree of plasticity—ethical and otherwise—is likely to define the person who wins the tournament, the ability to be a star at teamwork and loyalty, but adept at stepping ahead of peers when the finish line nears without the baggage of doubt or guilt. Recall Robert Trivers's point that those who deceive others most efficiently are those who first deceive themselves, for which there is some specific experimental support in the business context.[31] Power, in turn, seems to make people better liars.[32] When coupled with other "dark side" traits like Machiavellianism (the willingness to manipulate) or psychopathy, however, we see how executives can gradually edge toward the abyss; if that executive has strong internal power, the threat can be considerable. An experimental study offers evidence that "high-Machs" are particularly adept at rationalization, which makes corporate fraud more likely.[33] This leaves us with a disturbing suspicion that psychologically motivated deception—in the guise of utmost sincerity—is frequent enough to be something of a survival trait.

These are possibilities, of course, that may well be countered in organizations sufficiently worried about them, a subject we'll come to in chapter 4. But the upsides of these traits have to be kept in mind, as well as the connection to the cyclicality of corporate fraud—its tendency to spike during boom times. Boom times are precisely when aggressiveness risk-taking is rewarded (or less penalized, by either the market or legal authorities).[34] A sustained boom period will disproportionately mean that risk-takers gain power and influence. Personally, it inflates for each "winner" in the promotion tournament the sense of self-efficacy. Egos grow. Collectively, multiple winners sharing the same competitive ethic will signal to others the virtue of such traits and dispositions. Those signals are normative, and we're about to see, contagious.

The correlations between traits like overconfidence or high testosterone and an enhanced risk of corporate fraud derive from what has become a cottage industry of business researchers who search for causal connections between discernable traits in both executives and organizations and adverse outcomes like civil litigation, prosecutions, and SEC enforcement. Other discoveries about the antecedents of risk-taking and wrongdoing are fascinating as well, again subject to the earlier caution that individual studies have to be used gingerly in deriving legally useful insights. Examples: Companies led by a CEO who has at least one daughter are less likely to be sued (and take less risk) than those who don't.[35] Firms whose executives lean Democratic politically are (slightly) more likely to be accused of securities fraud than Republicans, although Republican firms are more likely to be sued for employment or environmental violations.[36] Companies are more likely to commit fraud the farther away their headquarters is from the SEC, and more likely to move the headquarters even further away in the midst of a sustained fraud.[37] As this body of research grows, maybe we're beginning to see the outlines when the law's message is more likely to be cognitively distorted or not. There will be more on fraud's predictability shortly.

CULTURE AND FRAUD

So far, we've been focusing mainly on CEOs and CFOs as autonomous individuals, as if they had the capacity to pull off corporate fraud on their own. But corporate misrepresentation is usually a conspiracy involving a number of individuals, any of whom could blow the whistle if so motivated. Employees suffer when corporate wrongdoing is detected, and are thus a countervailing force in controlling the behavior of higher-ups.[38] If so, then the unrealistic beliefs of any one leader, whether from overconfidence or self-interest, might lead to nothing because the bias is countered by the more realistic sense-making or restraint on the part of other powerful people in the organization. That takes us to the social dimension of adaptive beliefs.

Why people in organizations believe what they do ("sense-making") is one of the most interesting challenges in the study of organizational behavior. Many organizations—especially large corporations—are so complex that no one person can truly know everything about them. Information is widely diffused. And information systems don't always bring it together in an accurate or understandable way, especially in terms of forward-looking implications.

But organizations don't work very well without some agreed-upon sense of what is going on. While there may be many ways that sense-making occurs, culture plays a central role. Corporate cultures are the shared explanations that individuals and small groups take for granted about what they are doing, how they are doing it, and why. The more powerful the culture is, the easier it is to coordinate the actions of the many people that it takes to make the business work. The less disagreement there is, the less time and effort people have to spend negotiating their conflicting interpretations of what is happening, and can get to work with a sense of direction.

If that description is right (and it is pretty much a given among organization researchers), then the content of the corporate culture matters. A pessimistic, cynical culture, for example, will induce doubts about both individual and collective futures, leading to what economists in game theory call "last period" behaviors—low cooperation, high selfishness. There isn't enough of a future worth investing in. By contrast, the message of an optimistic corporate culture is that there is ample reason to cooperate, be focused and enthusiastic. The optimistic, confident corporate culture, in other words, promotes the same virtues of persistence, aggressiveness, and willingness to take risk that we saw at the individual level. But it operates more powerfully, by spreading those virtues among many. Better teamwork and loyalty ensue, a melding of the identity of the individual with that of the group. George Akerlof and Rachel Kranton point out that such perceptions help solve an otherwise daunting agency cost problem, creating high-grade grease for the corporate engine.

That grease is powerful stuff. Neuroscientists find that the "feel good" hormone associated with cooperation within groups (oxytocin) also promotes aggression against those who threaten the group.[39] Precisely because of that power, emotions and beliefs can start the slide down the slippery slope to large-scale fraud. Desire is magnified, competitive instinct aroused, fear suppressed. The "can do" culture makes stretch commitments, and when obstacles are encountered (at least initially), they are marginalized. Dependent on resources like external funding in the debt markets, the company creates a representation of its current situation that is "true" in its own rosy view of reality, even if it doesn't necessarily follow the financial reporting rules religiously. As we've just seen, those who have drunk the Kool-Aid are more likely to get promoted and able to set the tone at the top, privileging those perceptions.

That kind of belief system can persist for quite a while, as a self-fulfilling prophecy. If the stock market buys into the story, as it did with companies like Enron and WorldCom, the financial markets reinforce the collective corporate ego; the managerial labor and product markets may as well. Acquisitions of other companies are easier because of the stock price and favorable borrowing conditions, enabling further growth and momentum.

Taking this story to the social level of the organization rather than just one or two key executives is both more realistic and more troubling.[40] It is more realistic precisely because information is so diffused and compartmentalized in organizations, and because there are such massive pressures to accentuate the positive in attracting the resources necessary to succeed in a winner-takes-most world. It is more troubling because, as we are about to see, it blurs the assessment of both individual and corporate culpability for the large-scale harms that fraud causes, and makes corporate fraud that much harder to deter in the first place. Not surprisingly, many researchers think that dysfunctional corporate cultures are a main reason that frauds occur.

The motivations for fraud cross firm boundaries, too. One study demonstrated that within urban geographic areas, the incidence of financial fraud by one company makes it more likely that others there will commit fraud as well, even if they are in entirely separate industries.[41] The options-backdating scandals during the last decade spread contagiously through interlocks on corporate boards of directors—apparently, boards learned to play accounting games from other boards.[42] The more the rationalization of fraud spreads among business elites, the more powerful the competitive pressures to conform.

All this adds something important to our story. Obedience to the law depends on many things, including the perceived legitimacy of the legal demands.[43] As the likelihood of detection diminishes, that factor grows in importance. Cultures enable beliefs about the law's legitimacy that can be either positive or negative relative to other values, and when the latter, compliance falls. Put that together with all the other self-serving filters we've encountered and one can readily see how investor protection messages get lost in translation in high-velocity business settings.

SUE THE BASTARDS

So what does all this mean for the law? In the aftermath of a large fraud, the public wants there to be punishment that reflects the apparent severity of the harm. When executives have acted badly, it's tempting to want them left "naked, homeless and without wheels," to use a memorable phrase from former SEC chair Richard Breeden. Some of this is a desire for retribution for the pain caused, but usually it also stresses the need to deter.

When the SEC brings a fraud case, it tends to use Section 10(b) of the Securities Exchange Act, pursuant to which the Commission has adopted a general antifraud rule, Rule 10b-5. Rule 10b-5 prohibits misrepresentations, half-truths, and schemes to defraud in connection with the purchase or sale of a security. Neither the statutory provision nor the rule says anything about state of mind. That silence left the matter to the courts, which have had much to say on the subject but not always spoken with a great deal of clarity. Drawing from words in the statute like "device" and "contrivance," the Supreme Court has ruled that the enforcer in an action charging a violation of Rule 10b-5 must prove *scienter*—some form of intentionality—and not simple carelessness.[44] That would include actual knowledge that what was said was false and misleading, if not a desire that the trickery succeed. According to most courts (though the Supreme Court has not yet spoken on this), scienter also includes "recklessness," a familiar legal concept that can be expressed in a number of ways—an extreme departure from ordinary care, perhaps, or the conscious disregard of a risk that what you are saying is untrue.

Criminal prosecutors have a number of statutory provisions they can invoke in investment-related cases, but 10b-5 is a preferred weapon for them, too. They have a double burden on state of mind. They have to prove scienter as well as "willfulness." What, if anything, differentiates those two is something on which the courts have been extremely unclear. At most, willfulness connotes an awareness of wrongdoing that goes beyond the awareness of the risk of falsity (and if that distinction escapes you, you're in good company even among well-trained lawyers).

The Awareness Conundrum

What I've presented is greatly oversimplified, of course—we could go on for pages documenting the conflicting ways courts have talked about state of mind in securities fraud actions. But you have more than enough to see the problem. The word that ties together the legal standard is *awareness*—of the departure from the truth, or disregard of the risk of falsity, or of wrongfulness. You can get someone for looking the other way, but only if it is deliberate disregard or conscious avoidance. As Sam Buell has pointed out in his wide-ranging study of white-collar crime and securities enforcement, judges and juries expect to hear evidence of moral blameworthiness. And it's not at all clear that executives have that awareness when there are mental blind spots.

If so, we should worry about the law being too constricted, preventing successful enforcement. I do worry about that, and this is the source of much of the public argument today about why we don't see more executives in jail after a scandal. But we shouldn't overstate this concern, for two reasons. First, we've seen that many frauds go through stages of awareness, so that toward the end, at least, there is a guilty state of mind. That may be enough for a conviction, even if blind spots created the trap in the first place. Second, even when a cognitive blindness defense might be available, it may not be credited by judges or juries. Those charged with determining guilt or innocence at the various stages of enforcement must *infer* state of mind, in hindsight. Given the complexity of the human mind, that is tricky enough. Financial reporting and disclosure are not subjects on which most judges or jurors have much background or experience to draw from in making sense of the conflicting claims. The defendants' story of good-faith blindness thus has obvious credibility problems—people always have an excuse. In assessing blame, we tend to overweight perceptions of character as opposed to situational forces. If enough doubts about character can be introduced, juries may convict regardless of what was going on in the defendant's mind.

Hindsight is especially a problem for white-collar defendants. Enforcement usually only follows when something truly bad has happened to the company. The defense is essentially saying that defendants did not appreciate the risk, and were just doing the best they could under ambiguous, fast-moving circumstances. While we might sympathize in principle (or at least acknowledge that problems are often difficult to foresee), knowledge that the bad event actually happened strongly biases the assessment of the likelihood that that event would happen at the critical time. It's the hindsight bias, a well-documented psychological tendency familiar enough to anyone who has lamented (but probably also engaged in) Monday morning quarterbacking. And warning judges and juries about the hindsight bias rarely eliminates it. If they're motivated for some reason to assign blame, hindsight makes it much easier.[45]

Enron in the Courtroom

Thus it's entirely possible that juries, in particular, will ignore the cognitive blindness and find liability anyway. In high-stakes trials, it is not clear how much attention is paid to precisely evaluating state of mind. Ken Lay at Enron received a long jail sentence. It would take a book-length treatment of the Enron story to sort through just Lay's state-of-mind defense that he, as CEO during part of the relevant time, was so focused on other matters of Enron business that he never formed any culpable awareness that the company's accounting for the complex web of financial transactions engineered by subordinates might be bogus. Given how the human mind works, it's entirely plausible that he never did, and that the psychology of the setting he was in (in contrast, perhaps, to other Enron insiders) was especially ripe for both denial and cognitive blindness. One of the side issues at Lay's cross-examination at trial was an investment with another defendant in a small company that did business with Enron, contrary to the company's code of ethics. That no doubt laid the groundwork for a greed narrative, especially when coupled with Lay's predictably large compensation at Enron and cavalier dismissal of the ethics rules as worth slavish adherence. But even if true, that investment wasn't very probative of what Lay knew or suspected about accounting fraud.

Those kinds of storylines can influence juries. Indeed, when members of the Enron jury who voted to convict Lay explained their decision to the press (as typically happens these days after high-profile criminal trials), they said nothing about evidence of awareness.[46] Instead, the familiar "captain of the ship" image was offered: people at the top *should* pay attention to what's going on, and not let dangerous things happen. But as a matter of law, that's not the question. If it was the jury's motivation (perhaps bolstered by a combination of character judgment and hindsight), Lay was sent to jail improperly, a serious due process issue. I don't know enough to come to that conclusion—and the Enron prosecutors emphatically think they presented a solid legal case[47]—but there is enough here to be troubled. Prosecutors and SEC enforcers are hardly immune from their own self-serving inference and the cognitive dissonance that comes once there is a commitment to the case.

Filtration and Deterrence

Whether or not cognitive blindness works as a defense in particular cases, however, the much more serious problem is deterrence. For the threat of enforcement to work in deterring fraud, it has to register at the time the wrongdoing begins. If overconfidence, optimism, and self-serving inference distort judgment and risk perception, especially in the early stages of the slippery slope, deception will occur notwithstanding the law's best intentions. Legal risk does not register accurately when cognitive bias filters the law's message. For the law to tell someone to "tell the truth" or "act reasonably" will not necessarily have much impact if the person has—unrealistically—become convinced that what she is saying is truthful and what she is doing is reasonable. All the more so when the culture bolsters those perceptions.

In response, of course, we could ratchet up the penalties for fraud to a more draconian level to try to get the attention of executives, but that raises hard questions of proportionality in punishment and might still not work as hoped at relatively low levels of detection. Moreover, any such fear would introduce greater precaution costs—costly steps taken to avoid liability. And it's hard to believe that such prosecutions would ever become so routine as to gain true clarity. The roulette wheel nature of enforcement inevitably reflects a mix of forces: political and media attention, the sheer volume of potential cases, prosecutorial resources, and so on. The predictability of detection and prosecution that is needed for solid deterrence is sadly lacking.

There is more to say on all this, and we'll come back to the legal question in chapter 6, on why so few corporate executives were indicted for their roles in the financial crisis. For now, you see the problems associated with deterring powerful people who are steps removed from day-to-day operations and subject to large blind spots. It's the most important lesson for law so far from all the social science we've been surveying.

DETECTION AND ENFORCEMENT

The SEC's Enforcement Record

Whether corporate misrepresentations are the product of greed or blind spots, deterrence will fall short if the SEC isn't a good enforcer, and the SEC's enforcement program has more than its share of critics. From within the business community, there are claims of too much aggressiveness, even abuse of authority—reputation-damaging actions brought without enough evidence of serious wrongdoing. Part of this, they say, is pressure on the enforcement staff to "make their numbers" by meeting or exceeding expectations about how many cases they close.[48]

But the much more common criticism is just the opposite: that the SEC is simply too soft on Wall Street and corporate America. Recall once again the claim that the SEC knows to "keep sweet the Wall Street elite." Common complaints about the SEC's weak will are that it (1) settles too many cases for sums of money that are far less than either the harm caused or profits gained from the behavior in question; (2) tends to impose monetary penalties on firms (and thus their innocent shareholders) more than on their wrongdoing executives; and (3) too rarely demands damaging admissions of guilt, and waives the painful collateral consequences that are sometimes supposed to accompany a finding of wrongdoing in order to let the wrongdoing firm keep doing business as usual.

There are also more subtle claims that the Commission brings too many "little" cases that distract attention from larger and more systemic abuses of law and power that continue on Wall Street and in corporate executive suites and boardrooms. Recent chair Mary Jo White fueled some doubt by heralding a "broken windows" enforcement philosophy: going after low-level violations as part of a campaign to clean our financial markets of the markings of misuse. That makes some sense given that the opposite (no enforcement of little things) likely leads to an excess of small violations, and that many big frauds start out as little matters before descending the slippery slope. As we've seen, securities violations can be contagious. But such an emphasis can also be a distraction. There is something of a broken windows cult in policy circles because the program was implemented as a criminal deterrence in

New York by Mayor Rudy Giuliani in the 1990s, when the street crime rate dropped. Many scholars today doubt that the program was all that impactful (demographics and a sharp increase in the number of police may have been more important). But the rhetoric seems to thrive because of the bad connotations of urban blight. Whether it has much to say about white-collar crime is doubtful, with the risk that, absent a sharp increase in the total volume of enforcement, bigger, harder cases get crowded out.

If the SEC is too soft, why? Many blame the revolving door—the movement of star lawyers back and forth between elite corporate practice and the SEC. Some research does show a lesser likelihood of SEC sanction against companies that are active lobbyists and campaign contributors.[49] Bigger firms do get more flexible, lenient treatment than smaller ones.[50] On the other hand, research also shows that stars on the enforcement staff—based on the size of the notches on their belts—do especially well in the job market after they leave.[51] Aggressiveness (within reason) seems to be attractive to Wall Street and law firms. Whatever the right strategy for career success, SEC enforcement staff members are surely prone to self-serving biases, too, and unconsciously conflate what is best for investors (or the best that can be achieved under the circumstances) with self-promotion.

An alternative explanation for what might appear to be a toothless SEC is simply one of scarce resources: the SEC has been forced to live in relative poverty given what is being asked of it. To be sure, enforcement intensity is higher in the United States than anywhere else, but that is simply relative. Settlements on somewhat favorable terms to the subjects are a necessity if the Commission can't credibly threaten to litigate, because defense lawyers know that the staff can't afford to take more than a handful of cases to trial each year. That also results in corporate fines rather than the more challenging individual enforcement actions, especially aimed at corporate higher-ups, and fewer admissions of guilt. There is a natural reluctance for the SEC to get involved in too many complex investigations in the first place, where the costs in terms of manpower and technology can be massive. No one wants the SEC's equivalent of Vietnam or the Middle East wars—discouragingly massive and costly efforts that produce no readily definable victory anyway.

Madoff

The SEC's failure to catch Bernard Madoff notwithstanding the efforts of whistle-blower Harry Markopolos to alert the SEC to his massive Ponzi scheme is another familiar indictment, loudly invoked both by those who want to cut the SEC's budget further (why give more money to the inept) and by those who want more toughness but doubt that it will ever come from a government bureaucracy. Madoff was a well-known and well-respected Wall Street broker—with close contacts at the SEC and elsewhere—who gradually built a separate private money management business by promising that he would engage in proprietary options-based investment strategies that would make solid (if not spectacular) returns in all kinds of markets, the kind of consistency many investors covet. And to most, the reported returns were just as promised. But the essence of a Ponzi scheme is that the returns aren't real—the schemer is simply creating the illusion by constantly prospecting for new money that is then used to pay off the first rounds of investors. Madoff created what was probably history's largest such scheme, right under the SEC's nose.

Most accounts of the SEC's fault for the Madoff scandal suggest that the staff essentially blew off Markopolos, but that is not quite right. The Commission did open multiple investigations and questioned Madoff. Their failures to understand Madoff's unusual trading strategy, communicate with each other, and ask Madoff the right questions were all inexcusable. But there was a backstory: key people who had been detailed to the Madoff investigation were told to move on when Eliot Spitzer publicized the mutual fund market timing scandal, because the SEC felt pressured to show that it was fully deployed on that particular issue. This was not a good choice, but more understandable when resources are painfully thin, when (cognitively) there were reasons to doubt that anyone as prominent as Madoff could be pulling such a stunt, and when the press and politicians can dictate what gets attention without realizing the opportunity costs. The SEC's enforcement motivations are always complicated, especially when it has to make do with less than any reasonable estimate of what it takes to police our financial markets.

The SEC as Robo-Cop

One of the big questions of the moment is whether technology might help the SEC be a more productive enforcer—a "Big Data" opportunity in the public sector. We've already seen that many quantifiable factors seem to correlate with fraudulent activity. There has been booming scholarly interest in finding "tips and tells" in corporate disclosures, press releases, and conference calls that might signal that management is hiding something. Managers who are trying to conceal demonstrate much more positive emotion and avoid anxiety words when speaking to investors. Cues like tone of voice and the use of particular words in conference calls generate immediate stock price reactions, in one direction or the other.[52]

Though this prediction research is still in its infancy (and filled with methodological squabbling), it is intriguing in its connections to fraud prevention. For example, research by Craig Lewis (formerly the SEC's chief economist) found substantial word clustering in financial disclosures by firms later found liable for fraud in government enforcement actions as compared to nonfraud firms. These wrongdoers were light on discussions of managerial characteristics, financial liquidity, and thorough explanations for financial performance; unusually heavy on highlighting mergers, new products, and growth strategies. Like magicians, they want you pay attention elsewhere, not where the trickery is taking place.

The SEC has shown an interest in developing this surveillance capacity in-house,[53] which some referred to as its "robo-cop" program (and the SEC does successfully use sophisticated data analytics in inspections of securities firms and detecting insider trading). There is some low-hanging fruit—in the related area of fraud by investment managers, for instance, one study used risk profiling to identify a 5% segment of advisers responsible for 40% of the total dollar losses from fraud during the period studied.[54] But the prediction of corporate fraud is daunting, partly because our knowledge is so primitive. The discoveries are statistically significant, but at relatively low levels—in other words, any results will contain numerous false positives. Time will be wasted tracking down many false leads. In addition, linguistic patterns of fraud are dynamic, changing in response to new conditions and opportunities. The SEC's artificial intelligence capacity has to be constantly learning and adapting, which is extraordinarily expensive and requires sustained technological sophistication and resources. Government agencies rarely get the budgets to keep abreast of the latest developments. Hedge funds and analysts are likely to be the more successful innovators in this area, with the computer power to dive deep and quickly into the data and exploit any edge this gives them. They supposedly have already asked former FBI agents and others to help them learn to detect corporate lies and will no doubt find this analytic potential increasingly attractive, maybe even be willing to share their findings with the SEC.

FRAUD-ON-THE-MARKET CLASS ACTIONS

Public authorities do not have a monopoly on enforcing the securities laws. The idea that victims themselves should be able to sue fraudsters to remedy their own losses makes sense. For those worried about bureaucratic incentives, letting victims sue is an appealing alternative, and also does justice: a mechanism for compensation as well as additional deterrence. In the securities statutes, Congress sometimes creates an explicit right of action for victims, as with respect to public offerings under the Securities Act. For the venerable Rule 10b-5 there is no explicit remedy, but—long ago, in a time when the virtues of securities regulation were largely taken for granted—the courts implied one anyway. Ever since, they have had to figure out without help from Congress or the SEC what the standards for recovery should be. As we'll see, it didn't take long for private litigation, too, to get bogged down in claims about ambition, motivations, and politics.

The Class Action Debate

Think about a large-scale corporate fraud, like Enron. The intuition is that the harm to investors must have been massive—all shareholders suffered losses when the company collapsed. But normally in the law of fraud, a victim has to show reliance on what was misstated, so that there was a causal connection between the lies and a decision to buy or sell the company's stock. That narrows the class of victims considerably, and introduces a procedural complication. If private securities litigation forced each investor to prove reliance individually, the lawsuit would get bogged down and exceedingly costly—it's hard to imagine how the case could be managed, given thousands of investors and millions of trades.

In the late 1980s, in *Basic Inc. v. Levinson*,[55] the Supreme Court embraced a solution to this that some lower courts had fashioned, with momentous—and in many ways unexpected—consequences. The Court determined that reliance on a material misrepresentation could be *presumed*, so that it didn't have to be demonstrated, so long as the stock in question was traded in an efficient market (the tricky concept we encountered in chapter 1). The idea was that most investors trust the market to impound information rapidly and efficiently, rather than do that work themselves. So reliance on the market was reliance on the fraud.

By making it easy for investors to form themselves into a class, the Court created a stunning corporate liability risk. Today, claim damages in these kinds of "fraud on the market" cases easily run into the billions of dollars. For a variety of understandable reasons, companies and their executives are loath to go to trial in the face of such exposure, even if they think they probably would win the case. Juries, after all, are never predictable. And the costs associated with taking the case to trial—legal fees and the like—can be in the tens of millions of dollars in a complex case even if defendants win. The bad publicity and distractions associated with the lawsuit add to the reluctance to litigate to the end. As a result, the bulk of these cases settle unless defendants can get them dismissed early on. Settling a case for $100 million is a lot, but not when there was a risk of a billion-dollar verdict, especially if insurance obtained by the company covers some or all of that settlement. Most companies have lots of insurance.[56]

With the ease of settlement comes temptation to bring more and more lawsuits, because this is a lucrative business. When the lawyers for the plaintiff class win at trial or get a settlement, they have a right to compensation for their efforts. Typically, the figure is somewhere between 15% and 30% of the amount recovered for the victims. So with a $100 million settlement, the lawyers can expect $20 million or so. In the last fifteen years or so, securities class action settlements in the aggregate totaled some $70 billion. For these, plaintiffs' lawyers took some $17 billion in fees and expenses. Most of these were 10b-5 fraud-on-the-market cases.[57]

Not surprisingly, corporate officers and directors decry this litigation as legalized extortion. Revelation of bad news that causes a company's stock price to drop leads to the filing of a lawsuit, as plaintiffs' lawyers comb through all the company's prior filings and press releases to find something that led investors to believe that all was well. Psychology, as we saw, teaches that even innocently optimistic statements can look like a lie in hindsight. Critics claim that many dubious cases are brought only because the plaintiffs' lawyers are confident in extracting a settlement, with fees that more than justify the effort. The story, in other words, is of lawyerly greed. Supporting this impression (though maybe just a continuation of the nasty politics) is that some of America's best-known securities class action lawyers of the 1990s went to jail for how they incentivized clients to pursue securities class actions.

Plaintiffs' lawyers say the claims of greed are nonsense. The large volume of cases simply shows how much some corporate executives are willing lie to protect their power and compensation; the eagerness to settle on the defense side is a demonstration that the cases have merit and that the defendants are afraid to go in front of a jury to defend themselves. Their story, in other words, is of widespread executive corruption, against which the lawyers (not the SEC) are the investors' best champion.

This is a very bitter battle, played out both in Congress and the courts, with lots of money at stake. The business community got Congress to pare back on fraud-on-the-market cases in the Private Securities Litigation Reform Act in 1995, but to a far lesser extent than its lobbyists hoped. *Basic* was saved from being overturned, but a host of new procedural hurdles made these kinds of cases harder to bring. That legislative compromise sits uneasily among federal judges who lean hard toward one side or the other. Once, as we saw, the judicial voice consistently favored strong investor rights. In the mid to late 1970s, however, there was a shift to the right and greater sensitivity to regulatory costs and business interests. The Supreme Court rejected the idea that judges should freely imply rights for victims; that's for Congress, not the courts. But the holdings from earlier days live on. Today, some conservative judges see the surviving remnants of the earlier era as the illegitimate children of judicial activism, perhaps with a right to life but little cause for sustenance. Fraud on the market is one of these juristic bastards.

Who's Hurt and Why?

Judicial ideology aside, what should investors think about these cases?[58] The fraud-on-the-market theory (which the Supreme Court reaffirmed in 2014, with a tweak)[59] says that all purchasers or sellers who relied on the fraud in an efficient market in the expansive way we've just described—in other words, nearly every purchaser or seller during the time of the alleged fraud—should recover the loss suffered. This is based on the idea that the investor was harmed in buying the stock at an inflated (i.e., distorted) price. So if you bought Tyco stock at, say, $95 per share and then watched it collapse, you'd claim compensation for the difference between $95 and wherever the price ended up when the fraud was revealed. That's the per share recovery. Given the extraordinarily large amount of trading that happens in the stock of a widely followed company, those numbers aggregate into extremely large sums. As we saw, class-wide claims in a single case often go into the billions of dollars.

Not surprisingly, there are many obstacles standing between your demand for compensation and a check in the amount that makes you whole. But let's put those technical litigation questions aside for a moment and think about this approach to compensation, particularly for investors who did not rely in the eyeball sense on the fraud. For these victims, as we've seen, what we have is largely a system of fraud insurance. And thinking about this as insurance delivers some important insights.

There are two eye-openers, which legal scholars have been debating for some time. First, there is no doubt that you "lost" by buying stock at an inflated price. But all securities trades are two-sided, so that your loss was somebody else's gain. Who, then, was the winner on the other side of your trade? Although it could have been an insider who knew about the fraud (and hence insider trading), probably not. The vast majority of trades during the time of a fraud are between investors who are oblivious to it, so that marketplace activity actually generates almost as much windfall for investors as losses.

Keep that in mind. If you're an active trader, you have pretty much the same chance of being better off by the fraud as being harmed. And over time, therefore, your gains and losses from fraud should average out to about zero. If you're worried about the losses being particularly devastating when luck runs against you, remember that most investors are well diversified. For them, financial devastation is unlikely. (This is why, in big frauds like Enron and WorldCom, the investors we should feel the most sorry for are employees and retirees whose holdings are heavily concentrated in that one stock.) The netting effect is important because it makes little sense to buy insurance for issuer-specific risks when you're well diversified anyway, and are likely to have fraud gains as well as fraud losses. Indeed, if you get to keep your windfall gains and are compensated for all your losses, you end up being *better off* as a result of corporate fraud.

But this idea by itself doesn't eliminate the case for fraud insurance.[60] You can think of many kinds of investors for whom netting doesn't quite work—long-term investors who habitually buy and hold their stock, for example, or index funds whose holdings expand over time, systematically buying more than they sell. And of course there are employees and retirees locked into buying company stock but prevented or dissuaded from selling it. In other words, netting works for active traders; not so much for long-term investors.

That's where the second eye-opener comes. As noted earlier, the vast majority of investors in the stock of a company that commits fraud have no right to sue. Every investor in a company that has misrepresented the truth feels victimized when he or she watches the value of holdings plummet after a fraud is revealed. But the only shareholders who can sue are ones who bought after the lies started, and still held after the truth came out. Others didn't buy at a distorted price. Rule 10b-5 is a remedy for deception, not corporate mismanagement. Some time ago, the Supreme Court said that there is no right of action for people who said they held onto their stock in reliance on what turned out to be fraudulent.[61] While that holding was justified as pragmatic (avoiding nightmarish proof problems), it makes sense conceptually as well. If all shareholders learn the sad truth at once and try to sell in anything approaching an efficient market, the price will collapse anyway.

When there is a judgment or a settlement of a securities fraud class action, that sum of money is almost entirely paid out by some combination of three sources. The first is the corporation itself, if it's still solvent. But as with SEC enforcement actions that fine the company, taking money from the company treasury to a large degree comes out of the pockets of the current shareholders. So to this extent, money shifts from the pockets of current shareholders to the smaller subset of investors (who may or may not still be shareholders) who were relatively recent purchasers. Think about the buy-and-hold investor. While such a person could be in the victimized class (and probably be a net loser to fraud over time), it's just as likely—if not more—that most or all of his or her purchases occurred before the fraud. In other words, it's more likely that that typical kind of investor ends up (indirectly) paying damages rather than receiving them, or both paying and receiving, but more the former.

There are two other potential sources for funding a judgment or settlement. As noted, most companies buy insurance to cover the risks of lawsuits. Settlements in fraud cases, at least, can be partially or fully paid by the insurers rather than the company. But these insurance policies are paid for by companies, and so the insurance system—as a whole—is also funded, indirectly, by investors. The same pocket shifting still occurs, albeit from a greater number of investor pockets.

The third source is third parties—investment banks and accounting firms, usually—who assisted the fraud. Those firms pay out of their own pockets (and indirectly, if they are publicly held, their shareholders' pockets). We have far less circularity here, to be sure, even though investment banks and accounting firms charge prices that reflect their litigation risks (it's a cost of doing business), so that these costs are at least partly passed on to the corporation (and shareholders) paying those prices. However, this kind of third-party liability is now relatively rare. In a series of cases, the Supreme Court made clear its distaste for third-party liability in implied rights of action, meaning that liability is least available where it's most useful.[62]

The Dilemma of Compensation

So where does this leave us on the main question: does fraud-on-the-market compensation help investors, hurt them, neither, or some of both? In the aggregate it's largely a form of pocket shifting, though we shouldn't take the idea of shareholders bearing the entire cost as literally true. Instead, it is a form of insurance that many shareholders—the more active traders and the well diversified—don't need all that much. Longer-term and indexed investors are more exposed to loss, but only to the extent they traded during the class period. Company shareholders who didn't trade during the class period get nothing, and foot much of the bill.

The best way to answer the question, then, is to ask investors how much they would pay for this kind of protection. I suspect that many would decide they don't need it at all given the point about the netting of gains and losses and the effects of diversification. Others might see it as potentially useful, but then comes the question of cost. Indirectly, shareholders pay for the attorneys' fees for both sides, the steep premiums paid to the insurance companies, and the uninsured amounts transferred to injured investors. Even if we just consider the attorneys' fees, we're talking about 15%–30% of settlement amounts on the plaintiffs' side and at least that—some say much more—on the defense lawyer side.

That makes this very expensive insurance, for risks that most victims can bear. There doesn't have to be complete circularity (100% pocket shifting) to conclude that—from a compensatory standpoint—this product has an excessive markup. The SEC and consumer advocates are usually suspicious of the sale of securities or insurance that have such high costs and fees embedded in them, and offer relatively little in return. And there is evidence that some investors, at least, don't care much. A study found that a large number of institutional investors—the ones with the largest losses—never bother to claim their compensation after a case is settled and the money sitting ready to be paid out. They identified billions of dollars left on the table as a matter of either ignorance or disinterest on the part of the money managers.[63] And after the Supreme Court surprisingly declared in 2010 that this cause of action was not available to investors who buy or sell stock outside the United States (e.g., on a foreign stock exchange),[64] there was little immediate evidence that sophisticated investors sought to trade in the United States rather than on a foreign exchange when that choice was available. As Robert Bartlett puts it, "That the presence or absence of the Rule 10b-5 private right of action has such little consequence on institutional investors' trading would thus seem to call into question the value of exporting the current system of private 10b-5 securities suits as a primary means of encouraging greater capital formation."[65]

And then there is the matter of stock market efficiency. When the fraud-on-the-market theory was set in place in the 1980s, conservative academics, judges, and policymakers were surprisingly enthusiastic about it. It was not that they were all of a sudden plaintiff friendly. Rather, they were intrigued by the science of testing when it is that efficient markets are distorted by fraud. They believed that sophisticated statistical techniques could do much better than the subjective inferences of ordinary judges and juries in determining the merits of these cases. By looking carefully at how the market price of the stock responded to the alleged misrepresentation (or how it responded later on when the truth came out), we'd know whether the information was important and unexpected, whether that price was distorted, and how much loss investors suffered. One of the pioneers was a law professor at the University of Chicago, Dan Fischel, who both synthesized the idea of fraud on the market as good science and founded a consulting firm to provide expert analysis on these questions in court. The latter earned him a fortune, which may have bolstered the enthusiasm he felt for the doctrine even as other conservative scholars later started turning against it.

Today there is more doubt about how efficient the markets really are, perhaps subject to mood swings, overreaction, and underreaction. As the Supreme Court said when reaffirming *Basic* in 2014, this evidence is not necessarily fatal to the idea of fraud on the market: fraud predictably distorts prices, even if we doubt that the reaction to the misinformation will necessarily be instant or precise. (Some of the country's most distinguished financial economists filed an amicus brief in the Court to stress that point.) But it does make one wonder precisely what it means for an investor to *rely* on market "integrity" in an all-too-human, noisy financial marketplace. More importantly, these doubts challenge the confidence we once seemed to have in our ability to measure distortion with scientific precision, so that damages accurately capture the difference between what innocent investors paid for their stock and what their wealth would be in the counterfactual world where no fraud had been committed. Even in a perfectly rational market, that's much harder than the enthusiasts anticipated. In a messy world where price reactions vary based on sentiment, it's guesswork.

DETERRENCE

The foregoing leads many people (including me) to doubt that our costly system of fraud-on-the-market class actions can fully be justified on compensatory grounds, even if we concede that some investors clearly deserve a remedy. But that's only half the story. Perhaps the greater value of such litigation is in deterring misconduct, so that less fraud occurs in the first place because of the threat of such high-dollar lawsuits. As we've seen, fraud surely causes harm to some investors, along with much social harm. Plaintiffs' lawyers have for a long time insisted that they provide more focused, relentless advocacy when allowed to pursue cases on behalf of investors. They point to high-dollar settlements where the SEC got much less or nothing, and came late or not at all to scandals that they uncovered.

The question is how much value class actions add to the deterrence that already exists.[66] Maybe a great deal—no one can ignore the threat of the multi-billion-dollar liability we've just described. Here, the main question becomes one that is also raised by SEC enforcement: how well does deterrence work when the main (and sometimes only) defendant is the *corporate* wrongdoer.[67] The problem isn't hard to see. A large fine by the SEC or billion-dollar settlement by the corporation of a class action suit comes not from the pockets of the wrongdoing executives, but out of the corporate treasury or (in the private litigation setting) insurance. That's indirectly money from the shareholders' pockets, which doesn't seem quite right given that investors are usually thought of as the victims of fraud rather than its perpetrators. Critics of the SEC's campaign of big corporate penalties and of the class action apparatus say that both are abusive, ways of generating headlines and taking advantages of management's anxiousness to settle so long as other people's money will fund an end to the unpleasantness.

At least for SEC enforcement, we shouldn't overstate this concern. Shareholders often benefit from the kind of dishonesty we've been describing; as we've seen, the motivations for hiding or avoiding bad news often come from intensity, passion, and competitiveness. Or the dishonesty is directed at preserving access to the debt markets, which also benefit equity holders. Cover-ups almost always try to protect the corporation and shareholders (and executives, to be sure) from the immediate devastations of revealing the truth. Given that, a corporate penalty for the fraud is not entirely unjustified as a matter of corrective justice.

The deterrence issue is made more difficult with respect to class actions, however, because of insurance. The SEC will ordinarily bar any insurance coverage of fines or penalties, for obvious reasons. But plaintiffs' lawyers are simply anxious to maximize the payout, from whatever source. Individual contributions to settlement amounts and judgments are rare.[68] In a study of the role of insurance in private securities litigation, Tom Baker and Sean Griffith showed the extent to which insurers go to satisfy the officers and directors who make the decision to buy their policies. As a matter of law, intentional harms are not insurable (one reason that executives are so anxious to settle—no one wants to be left without protection after trial). Settlements, on the other hand, can be funded without much risk of criticism. Insurance softens the blow to the shareholders, but also lessens deterrence. We might hope that insurers would take steps toward fraud prevention so as to manage their own risks, but there is little evidence that they do so. Companies and their executives want platinum coverage (at company expense), which means deferring to management's wishes both before a claim and after. Fortunately from a deterrence perspective, if not the shareholders', policy limits mean that the company ends up paying some of the settlement. But the bite is almost surely diminished. As a result, the cost-benefit calculus of deliberate wrongdoing tilts further in the direction of doing it and letting the company and the insurers bear the risk of the lawsuit—a classic moral hazard problem. The same would be true if we see corporate fraud as a "last period" problem, where the executives are motivated by trying to save their careers by concealing the sorry truth.[69]

Another reason not to put too much faith in deterrence from corporate liability via fines, judgments, or settlements is the one we've stressed. Where cognitive blind spots and information diffusion distort perception and delay recognition of the risk of fraud, the awareness doesn't come until too late. Liability risk is also somewhat manipulable, which may kick in the illusion of control. When there is corrective disclosure after discovery of some prior falsity, bad news will often be bundled together with other bits of information about the company that make it hard to disentangle the portion of the stock price drop attributable to revelation of the fraud from the impact the other information that was disclosed that day. Indeed, there is a fairly obvious message to company officials who want to bury a corrective disclosure: bundle it with lots of other news, either separate bad news or separate good news that offsets the effect. Maybe even lie again to mask the effects of the previous lie. There is evidence that corporate managers have learned to bundle their disclosure of bad news with other announcements in order to muddy the effects of disclosing the truth on the prevailing market price of their stock.[70]

Notwithstanding all this, there has to be *some* deterrence value to corporate liability, and this is the best argument for the social good of corporate fines and fraud-on-the-market lawsuits. The threat of large-dollar lawsuits is very salient as a general matter, and may incline lawyers, accountants, independent directors, and others who play a role in the disclosure process toward more caution and candor than reigns in the exuberance of the executive team. Big settlements send a message that many hear. In this regard there is some helpful (though inconclusive) empirical evidence.[71] Notwithstanding insurance, variations in settlements do seem to reflect that the lawsuits have some merit.[72] When a company settles a financial reporting case, we observe other companies in the same geographical area becoming more cautious in their accounting and disclosure, compared to ones further away. And after settlements, companies do make changes to their corporate governance and disclosure practices that seem to be valued by investors as reflected in the company's market price. Some message seems to be getting through.

So back to the question with which we started this section: does the fraud-on-the-market lawsuit make investors better off? Perhaps the best way to pose the question is the way Bill Bratton and Michael Wachter do.[73] From investors' standpoint, would you agree to an abolition of such class actions in return for a doubling or tripling of the SEC's enforcement budget? It does go back to the incentives problem, but as we've said, people raise incentives problems with respect to class action lawyers, too. I'm sure there is some figure at which the trade-off would be worthwhile. But no one is currently offering that deal, and if you're concerned about too much corporate fraud and convinced that the system of weeding out low-merit cases is working, the system of private securities litigation may do just enough deterrence work to earn its keep.

Whether or not that is so, we could no doubt design a better system for investors. For now, however, no one with political muscle has an overwhelming incentive to change the law too radically. Plaintiffs' lawyers benefit from fraud-on-the-market lawsuits and the strong settlement incentives they create, especially with such extensive insurance funding. They know that going after the executives makes settlement more difficult and less likely, and so go easy on them. Executives and directors, in turn, hate fraud on the market but recognize that it's insurable and not much of personal threat at all. Defense lawyers may shed some tears on their clients' behalf, but make the most money of all from the system. Sadly, then, we have a fairly stable political equilibrium, changeable only with a strong power shift that is unlikely to make investors' best interests (whatever they are) the point of major concern.

HALF-TRUTHS, PUFFERY, AND PROTECTIVE DISCLOSURE

We now have a list of reasons why the enforcement of the antifraud rules is not as potent as it could be, frustrating the ability to deter. To this we can add one more: the law itself creates opportunities and incentives to conceal and dissemble, further enabling the self-serving inferences that make it seem that all is under control. We've already seen the psychology of this—frank reporting is often an admission of failure, which managers resist, rationalize, and often enough avoid. When disclosure happens, it's often downplayed, attributing failures to situational factors, just as success is ordinarily portrayed as the result of skill and foresight.

As we'll see in more detail in chapter 4, the securities laws impose extensive periodic disclosure responsibilities on public companies and their managers. These are supposed to overcome the reluctance to divulge, and bring lawyers and others into the disclosure process. Yet while these obligations are frustratingly extensive in many respects, they are also strikingly limited when it comes to many of the most sensitive things that may be going on inside the business. Our full disclosure philosophy turns out to be much less than it first appears, which weakens its normative punch.[74]

Suppose that information is percolating up inside a company about slowing sales and glitches in its next-generation product line. There is no real time obligation to disclose this kind of bad news. Every quarter, financial results will have to published, but those look backward to fiscal periods already closed. (And revenue recognition practices might give management some discretion that can be used to smooth things out even there.) Management does have an obligation to explain about known trends and uncertainties that are "reasonably likely" to happen, as a heads-up to investors still relying on positive past results. But deciding what's "reasonably likely" involves an exercise of judgment that is difficult to make without bias.

The Discourse of Disclosure

So how do managers speak to the market when they have something to hide and no clear-cut duty to disclose? This is unstable territory. The markets have a thirst for information, and "no comment" is a signal of something you want to hide, especially if the company is usually more forthcoming. It may simply pique the interest of journalists, analysts, investors, and regulators, making them press harder to figure out what's going on. There has been a lively debate among legal academics, at least, about whether if we're serious about letting companies keep secrets for competitive reasons, we shouldn't let them lie to preserve that secrecy to the greatest extent possible.[75] That would involve some difficult line-drawing problems as we move away from true competitive secrets (strategic plans, mergers, etc.) to that which management wants to conceal mainly because the truth would be harmful to the company (and to the managers). As a result, the law sticks to a duty of candor if the company chooses to speak.

The liability threat is somewhat enhanced by the half-truth doctrine. When executives speak, they can't hide behind technicalities in order to mislead. Think of a pharmaceutical company that has been challenged by the Food and Drug Administration for some safety issue at two of its manufacturing plants. There was a more minor deficiency at one of the plants, which has been settled with the FDA with a minor fine. There are still pending negotiations about the bigger problems at the other plant, with a good chance that the fine and the remedial obligations will be painful. If the company were asked about rumors of problems with the FDA, it would be technically true to say that "the issue at Plant 1 has been resolved without material penalty to the company." But it would also be a half-truth, and thus fraudulent, because omitting the other, bigger problem renders the response misleading. Plaintiffs' lawyers would be all over that statement after the bigger bad news about FDA sanctions later came out. (That said, psychological research suggests that "artful paltering" of this sort is perceived by speakers as far less blameworthy than outright lies, and thus more common.)[76]

But like the duties with respect to risk disclosure, the half-truth doctrine is restricted to cognizably "material" developments, which in the face of uncertainty involves a managerial assessment of the probability of the bad event happening (and the magnitude of the impact if it does). When biases suppress the perception of risk, the assessment of materiality becomes biased as well.

Puffery

What if company officials said, "We're comfortable in where are with the FDA"? Given the good chance of a bad outcome with regulators, this doesn't seem particularly honest. Yet in the eyes of many judges, that might not be fraud because of something called the puffery doctrine. General statements of optimism, even in response to private signals of trouble, are lawful because reasonable investors don't pay attention to corporate happy talk. A good illustration involved Centel Corporation, which was faced with financial distress and forced to auction off most of its valuable cellular properties, if not the whole company.[77] Privately, the company was concerned about the underwhelming interest bidders were showing in those properties when they came to do their due diligence inspections. But when asked about how the auction was going, the company's official response was that it was going "very smoothly." Later on, the auction was pretty much a failure.

The court held that there was no fraud on the market. The opinion for the court of appeals was written by Judge Richard Posner, well steeped in law, economics, and finance. He invoked the efficient market hypothesis and said that the smart money understands the language of business, and wouldn't read "smoothly" as anything but a weasel word that could cover a range from disappointing to excellent. (In a departure from how many judges would handle this, he did say that "smoothly" would have been misleading had the truth been totally disastrous.) In explaining his nuanced reading, Posner suggested that corporate speech is like the letters of recommendation he gets when he's about to hire someone. The word "outstanding," presumably, actually means good. Calling someone good means you probably shouldn't expect all that much. The truth is not expected, so that if a recommender were to be honest (saying good when she really means good), the reader would be misled and the applicant judged too harshly. When "puffing is the order of the day," Posner said, "literal truth can be profoundly misleading." And he's quite sure that puffing is the order of the day in corporate America.

What a disorienting idea—yet very much the law, and often applied by judges far less sophisticated than Posner. What this does is create a corporate free speech zone, free of fraud liability, so long as it stays in certain confines of contextual ambiguity. The puffery defense (which applies in many settings besides the securities markets) makes ample sense if there is a common skepticism of the sort Posner assumes: market actors who simply ignore such language and whose behavior constrains the market price so that it isn't moved by the countervailing forces of either emotion or gullibility. As a result, there is no price distortion.

But is he right?[78] To some extent this takes us to the more skeptical current understanding of market efficiency, in which sentiment might play a role so that hype works. Yet even if we stick fairly closely to the assumption that rational forces drive market reactions, there is room to wonder about such strong faith that rational actors pay no attention to generalities. There is evidence, for example, that management's reputation for credibility is *priced* in the market—part of why a stock price drops after the discovery of fraud is the loss of credibility. (There is an interesting debate about whether this "credibility discount" should be part of the class's recovery in a fraud-on-the-market lawsuit.) If managers have built up a reputation for credibility, maybe the market takes them at their word that "smoothly" really does mean "well" rather than some less positive assessment. Managers speak repeatedly to the market, and what they say should be taken in the context of ongoing dialogue. So, for example, saying, "We're pleased with what's happening" might seem very vague and general in isolation, but seems more reliable if it comes after a more specific disclosure of an exciting new product development and implies, in essence, that everything is still on track to meet expectations. If that is how markets interpret management's disclosures, the puffery doctrine is much too simple-minded because it misses the importance of both credibility and context. And again, most judges applying the doctrine are less careful than Posner, dismissing cases simply by reference to the generality of the word choice.

Though many judges are being overly simplistic in puffery cases, there probably is something important driving the instinct to create a fraud-free zone. First, note that general statements of optimism may be habitual in executives chosen for that trait. In other words, this category may be one where there are particularly strong doubts about whether what was said was deliberately wrong as opposed to well-meaning even though not entirely realistic. The puffery doctrine may be a buffer where the risk of erroneous scienter inferences is particularly high.

Second, this is precisely the context in which event studies and related statistical techniques are unlikely to be of help—most corporate speech that uses generalities is of the confirmatory sort, not a way of signaling significant change. So we wouldn't expect to see distinctive stock price reactions to it. If we let the case go forward anyway, we're asking for a good deal of speculation from the judge or jury. And precisely because credibility has to be important here, allowing cases of puffery to go forward means that company officials would have no liability if their credibility was low, whereas precisely the same words uttered by some other executives would be actionable because they were more trustworthy. Those are slippery distinctions on which to base judgments involving millions of dollars of liability. I suspect that what many judges are doing in cases like these is to say, "I wouldn't be a damn fool to rely on language like that" and project that self-assessment onto the marketplace as a whole.

Finally, and almost by definition, puffery cases arise when there is no duty to speak with clarity. That is to say, the SEC makes companies disclose quarterly results in accord with generally accepted accounting principles, producing hard numbers. When there is a duty to disclose, puffery provides no opportunity for protection from liability. So when puffery happens, it's usually a way of concealing some unpleasant facts that the company was not, at the time, obligated to disclose. That important because of how the fraud-on-the-market doctrine works. Recall that the idea behind fraud on the market is that investors should be compensated when they buy or sell at a distorted price, one higher or lower than it should have been. The key here is "should have been." To use an example from before, assume a stock price around $20, reflecting the market's expectations about the company's performance. Inside the company, some bit of bad news emerges, but not such that there is any immediate duty to disclose. If the company remains silent, investors who buy at $20 are hurt (the price doesn't reflect the hidden truth), but they have no right to recover, because the company's silence was lawful.

Then why should it make a difference if company executives puff? The puff might (falsely) confirm the market's erroneous impression than nothing had changed, but doesn't necessarily cause harm above or beyond what would have been suffered by investors had nothing at all been said. No harm, no foul. There is the possibility, of course, that the puffery disarmed the market, lulling it into thinking all is well when, but for the puffery, there would have been more skepticism. Maybe, but that counterfactual inference would be very hard to be sure about. What the puffery doctrine does is to create a tool to enable the concealment of information when the law does not otherwise insist on its disclosure. Management only takes on the duty to reveal the truth only when it speaks to the issue with greater specificity, so that the risk of lulling or misleading is more palpable.

Bespeaking Caution

We can compare puffery to a related doctrine that also deals how corporate executives speak to the market: the "bespeaks caution" defense. The statutory form of this was adopted by Congress in the 1995 Reform Act, and was the reason President Clinton vetoed the bill, only to be overridden by supermajorities in Congress. Essentially, it says a company can make projections and estimates about its future performance without fear of liability, so long as the forward-looking statement is accompanied by meaningful cautionary language warning investors of important factors that might lead the projections or estimates to be wrong.

That sounds sensible, but think about it. Imagine that, for the worst of reasons (a short-term desire to pump up the stock price), management makes an earnings estimate for the next year that far exceeds what it privately believes is likely. In terms of liability, why should it matter that what follows the false estimate is a statement that the expectations might not come to pass because, for example, a competitor might introduce a new product that renders one of the company's key products obsolete (a fairly standard cautionary warning)? Or even ten or twenty similar warnings? Cautionary language might counter an investor's naive belief that projections and estimates are dependable. But intelligent investors already know that estimates about the future are only that: best guesses that are inevitably subject to change. In anything resembling an efficient market, such warnings are unnecessary and entirely useless unless they convey something about management's assessment of the probabilities that something may go amiss, not just the possibility. But there is no requirement of that in the statute.

So what Congress seemed to do was create a low-cost right to lie about future expectations. That would make sense only if smart investors pay no attention to projections and estimates anyway, so that we lump them together with puffery. The empirical evidence, however, is that earnings estimates matter to the market. Even though smart investors presumably understand the potential for optimistic bias (deliberate or cognitive), the market reacts—often sharply—to estimates that exceed or fall short of expectations. To be sure, management pays a price in its reputation for credibility if it too often overestimates performance. But in the face of some "last period" pressure or an optimism-commitment whipsaw, managers might lie anyway and hope for a miracle.

The question for Congress was whether guarding against that risk was worth more than giving honest (even if optimistically) inclined managers the sense of freedom that they can make whatever estimates they want without fear of a big-dollar fraud-on-the-market lawsuit if the estimate was off the mark. Given the other changes made by the Reform Act, particularly the heightened pleading standard that requires plaintiffs to have compelling enough evidence that the fraud was deliberate, maybe this was too much protection for managers.

Interestingly, many judges have reacted skeptically to claims of this safe harbor from liability. A handful have simply ignored the plain language of the statute and held that no amount of cautionary language can protect managers when there is enough evidence that the projection was a lie. Others have been more clever, acknowledging the availability of the harbor but denying its safety in the particular case because the cautionary language was just not "meaningful" enough. Even Judge Frank Easterbrook—inclined to think much like Posner (though they don't agree on everything)—wrote an opinion that infuriated the business community in saying that cautionary language would not immunize fraud unless it were determined by a judge that it represented the known risks about the future that management considered the most important.[79] That would be hard for management to show if they were hiding things that were likely to throw the projection off course, which was exactly Easterbrook's point.

Not all judges do finesse their interpretation of the law—others adhere faithfully to Congress's text, consequences be damned. The resisters seem to prefer the line drawn in the puffery cases. Where there is no duty to disclose—and there is no duty to make projections or estimates—management has a right to silence and the ability to speak in generalities without fear. But when what is given to investors is specific and important enough, reliance by informed investors is likely, and the market will move, we have real distortion, feeding the concern on which fraud on the market is based.

To nonlawyers, these references to duty, materiality, cautionary language, and the like might seem unduly refined and totally mystifying. But think of these as rules of discourse that corporate managers and investors are expected to learn and put to use. Some things can be kept secret, while other things can't. This muddiness in the law allows self-serving managerial biases to flourish, because there is so much wiggle room. So where secrecy is permissible, take what management says with a grain of salt—Posner's reminder of how letters of recommendation work—unless management signals by its clarity and specificity that it is saying something on which investors can rely. Beware of words of opinion and statements that come with an abundance of cautionary language attached, because the liability risk there drops considerably and managers get little negative legal feedback from pushing the lines in displays of optimistic exuberance and competitive posturing. Indeed, remember that this can be a trap in which managers get caught as they feel pressured to do things to live up to their commitments and predictions. For better or worse, the law tolerates hype until the truth eventually gets revealed in the form of disappointing hard numbers. Investors who chase the hype (or the price movements caused by other investors doing the same) rarely get compensated if they later decide that their trust was abused, even when it was.

3

The Insider's Edge

Insider trading touches a very sensitive nerve, and not just among investors. Perhaps there is a bit of envy or jealousy that there are people (not us) who get access to and the opportunity to trade on corporate or financial secrets. Perhaps it's resentment about the very uneven playing field in our financial markets, notwithstanding the pretense otherwise. Whatever the impulse, insider trading fascinates. It has been the plot line of many movies, TV shows, and books, fiction and nonfiction. When there is a criminal prosecution or big SEC case, media coverage is intense and, for the subjects, brutal. Insider trading enforcement blossomed in the 1980s with high-profile actions against Ivan Boesky (who said, "Be greedy and still feel good about yourself," and so was the model for the Gordon Gekko character in the movie *Wall Street* who shouted "Greed is good" at business students) and numerous confederates. It has continued unabated to the present, as hedge fund mogul Raj Rajaratnam and his friend Rajat Gupta—a particularly distinguished and respected man—took their unwanted star turns in the criminal docket and got sent off to jail. In between were many others in the enforcement crosshairs, including some big names like celebrity homemaker Martha Stewart and entrepreneur Mark Cuban. The press obsessed over the New York City federal prosecutor's for-a-time undefeated record in insider trading cases as if covering a sports phenomenon.

The reality is much more complicated. When they sentence convicted insider traders to what are often very lengthy jail terms, judges feel compelled to condemn the crime by calling insider trading an "assault on our free markets" or a "virus on our business culture." But listen closely and you can sometimes hear more ambivalence. The very thoughtful judge Jed Rakoff, from whom we will hear more later in the book, was clearly pained by the sentencing decision involving Gupta.[1] Gupta was convicted for conspiring with Rajaratnam by passing on information that he learned by being a director of Goldman Sachs (including, in the midst of the financial crisis, that Warren Buffett was investing needed equity in Goldman). The US sentencing guidelines, to which judges are expected to adhere, specified a long jail term, calculated largely on the harm caused by the offense, which would be measured by the gains of Gupta's contact, Rajaratnam, made trading with investors. Rakoff acknowledged that it was a strange version of harm, especially since Congress, the courts, and the SEC had not said that the kind of insider trading offense involved here assumed any harm to investors. Instead it was a breach of trust as to the source of the information, Goldman

Sachs, which might have suffered *no* tangible harm at all. And when he turned to Gupta himself, Rakoff found him almost saintly:

> Thus, at the very outset, there is presented the fundamental problem of this sentence, for Mr. Gupta's personal history and characteristics starkly contrast with the nature and circumstances of his crimes. All the evidence before the Court—not just the letters written on Mr. Gupta's behalf but also the objective facts of record—establish beyond cavil that Mr. Gupta has selflessly devoted a huge amount of time and effort to a very wide variety of socially beneficial activities, such as the Global Fund to Fight AIDS, Tuberculosis and Malaria, the Public Health Foundation of India, the Indian School of Business, the Pratham Foundation (which provides quality education to underprivileged children in India), the Cornell Medical School, the Rockefeller Foundation, and many many more. As well summarized in his counsel's sentencing memorandum, such activities are but illustrations of Mr. Gupta's big heart and helping hand, which he extended without fanfare or self-promotion, to all with whom he came in contact.[2]

We'll come back to why Rakoff thought Gupta did what he did (and to be clear, he did blame Gupta for a serious breach of trust). But the uneasiness of sending a good person to jail for a long time based on a very abstract definition of harm was tough to swallow, especially because Rakoff understood the intellectual disconnects very well. There was a special irony in invoking a doctrine designed to promote an even playing field for public investors in a case where the role of poor victim is played by Goldman Sachs.

Insider trading enforcement has become the symbol for the US brand of investor protection, the most emotionally resonant setting for assuring investors that someone is working for them against the forces of greed and arrogance.[3] It's an advertising campaign as much as a legal one, in which regulators and prosecutors proclaim their value and importance in pursuit of both legitimacy and scarce public resources. The guilty pleas and trials are morality plays where we can watch elites and their friends get their comeuppance, maybe forgetting for a brief moment that most investors are still on the downhill half of that still-steep playing field. The more the SEC and criminal prosecutors feel embattled, the more expressive value these cases have. And they offer very good theater indeed.

DECEPTION AND HARM

The usual intuitive sense of the harm from insider trading is that the victims are other investors who were buying stock when the insider was selling on bad news, or selling when the insider was a buyer on good news. Had they known the secret, they wouldn't have traded at the prevailing market price. In efficient market terms, the market would have adjusted on public availability of the news, making the price at which they traded a fair one.

While the instinct makes sense, those same investors almost certainly would have traded anyway, even had there been no insider in the market at the same time. Unless those "victims" can somehow say that they were induced into the market by the insider, there is no way to say that the insider *caused* that damage. And such inducement is unlikely. Most of the time the insider's trades are just a small, unidentifiable piece of the much larger anonymous trading going on in the market at the moment, signifying nothing. There are circumstances where the trade could be large enough to move the price a bit, but even then it's unlikely that any other traders place an order because of that. And—importantly—even if they do, they're not relying on any information beyond the highly uninformative fact of the trade itself. They don't know, usually, who is trading, or why. Markets are impersonal and anonymous. What caused the uninformed traders' loss was the failure of the holder of the secret (usually the company whose shares are being bought or sold) to reveal it publicly. But securities regulation makes clear that companies can keep secrets absent a duty to disclose. So either there was nothing wrong with nondisclosure or there was a violation for which the company and its executives should be blamed, but for the nondisclosure, not the trading.

That disconnect between the insider's trade and the trading of other investors undermines the standard harm story—especially if we are thinking in terms of fraud or deception. When federal insider trading enforcement first started in the 1960s, there was an intellectual counterattack launched by Henry Manne, mentioned earlier as a founder of the law-and-economics movement in securities regulation. Manne claimed that, if anything, insider trading is *good* for markets. To the extent that the trading moves the market price at all, it moves it in the right direction, toward a fairer price, enhancing market efficiency. Someone selling at the same time the insider was buying may get a somewhat better price because of the market move, compared to the price had there been no trading or no impact. (And anyone who buys to jump onto the uptick as an early sign of momentum benefits even more.) Manne stressed another point, too. Allowing insider trading gives executives a source of profit from their positions that should allow companies to pay them less in the form of salaries and bonuses, another benefit to companies and investors.

That seems devastating to the case for heavy-handed regulation of insider trading. But the SEC's obsession and Manne's critique simply started a debate that continues to this day. Those on the proregulation side make some good counterpoints.[4] Let's go back to the claim that what causes harm is the nondisclosure of the information. To the extent that the law does not impose an affirmative disclosure obligation, it's a matter of business judgment whether to disclose or not. And if insiders were free to profit from the secret by trading, they'd have an incentive to delay disclosure that might otherwise be made, so as to suck all the available profit out of the market while they can. Conversely, insider trading might threaten the secrecy where keeping the secret is important, by calling attention to the trading and making others in the market wonder why it's happening. Managers might also have an incentive to run the company in a way that simply makes its stock price more volatile, because insider profits come whether the news is good (buy the stock or call options) or bad (sell, or short the stock).

There is also a fairly technical debate about the cost of capital. If you are a frequent trader—especially a regular provider of liquidity to the market—you have to worry about being exploited by others who know secrets that you don't (what economists call adverse selection). In the extreme, you won't trade at all if the risk of exploitation by informed traders is too high. More likely, you'd take precautions, expanding the spread between what you're willing to buy and sell at to reflect the risk you're facing. You might also look for markets that are structured to shut out insiders and other informed traders to the greatest extent possible. None of these fear-driven precautions is good for the markets, and so maybe prohibiting insider trading helps lower the cost of capital.

All this eventually led to some revisionism by those on the Manne side of the debate.[5] If insider trading has a mix of costs and benefits, let the company decide what to do about it. In other words, treat secrets as a form of intangible property that belongs to the company. The company might choose to bar or limit trading in the name of lowering its cost of capital, preserving secrecy, or incentivizing its managers. Or it could allow trading. This idea led a fair number of economics-oriented thinkers to the conclusion that this property-rights approach justified a presumption against the permissibility of insider trading, but with the entitlement being in the company's hands, subject to waiver or modification if the board of directors so chooses. We'll see one way in which this idea has influenced the law very dramatically.

Even though it's largely illegal, insider trading is common enough, maybe even rampant in some settings.[6] Investors know that; hence the fascination and envy. Yet no one has ever been able to show that the public's investment enthusiasm is severely dampened because of fear of that trading. Our study of investor behavior has given us ample reason to believe that the motivations to invest are extremely robust, even when a triumph of hope over experience.

Insider trading enforcement is a big part of the "publicness" story we've been telling in this book. The capitalist system affords extraordinary power, privilege, and wealth to the private sector. Given the growing inequality of wealth in our society, the political bargain that supports that deference is an uneasy one. We've seen many ways that investor protection turns indistinguishably into demands for transparency and accountability that serve broader social and political ends. That's controversial, especially among enthusiasts for economic freedom, but an inevitable and necessary part of the bargain. The morality plays produced by prosecutors and the SEC are occasional but especially memorable reminders that there is *some* public accountability for hubris and greed that steps over the line from tolerable to not. I'm persuaded that insider trading should be regulated, for good policy-based reasons. But those reasons are hardly self-evident, and shouldn't produce religious-like fervor. I would have been no happier than Judge Rakoff in sentencing Rajat Gupta to even a medium-length jail term.

The contemporary law of insider trading—most all of which is judge-made, not statutory—derives heavily from a case involving Vincent Chiarella, who worked for a financial printer and was able to buy stock in companies about to be takeover targets by decoding documents for which he was helping set the type. For twenty years prior, the SEC and the courts had agreed that insider trading was fraudulent, and thus a Rule 10b-5 violation, but had done poorly at explaining when or why. There were hints that the related norm was egalitarianism—no one is supposed to have an informational edge. The resulting vagueness of the law was unsettling, especially once criminal prosecutors started trying to send people to jail for insider trading.

The criminal case against Chiarella came to the Supreme Court at a time when the Court had shifted to the right in political ideology. There were fears (or hopes) that the Court might simply say that insider trading wasn't deceptive, buying into Manne's idea that it should be encouraged, not thwarted. But by this time insider trading law had entered public discourse as an expression of fair play as against the forces of greed, communicating to the average investor that he or she gets the role of aggrieved principal in the morality play, not that of the chump. One can imagine the Court being reluctant to rule, effectively, that greed wins.

The Court's opinion was written by Justice Lewis Powell, a courtly, conservative Virginian who was the only justice with a corporate law background.[7] Powell wanted clarity to the law, and understood that in the common law, fiduciaries owe a duty of candor to those whom they are charged to serve. Drawing from this, his opinion upheld the idea that insider trading was fraudulent under Rule 10b-5 if (but only if, it seemed) the trader owed a preexisting, fiduciary-like duty to those contemporaneously trading in the marketplace—in other words, an obligation to put their financial interests ahead of his own. Chiarella didn't have any such duty to those from whom he was buying stock, and so he won his appeal.[8]

The decision was oddly awkward in a number of respects. Under state law there were many exceptions to caveat emptor, not just a fiduciary one. To the extent that the Court was drawing from this body of law for precedent, the limitation to fiduciary duty was hardly necessary or inevitable. Three of the dissenting justices, including the equally conservative Chief Justice Burger, said that the duty to abstain or disclose could and should be extended to Chiarella's wrongful theft of confidential information. Moreover, the fiduciary logic breaks down in a case where the insider-fiduciary is selling based on bad news, because there he or she is trading with someone who is not yet a shareholder, and thus not a beneficiary of any duty of trust. (To that point, Justice Powell simply said that it would be a "sorry distinction" to have different rules for insider buyers and sellers, as if that observation made analytical sense.)

The category of "fiduciary-insider" has some elasticity in terms of who is a fiduciary, but seemed limited to cases where the defendant was trading in his own company's stock. That was troubling to those convinced of the insider trading blight, because profit often comes from buying or selling stock in a company with which you have no direct connection. So the SEC and criminal prosecutors started making a new argument when they came to court, drawing from some dicta in the Supreme Court's opinion and a concurring opinion. Let's take the merger example. Someone can work at an investment bank or law firm representing the acquiring company, and know the secret as a result. But the profit comes from buying stock or options in the target, so that's the trade. What the government started arguing is that you deceive *the source of the information* when you pretend to be a loyal fiduciary but instead act corruptly by secretly buying or selling stock, no matter with whom you're trading. You're feigning loyalty, but acting selfishly. You've tricked the source, which thought it could trust you. And if that's fraud, the only other thing that Rule 10b-5 requires is that it be "in connection with" the purchase or sale of a security. That seems easy, since the whole point of the misappropriation was to trade. Courts gradually started agreeing with this analysis, and both prosecutors and the SEC had a run of success against such "misappropriators."

As it turned out, this argument turned out to be extraordinarily expansive. Trust is often present when secrets are shared, and any time that seems plausible, the trading can be characterized as a secret breach of trust—not just in employment settings. A psychiatrist could be seen as a misappropriator if he trades after hearing an angst-ridden story from the therapy couch that contained some financial nugget, as when the wife of famous banker Sandy Weill allegedly shared a bit too much about her husband's interest in Bank of America and the stresses at home it was creating.[9] Journalists could be accused of trading in advance of stories, deceiving their publisher-employers. And then the obvious: family relationships. Numerous misappropriation cases claimed that fathers feigned loyalty to their sons (or husband-wife, brother-sister, etc.) when they traded after some innocent shared conversation after a hard day's work.

There is a logic to this argument (similar arguments had successfully been made by criminal prosecutors for years in the law of mail fraud). Certainly it tells a story of betrayal and theft that resonates with those appalled by greed and opportunism. But there is something odd about basing a securities law violation on the harm that comes to patient-physician trust, or journalistic integrity, or the sanctity of family conversations. The securities laws don't exist to protect those things—indeed, they're not normally a subject of federal law interest at all but rather left to the states (a point that Justice Powell would have found particularly damning, being such a states-rights enthusiast).

The misappropriation issue first came to the Supreme Court in a case involving a reporter for the *Wall Street Journal* who traded on advance knowledge of the "Heard on the Street" column, and the Court split four to four on the question, with Powell's seat on the Court recently vacant.[10] That left the doctrine in limbo. It took a few more years, but another test case came up. A partner in a law firm, James O'Hagan, learned that his firm was engaged in assisting a still-secret takeover bid, this one on behalf of Grand Met for control of Pillsbury. He had embezzled money from the firm, and nervously was looking for funds to replace what was missing before he was caught. The Pillsbury bid was a godsend for him, and he made enough money from the trades to hide his wrongdoing. But then he got caught, and was in double trouble with criminal prosecutors. The misappropriation case was straightforward, but only if the misappropriation theory was a legitimate interpretation of Rule 10b-5. To the consternation of prosecutors and the SEC, the lower appellate court said it wasn't.

The Supreme Court decided that it was, and reinstated the conviction (which meant that Vincent Chiarella had violated 10b-5 as well: he just hadn't been prosecuted under the right legal theory).[11] The makeup of the Court had shifted via some Clinton-era appointees—Justice Ruth Bader Ginsburg wrote the Court's opinion. She accepted the basic premises of misappropriation, that it is an intangible property-based idea that gives the owner (the source) the right to exclusive use of secrets in its possession. What she insisted, however, is that these interests are not just state-law matters, but go to the heart of securities law: investor confidence depends on a belief in the integrity of the markets, which fiduciary breachers pollute.

After the Court's endorsement of the misappropriation theory, the SEC and prosecutors had a doctrinal treasure trove with which to work. The goal was to expand the fiduciary concept as broadly as possible, short of its breaking point.[12] Professional and employment relationships easily satisfied the test, even when the employee had far from elite status. Close family settings were fiduciarized as well, which extended that insider trading obligation to a more intimate part of a person's life. By rule a few years later, the SEC *presumed* certain family relationships to be fiduciary: spouses, parents, children, and siblings. You could try to rebut this by saying that there is no trust in your particular family, but that is likely to cause you even more trouble (try explaining why you felt free to share secrets if there was no trust that they would respect confidentiality).

Could a fiduciary obligation be created for purposes of the misappropriation theory simply because the trader promised to keep a secret? This was very important to the SEC because many secrets are legitimately shared in the business and financial world between parties who otherwise are dealing with each other at arm's length. A good example would be a bank and a borrower: the borrower has to give the bank private information, but we don't typically call the bank a fiduciary. Once it promises confidentiality, however, the SEC says that it takes on a limited fiduciary duty simply with respect to that particular information. That is so even if the only word that is used is "confidential," which clearly implies that the secret will not be passed on to anyone else but doesn't necessarily say that the information won't be used quietly for trading purposes.

So came the SEC's highly publicized case against Mark Cuban, the owner of the Dallas Mavericks of the NBA and an enthusiastic tech investor and entrepreneur. Cuban owned a substantial (but not controlling) interest in a Canada-based search-engine company, Mamma.com. The company was quietly contemplating selling stock in a type of transaction (a PIPE deal) that was not likely to please Cuban. From this point on, the facts are in dispute, but according to the SEC, the CEO called Cuban but first asked if he would treat what he was about to say as confidential. Cuban allegedly agreed, learned of the deal, became angry, said with frustration that he now couldn't sell his stock in the company, inquired a bit more about the financing, and then sold anyway. He avoided losing money on his investment, because the stock price dropped after the news came out.

What is striking here is the use of the fiduciary principle. Cuban was an outsider, about whom Mamma.com management seemed worried—the company surely had no expectation of loyalty on his part, and maybe even assumed that he was an adversary given the likely disagreement about the financing (Cuban notoriously hated PIPE transactions). Indeed, it's not hard to imagine that the company official shared the secret to prevent him from selling, which might destabilize the market for the company's stock during the financing plans, by planting the inside information. In any event, he was obligated to refrain from trading, according to the SEC, just by uttering something to the effect of OK when asked if he would keep something confidential.

After considerable legal skirmishing, the SEC convinced a federal court of appeals that its theory against Cuban was on solid-enough ground.[13] Cuban later won at trial, however, presumably after convincing the jury that the facts were not as the SEC told them (he denied ever promising confidentiality), which was made somewhat easier for him because the only other person privy to the conversation, the CEO, had refused to come to the United States to testify in person. Cuban was harshly critical of the SEC and its insider trading campaign both before and after the verdict. He noted that he won because he could afford the best defense possible, but that others facing similar accusations have to fold rather than fight. What's different about this kind of fiduciary status is that it cannot be inferred by reference to status, the way an employee, attorney, or even family member might. On its face, the relationship is not fiduciary, but arm's length. Only a small, controverted bit of evidence—a conversation or phone call—was said to have created the duty.

Two other cases illustrate the elasticity of the contemporary insider trading prohibition. One takes us back to family relationships. Recall from the above discussion that while secretive fiduciary breaches are fraud, brazen breaches are not, because if the fiduciary is open enough about what is happening, the source may be angry and frustrated, but not fooled. Deception, crucial to finding fraud, is lacking. So in one SEC case, a wife traded company stock (through her brother and his friend) after learning negative confidential information from her husband, the CEO of the company, during normal end-of-the-day conversations. That wouldn't be a particularly hard case but for the fact that she said she told her husband what she was intending to do *before* the transactions took place.

Putting aside the credibility of that story, the SEC took the position that it didn't matter. Weeks earlier, she and her brother had hatched the plan to encourage the husband to share details of what was happening at work, which she would pass on. Presumably she then led him on into being particularly loquacious. That was the fraud, according to the Commission—tricking the husband into thinking that it was safe to be open and sharing, when it wasn't. The court agreed, and so found the confession of their intention to trade came too late to save the fiduciary breach by the wife and her brother.[14]

The other case had no fiduciary duty to it at all, which makes it especially interesting. From abroad, some computer hackers found a way to enter the computer system of Thomsen Financial, which offers an electronic distribution service to companies as a way to make their publicity widely available to the public. Accordingly, the computer system frequently has on its server sensitive corporate information, waiting to be released at the chosen time. The hackers were searching for these secrets, in order to buy or sell stock in the companies in question.

Hackers aren't fiduciaries. They feign no loyalty and have no preexisting duties of trust or confidence. They are thieves, of a sophisticated sort. And in going after them, the SEC didn't try to say that they were fiduciaries. Instead, it said—fairly profoundly— that the case law only uses breach of fiduciary duty as means of satisfying the deception requirement under Rule 10b-5. When there is an undisclosed breach of duty, that works, but it doesn't imply that there must be a breach of fiduciary duty for there to be deception. That is surely right. No one has ever seriously suggested that lies violate Rule 10b-5 only when there is some fiduciary duty on the part of the liar. So even if the hackers weren't fiduciaries, they committed fraud so long as they engaged in some sort of deceptive behavior in connection with the purchase or sale of a security. The SEC argued that hacking is inherently deceptive; to get into a secure system, you have to fool the host into thinking you have authorization. The host is a machine, to be sure, but we're well enough into the world of computerized trading not to think that human intervention is required for fraud. Again, the court essentially agreed with the SEC.[15] Deception was the key, not fiduciary duty per se. Mere theft may still not be a form of deception, but deception is a well-used device in the dark arts toolkit of most thieves. Thievery and knavery are kindred enough.

That's quite confusing, of course—theft of inside information by trickery creates liability, but brazen theft does not? Someone violates the law by breaching a hastily made promise to keep information confidential, but not if he breaks and enters an office in an act of commercial espionage? That is not sensible line-drawing—it is instead the consequence of judicial utterances in a disjointed conversation. At the same time, what the misappropriation theory does reach easily gets *labeled* as a form of theft. In cases of deceptive theft, the emphasis is on both of those words, making judges and juries think of a compound crime that involves both cheating and stealing, a violation of two of the sacred Commandments, not just one. The misappropriation pathway offers an especially good way for enforcers to frame their case in a way to takes what is often at best constructive fraud and makes it seem an act of financial violence. We are back to Judge Rakoff's sentencing dilemma, about which there is more to say. But before that we have another pathway—maybe the slipperiest of all—to look down.

TIPS

From the beginning, insider trading law has recognized the possibility that, instead of trading, an insider will pass on the information to someone else in the form of a tip, and that that person (called the "tippee") will trade. A person who receives a tip— much less a remote tippee many steps removed from the insider—is not likely to be a fiduciary, and so would seem to have no disclosure obligation or opportunity to feign loyalty. So does that mean tippees are free to trade (or insiders free to tip so long as they don't trade)?

The first major case to pose this question was not one of the SEC's finest. In the 1970s there was a great financial reporting fraud involving Equity Funding, the Enron of its day. A former Equity Funding employee (Secrist) wanted to blow the whistle on the fraud, but no one was listening to him. Secrist contacted Raymond Dirks, a celebrated investment adviser, and told him of the fraud. Dirks didn't believe him at first but had the good sense to ask for some supporting evidence, which Secrist was able to provide. Finally realizing that Equity Funding was corrupt—and that many of his clients had invested heavily in it at his urging—Dirks quickly did two things. He contacted the financial press to alert it to an important story, which it pursued and ultimately broke. He also called his best clients and told them to sell Equity Funding as soon as possible.

So Dirks was something of a hero (Secrist even more so) in exposing the fraud before even more damage was done. The SEC acknowledged that. But the SEC concluded that Dirks had also committed unlawful insider trading by tipping his clients, and brought an enforcement action against him. This didn't have to take him to court because the case involved a securities professional, and in the administrative proceeding the SEC argued that the conspiracy theory articulated by the Supreme Court meant that any time someone receives inside information from an insider, that person inherits the insider's fiduciary duties, plain and simple. The SEC's administrative proceeding found Dirks liable, but in light of the conduct in the case, there was no penalty, only a mild censure. Most people would have walked away, but Dirks was angry that his integrity had been called into question, and he appealed all the way up to the Supreme Court.

Not surprisingly, the Court—again in an opinion by Justice Powell—decided that the SEC had overreached.[16] The Court said that there can sometimes be tipper-tippee liability, but only when there is something resembling a conspiracy to breach the insider's fiduciary duties. The resulting test was in two parts. First of all, the insider-tipper must be breaching a fiduciary duty by passing the information on, and this must be a *selfish* act, involving personal benefit rather than in the best interest of the corporation. Second, the tippee has to know, or at least have reason to know, of that selfish breach of duty.

Powell noted that there are various kinds of corrupt acts—an insider might be selling the information (the easy case), or using the tip to bolster his reputation, or maybe just making a gift of the information to a family member or a friend. The latter is a bit strange as a form of selfishness, but Powell in his pragmatist mood observed that this was like the insider trading for himself and giving the proceeds to the loved one. True, but a strange use of the phrase "personal benefit" nonetheless. In any event, this test meant that Dirks had not violated the law, and so his censure was removed. The insider, Secrist, had not breached a fiduciary duty to Equity Funding for personal gain—he was trying to blow the whistle on corruption. Thus it didn't matter what Dirks thought or did; he was free to use the still-secret information as he wished.

This complicated the law of insider trading, creating circumstances where a person could blatantly take advantage of material nonpublic information so long as he was neither an insider nor a tippee. Not long after the *Dirks* case, the SEC brought a case against Barry Switzer (then the head football coach at the University of Oklahoma, later coach of the Dallas Cowboys), who supposedly overheard a couple talking about a secret business deal, figured out the company involved, and called his broker to buy to stock in that company. The court said no liability for Switzer.[17] That innocent, overheard conversation wasn't a tip that was meant for anyone's personal gain. Switzer just got lucky. (Never mind that the husband and wife were major football boosters at Oklahoma and had had dinner with Switzer the night before, according to evidence offered by the SEC. Maybe the strategic lesson is don't sue a local hero in his hometown.)

The SEC wasn't happy with this turn in the law; from now on, it had—at least in "classic" insider trading cases, and probably in misappropriation cases as well—to prove the selfish or greedy nature of the tip, and enough awareness of that on the part of the tippee. Subsequent cases have involved tips supposedly in return for cocaine, hard-to-get Broadway tickets, live lobsters, and an iPhone, among other items of value. And the insider could always claim the tip was a gift, requiring nothing in return.

Of course, the SEC had to show that there was in fact a tip. The alleged tipper and tippee will often deny that any secret was passed from one to another, offering some alternative explanation for why the tippee made the trade in question. Most tips are oral, with no tangible evidence to support the tip (in one proceeding, a tip was written on a napkin and passed on at a lunch, after which the tippee supposedly ate the evidence;[18] more sophisticated types use disposable cell phones, codes, and the like). Recognizing the proof difficulties, most courts allow the SEC or prosecutors substantial leeway in making a circumstantial case. Proving that the insider and tippee talked (phone records help with that) or had frequent contact gets coupled with evidence that the trade happened shortly enough thereafter that there must have been a tip. As long as it involves reasonable inference as opposed to mere speculation, this is acceptable proof—it's up to the jury to decide what really happened.

The other half of the Supreme Court's test turns to what the tippee thinks. The co-venture is completed if the tippee knows about the breach and (presumably) the personal benefit. But tippees don't always understand why they are being given the secret, and may well not know the details of any breach of duty. But the Supreme Court's language extends liability to situations where the tippee should have known, so that ignorance is not necessarily an excuse. It's a matter of what a reasonable person would think: is this information coming to me in a suspicious enough way that I shouldn't take advantage of it? There seems to be a great deal of flexibility for judges and juries in that question. It becomes very much like stolen property, and indeed that is an analogy (if not description) that judges sometimes use for insider trading. So we're heading into "theft" territory again, a world of tainted property that bolsters the apparent criminality of the acts.

These are the strange distinctions the law has created. If you're in an airplane sitting next to someone with an open laptop you can read (or are at a table in a bar next to well-dressed bankers or lawyers who are talking much too loudly), can you trade based on what you see or hear? Probably yes, because you're in much the same position as Coach Switzer. But don't be too sure: it's possible that you could be the beneficiary of a reckless tip, assuming enforcers could articulate some kind of benefit to the tipper. Moreover, there is also a different and more stringent rule for information related to a tender offer. To take the legal discussion any further than this would be too technical and tentative, because the law has shifted back and forth in recent years on these questions. The point is that you wouldn't necessarily sleep well at night thinking about such elasticity, or how your conduct would look to an envious jury of your peers.

HEDGE FUNDS

We tend to think of insider trading as when someone learns a secret that is a sure thing in terms of opportunity for trading profit, but much of the time what the trader learns is more speculative. There seems to be an instinct among business people that trading on uncertain information is lawful, but that is not where the line is drawn. We saw this earlier. Materiality comes from assessing the probability that something important will come along with the estimated magnitude of the impact on the company if it does. Long-shot odds are consistent with materiality if the effect would be big enough. So in the pharmaceutical world, for example, enough complaints about *possible* side effects of a new drug could be material if they are sufficiently predictive of a risk that the drug will lose sales or be withdrawn from the market entirely. In thinking about this—and materiality really is one of the hardest assessments made in securities litigation—remember that insider trading cases tend to arise after big news comes to pass. Judges and juries assessing probability and magnitude will usually be judging in hindsight, knowing that the event *did* come to pass, and thus psychologically disposed to overestimate the likelihood at the time of the trade that it would. Knowing how the story ends introduces a powerful bias, expanding the scope of materiality as applied, if not in theory.

That background gets us to the hedge fund story. Since 2009 or so, the headline insider trading cases have been against hedge funds and their often celebrity-status (in the financial world, at least) portfolio managers. The first major criminal prosecution focused on Galleon Capital and its founder, Raj Rajaratnam, and also brought down the revered Mr. Gupta; more recently, SAC Capital was a major target, though not its founder, Steve Cohen, notwithstanding obvious prosecutorial suspicions.[19]

These are fascinating case studies along a number of dimensions. The criminal prosecutions were notable as being some of the first securities cases to use crime-fighting tools associated with organized crime and drug cartels, like wiretaps and informants who wear a wire to elicit more incriminating evidence from unwitting conspirators. The Galleon cases, in particular, also raised uncomfortable questions about ethnicity and insider trading, given how many of the defendants were from India and other nearby countries.

Hedge funds, as we've mentioned, are private pools of capital managed to generate exceptionally high returns. They are lightly regulated (though more regulated in the last few years after the financial crisis), with the freedom to employ whatever investment strategies, at whatever level of risk, the managers choose. This light-touch oversight is given on the condition that they don't raise their capital via a public offering and limit their investors to a pool of qualified investors. In other words, hedge funds are accessible only to the very well off, who are very much expected to fend for themselves.

Hedge fund investors (the rich) put their money in the fund for a limited duration. The hedge fund advisor gets paid a management fee that is performance based. Part of the fee is ordinary (e.g., 2% of assets under management). But there is also a big incentive component, usually 20% of profits net of any prior losses, thus creating a "high-water mark" goal to surpass. The rewards to success in a large fund can be extraordinary. Top managers usually have skin in the game as well, investing their own money along with their investors'.

And that's the puzzle. In a word of relatively efficient markets, how can anyone expect to regularly beat the market by so much? It is difficult for retail investors to beat the market at all on a risk-adjusted basis through mutual funds or ordinary pension investments, except by random luck. Hedge funds have to outperform consistently, for investors with little patience for excuses. Leveraging (using borrowed money to invest) does some of the work, especially when interest rates low and financial markets booming, but it takes much more.

So if you're running a hedge fund, how do you do it? Partly, it's a matter of human capital and technology. High frequency and algorithmic trading is a big part of the business, the arms race toward advantages based largely on speed, quantitative skills, and computer capacity. A discrete segment of the hedge fund business uses activist tactics, presuming companies in which they invest to improve their (short-term) financial performance. But perhaps the biggest part of the business—and no one makes their strategies so apparent that others can copy them, so we don't know all the recipes—is research. It involves finding the absolutely smartest analysts in the world, offering them much more than they can be paid anywhere else, and creating for them much the same incentive structure—meet the hyperaggressive targets and become very wealthy, or fail and be let go. Only a tiny segment has that skill level; hedge funds have to find and keep them. One reason that mutual funds supposedly have disappointing performance over the long run is that anyone who shines as a mutual fund portfolio manager can find much better prospects in the hedge fund world, and will quickly be hired away.

For much of the last two decades, this seems to have worked—the financial media have reported breathlessly on the extraordinary wealth that comes from being a hedge fund manager, and on the market-beating returns to their well-heeled investors.[20] The financial crisis showed that being short in the market, through derivatives and the like, can pay off even in meltdowns (though most hedge funds had negative returns in 2008). Something powerful was happening, out of the reach of ordinary investors, much less ordinary citizens. To rub it in, hedge fund managers seem to get very favorable tax treatment on their outsized incomes.

So far as insider trading is concerned, we have the makings of a delicious story. The start to the plot is obvious enough. Competition among hedge funds is fierce; talent walks out the door each day and may not come back. The temptation to cheat in order to get an edge is strong. The hypermotivated hedge fund analyst is by definition a collector and user of information, with as much speed as possible in getting the best-quality data on which to devote all that brilliance. For that you need connections, and more than anything, the hedge fund insider trading cases showed how rich the web of connections can be to enable brilliance.

Some of this was top-end, like the Rajaratnam-Gupta connection.[21] Gupta was a remarkably successful management consultant at McKinsey, who had extensive relationships—including seats on boards of directors—at companies like Goldman Sachs and Proctor & Gamble. He was also prominent in charitable and political circles, enlarging his social and professional network. Rajaratnam cultivated him, drawing on the shared ethnicity and the sense of having successfully overcome the outsider status that so many immigrants, even if well-off, feel in making their way in America. He offered Gupta private investment opportunities (not entirely successful, as it turned out). Then came the slippery slope. Small shared confidences, and confidential information, gradually became bigger ones, including the tips that eventually sent both of them to jail.

In large hedge funds, most of the research is done by analysts at a level or two below the top. In the case against SAC, prosecutors focused in particular on a relationship between Michael Martoma, a young portfolio manager there, and Sidney Gilman, an elderly doctor at the University of Michigan who was involved in overseeing the clinical trials for a drug being developed jointly by Wyeth and Elan, in both of which SAC was heavily invested.[22] Gilman also was part of an "expert network," a group of people who—for a fee—provide briefings and expertise on technical subjects, mainly for hedge funds and other sophisticated investors. (These networks warn their participants against any consultation that would involve unlawful insider trading.) Again, it was a carefully cultivated relationship that started out with general background information and then gradually got into more specifics about the drug trials as Martoma demonstrated more and more interest and expertise in a subject that so fascinated Gilman. Gilman let his guard down and finally passed on key clinical findings that indicated that stock should be sold, quickly. SAC did so, locking in a big profit that was about to disappear. According to prosecutors, Steve Cohen made the decision to sell, but they had no proof that Martoma told him it was based on inside information. Martoma was convicted and sentenced to jail, apparently unwilling to turn on Cohen in return for leniency.

We'll come back to the psychology of all this in the next section. For now, note the legal challenges in building an insider trading case involving a hedge fund. Such funds do lots of research and often trade rapidly. It makes sense that if an average investor trades a large amount of stock right after a conversation with an insider, it's because the insider revealed some secret. Thus it's permissible to make that inference even without direct proof of the tip. But a hedge fund is different, with many reasons for trading at any given time. The fact that there was a conversation followed by a trade may not be enough. That is why high-level insider trading investigations in this area have turned to wiretaps and other devices, to overcome the weak inference problem in criminal cases where proof has to be beyond a reasonable doubt.

There are also hard issues relating to materiality. Private conversations can take place lawfully so long as they involve facts that fall short of market-moving potential. Hedge fund analysts believe that they can take advantage of many different facts that they learn from insiders (or elsewhere) that would not mean much to the ordinary investor but help the smart analyst make sense of the big picture and draw conclusions about what to buy or sell. Their lawyers call this the mosaic approach, on the assumption that even though pieces are contributed by insiders, the mosaic as a whole is the analyst's legitimate work product—the skill, diligence, and expertise that the market should reward with trading profits. So what's wrong with talking to some expert network participant who happens to work at Walmart about changes in foot traffic in key stores?

On its face, that makes sense, and there is case law to support the argument. But let's go back to the misappropriation theory for a minute. Remember, that's the idea that it's a fraud for someone entrusted with information to use it for personal gain while pretending to be loyal and trustworthy. Using money or other inducements to tempt that person to share information that he is expected to keep confidential is wrongful, no matter how much the analysts' brilliance matters in discerning the best trading strategy. Juries rightly smell something noxious about trying to get an edge by paying people who work for a company or a medical research facility, where the game is trying to get them to reveal as much as possible short of some poorly understood legal restriction.

In these hedge fund cases, all the dramaturgy is on the prosecution's side. Defendants like Rajaratnam and Gupta have gained immense wealth, either running or connected to an extremely lucrative investment vehicle whose doors are slammed shut to anyone of ordinary means. They may be ethnic outsiders (which itself touches a deep societal nerve) but are still immensely privileged. The pursuit of so much more wealth through the aggressive search for an edge suggests much too much arrogance, pride, and greed. The audience is primed for the fall from the sky into hell, and so it comes. This script needs only minor editing for a younger analyst like Martoma, who exploited the old doctor in his search for fortune and to please his boss. To this was added the convenient backstory that Martoma—then known as Ajai Mathew Thomas—had apparently been expelled from Harvard Law School for altering his academic transcript.[23]

In late 2014, the hedge fund world finally got some good news, perhaps because prosecutors themselves became overconfident.[24] The case involved earnings-related information at Dell and NVDIA, leaked by midlevel employees at those two companies to analysts who were friends (but not close ones) of the insiders. There was no tangible benefit given or expected in return for the information. The information ended up in the hands of two hedge fund portfolio managers, who had no direct knowledge of how the information came their way. A criminal case was brought against the hedge fund traders, who were convicted on the theory that in a friendship-type setting, at least, benefit can largely be presumed rather than proved, and that what they knew should have been enough for them to realize that this was deliberately leaked information.

On appeal, the court reversed the convictions. It said that in a criminal case like this, remote tippees have to *know* of a personal benefit to the tipper. And when the alleged benefit is based on friendship, the relationship must be close enough so that the tipper would naturally expect meaningful tangible value from the gift.

This clearly was a slap at prosecutors, and many defendants (including Martoma) quickly asked that their cases be dismissed because of what they said were similarly strained inferences about tipper benefit and tippee knowledge. We'll have to wait and see how much harder this makes criminal prosecutions and what impact, if any, it has on SEC enforcement actions, which proceed on a more lenient "preponderance of the evidence" standard rather than the "beyond a reasonable doubt" required for criminal prosecutions. Perhaps this signals a judicial turn against the insider trading crusade, or maybe it's just a one-time reminder not to substitute inference for solid proof when the defendants' freedom is at stake.

INSIDE THE INSIDER'S BRAIN

The law of insider trading requires a look into the state of mind of the trader or tipper, because fraud requires some level of willfulness, intentionality, or maybe recklessness. The SEC believes, and has adopted a rule to this effect (10b5-1), that all it has to do is show that the insider was aware of the information in question at the time of the trading decision. The extent to which the inside information actually motivated the trading is irrelevant. Some courts, however, have ignored this rule and impose a requirement that the information be the (or at least a) *reason* for the trade. This sounds technical, but it comes up frequently enough. A defendant will say that he had formed an intent to trade before learning some secret, or had independent reasons to trade so that the inside information played no role. One corporate director persuaded a court that it was relevant that he had decided to buy a big-rig truck for his son to go into the trucking business, for which he would have to sell some company stock, then attended a board meeting at which he learned bad news about the company's prospects. So he said that even though he profited from the time of the sales, the trading would have occurred anyway, so it wasn't insider trading.[25] A favorite defense of hedge fund analysts and other active investors is to say that even if they possessed some inside information, their research uncovered enough other reasons to buy or sell that they would done so have anyway without the alleged tip. (This argument does double work, as a way of contesting guilty state of mind as well as countering the inference that there was ever a tip at all.) This can make the enforcer's burden much heavier.

The legal disagreement here is actually quite telling. Courts that demand a showing that the inside information was actually used are connecting back to the image of insider trading as market abuse. Our image of insiders exploiting their position to gain undeserved wealth implies that they were actually taking advantage of the information, trading *on the basis of it* (a common phrase to describe the act of insider trading). On the other hand, the forbidden fruit / stolen goods narratives require no more than awareness of the secret, and so are popular among judges who have become accustomed to thinking about insider trading in those terms.

While the SEC endorses the possession test, that idea has created a bit of mischief for it. In adopting Rule 10b5-1, the Commission decided that the question of liability for insider trading should be determined by what the insider was aware of at the time of the decision to trade. So if the insider decided to sell, and after that learned some adverse inside information, it would be all right to complete the transaction. That has led to the immense popularity of "10b5-1 plans" among corporate officers and directors, whereby they adopt prearranged plans to sell stock in the company (sometimes purchases, but this is less common), allowing them to claim that the selling decision preceded any acquisition of bad news that made those sales particularly profitable. Some of the mischief is specific—canceling sales when good news is about to be announced, which the SEC reluctantly concedes doesn't violate insider trading law because there is no trading involved. The bigger concern is that this pushes on the murky line between material and immaterial. What if an executive puts a selling plan in place after seeing key people in the company becoming more anxious, or talking about moving on to other jobs? "Corporate bad mood" is a hard materiality argument to make, and very difficult to detect or prove. Empirical evidence is mounting that the creation or increase in 10b5-1 selling plans is predictive of a disappointing corporate future; in other words, insiders earn abnormal returns by putting them in place.[26] They seem, on average, to know that something makes selling wise, and then use the rule as a shield.

The discussion thus far is about the law as applied. But how well do we understand motivations for insider trading, whether in applying the law or in assessing insider trading as an act of economic violence? The conventional account, once again, is straightforward. Savvy insiders and tippees understand "in the moment" that what they are doing is wrong—even if they don't understand the law's nuances—and are simply taking a calculated risk for a large payoff. We have no idea how much illegal insider trading occurs, but the common assumption seems to be that there is a lot of it. The odds seem to be strongly against detection and sanction, especially if those involved avoid telltale signs (e.g., eating the paper with the tip on it).

It's hard to argue against deliberateness as the main story. Recall our discussion about self-confidence and overconfidence as survival traits in a hypercompetitive world. Testosterone feeds the appetite for risk, as well as the sense that the fight is there to be won by those with enough guts. Let an edge go by and your competitor will take it; let enough edges go by and you're out of business. One journalistic account of insider trading at SAC quoted people who said that in job interviews SAC interviewers would ask potential recruits what the riskiest thing was they ever did.[27] They weren't looking for extreme prudence. Many public companies have opportunistic cultures, if not quite so dramatic, that celebrate aggression and guile as keys to success. Risk takers who don't get caught can feel like heroes, their wealth a source of one-upmanship over their peers. In secure-enough settings, they can let others know about the edges they have: knowledge is power, and cachet. The driver may be ego (and subconscious insecurity) as much as the money itself.

The apparent infrequency of detection and prosecution inflates the sense of invulnerability. The SEC's mechanisms for detection of insider trading (managed in cooperation with its self-regulatory partner, the Financial Industry Regulatory Agency (FINRA)) are largely secretive and dimly understood by most people. FINRA operates a real-time market surveillance system that, among other things, watches stock price moves when the price pattern goes outside of normal parameters, a sign that the market thinks something interesting is going on. Unless a good explanation is forthcoming, the system records the suspicious activity to match it with any big news that comes about the issuer over the next days or weeks.

If that happens, the suspicion heightens. At that point, there is a request for all electronic trading data from all broker-dealers, indicating what orders—and for whom—were part of the suspicious activity. That is quite a data dump, on which another sophisticated computer program goes to work identifying any patterns of connection among the trades (e.g., trading heavily concentrated near the company's headquarters). Then, if a formal investigation is launched, enforcement people can subpoena anyone who turned up in the correlations, and leniency can be offered to those who cooperate and help connect the dots. More recently, the system has been programmed to allow for cross-sectional searches: taking multiple similar suspicious events and seeing what actors (particularly hedge funds) are systematically trading in advance of events and making big money.

This computer-aided detective work is quite powerful, and with enough time and resources the SEC can come close to a circumstantial case against anyone. But that level of effort consumes lots of resources, and is thus highly episodic. (Insider trading from foreign accounts poses special problems, which often requires cross-border enforcement cooperation between regulators, which is not always going to happen.) So it does come as a shock to people when their insider trading is detected when it looked to be well under the radar. If the savvy people start to sense that there is too much sunlight in some areas, they'll look for trading less likely to set off the alarms. A recent study shows that company insiders aware of news affecting their own company stock are less likely to trade on that stock, but may trade in the stocks of other companies (suppliers, competitors, etc.) that might be similarly affected by that same news.[28]

While appetite for risk and return describes much of the motivation for trading, some of it seems more impulsive. So we come to one of the most visible of all the insider trading stories from the last two decades, involving Martha Stewart.[29] Stewart was extremely wealthy, mostly from her controlling interest in Martha Stewart Omnimedia. But because of her prominence and connections, she was often invited to take valuable IPO allocations, which extended her portfolio to include quite a number of emerging companies. When the tech stock bubble burst in 1999–2000, she saw a dramatic decline in her portfolio's value, and said she was emotionally torn up for having held onto those stocks too long, a common investor mistake. But she had one stock left in the portfolio with a gain, ImClone. ImClone had a promising drug under development, awaiting word from the FDA about clinical trials.

When she was on a jet to Mexico, during a refueling stop Stewart received a phone call from her Merrill Lynch stockbroker's assistant. Her broker was also the broker for

ImClone's CEO, Sam Waksal (not entirely a coincidence; Waksal and Stewart were also friends). The message was that ImClone's price was dropping and the Waksals were selling their stock. Did she want to do the same was the obvious question of the call. She said yes.

That was exceedingly poor judgment. That phone message certainly sounds like a tip, if not from Waksal himself then from the broker. Brokers are supposed to respect the confidentiality of each client's account—that was certainly Merrill's stated policy. Given the money from the trade and the account, the pecuniary and reputational benefits from the tip seem obvious. Stewart had started her career as a young stockbroker, so presumably she'd understand the danger. And her account was at Merrill Lynch, so the connection to Waksal was in plain view for compliance people and regulators to find.

It didn't take long to find, either. Stewart and her broker apparently conspired to alter documents and make up an explanation for the trading. When Stewart was sent to jail, it was for that—obstruction of justice and false statements to government investigators. All because she sold stock to avoid a loss of about $47,000, which to her was a pittance.

What was she thinking? Actually, the insider trading case against her wasn't an easy one legally, which was the reason the prosecutors went after her for obstruction rather than the underlying offense of securities fraud (the SEC, on the other hand, did charge her with insider trading, which she later settled). One soft spot was the alleged fiduciary breach by the broker, who might argue that neither Waksal nor Merrill would really object to his taking care of a good friend and client like Stewart. So he may not have been feigning loyalty, as required for a misappropriation.

But the bigger soft spot goes to the substance of the phone call. What Stewart could have thought was that word was already out on the street that the FDA had slammed ImClone, which would explain why the price was already dropping. The reference to the Waksals would imply that the stampede to sell included the controlling family, not that the Waksals were selling in advance of any disclosure (which would surely be detected, she'd think, and so would be absolutely crazy). Her inference would not have been a careful one, but the decision to sell was made very quickly and under circumstances where this last profitable investment was about to go into the same negative territory as all her others, which had already made her sick. Psychology says that her judgment would be clouded by the loss frame, the regret and the desire to avoid any more pain. I don't know that to be sure, of course, but surely something was interfering with good judgment, and it was not the mere $47,000. (Ironically, ImClone's price later recovered as the drug in question made it back on track with the FDA, so she wasn't really avoiding a long-term loss at all.)

Impulsive bad judgment is commonplace. People make choices out of overconfidence or wishful thinking that they later come to regret, but feels normal and acceptable at the time. But once the first ethically compromised step is taken, it's hard to resist the second step because of the pressure to maintain consistency with our prior actions and beliefs (the familiar concept of cognitive dissonance). So begins the slide down the slippery slope, until there is no backing out with a confession of significant wrongdoing. We saw that pattern in the context of financial misreporting, and it applies here as well. Both Sidney Gilman and Rajat Gupta recognized after the fact that they had been sucked into compromising relationships, pained at how easy it was to pass on increasingly valuable information because of the private expectations that had been created based on deepening relationships. Gilman said that the first bits slipped out, even as he acknowledged that later on he became complicit in the deception.

I suspect that this aptly describes Gupta's state of mind, too. It's not entirely removed from the deadly sins of arrogance and pride, but shares that space with loyalty, insecurity and an excess of consistency. There is also the matter of gut feelings about insider trading advantages. We know from social science research that perceptions of legitimacy influence the inclination to abide by the law—under circumstances where the likelihood of detection is low, only a fairly strong feeling that the action in question is socially illegitimate will overcome countervailing impulses. We've already raised the possibility that in highly competitive business settings, informational edges are status symbols. No doubt Gupta had done much social good based on his connections, something that can subconsciously license an occasional act of opportunism. Being tired and stressed can also make resistance to impulse harder.

And then there is the awkward issue of ethnic culture. Survey evidence shows that Americans have mixed feelings about insider trading, but are instinctively opposed. Most sense that it is wrong, even if they admit that they might well give into the temptation if they had the chance (evidence of envy, in other words). That view is shared in some countries (e.g., the Netherlands), but much less so in others. Comparative evidence relating to insider trading shows that in certain countries—Italy, Turkey, and India, for example—significantly larger portions of the population consider insider advantages to be perfectly natural.[30] I agree with Anita Raghavan in her book *The Billionaire's Apprentice* that there were more compelling cultural influences, particularly the network of mutual support among Indian-American strivers who successfully overcame outsider status, to explain what Gupta did. But it's fair to note that Gupta was raised in a cultural setting where taking advantage of a privileged status might not feel very wrong, especially if you've earned that status, are causing no severe harm, and are habitually giving the tangible benefit to someone else.

So we come back to Judge Rakoff's sentence of two years in jail, a significant amount of time but less than what other convicted tippers and traders had gotten. Rakoff made his own assessment of motivation, finding that Gupta viewed his relationship with Rajaratnam "as an avenue to future benefits, opportunities, and even excitement," maybe a way of rejecting the straitjacket of responsibilities around which he had built his life. Gupta was simply a tipper, having made no money at all from any of the information in his possession. But gain was to be measured by his tippee's profits, and Rajaratnam was greatly enriched by the tips, so that a long prison sentence was called for under the sentencing guidelines. This pained Rakoff, causing him to observe that, while surely there was a breach of trust and ill-gotten gains, shareholders were not obviously the victims here at all. The judge said—as he had to in light of the conviction—that Gupta willfully committed a bad act, a serious breach of trust. So it was. But Gupta was a particularly complex protagonist in the heavily watched morality play, and the common greed-based script didn't lead to a comfortable ending. Rakoff understood that not a single penny of pecuniary harm had been alleged or proved, and in all likelihood there was no substantial harm (in the "proximate cause" sense of the word) from what Gupta did. In the end, he gave Gupta the lowest sentence he could possibly justify in light of the crime of which he was found guilty, and seemed pained by even that. Rakoff understood what insider trading prosecution had become, more than he could publicly say.

FAIR DISCLOSURE AND THE RACE FOR SPEED

One issue has long bothered enthusiasts for the campaign against insider trading, particularly at the SEC. Suppose an investment analyst contacts a high-ranking company official to troll for useful secrets. If the official passes on inside information, that would seem to be a tip. But once we define a tip as involving a breach of fiduciary duty for personal benefit, where's the breach if the insider concludes that it's in the best interests of the corporation to share the information with that particular analyst? That might well be the case if, for example, the analyst was a major booster of the company's prospects, and the insider's tip might reinforce the enthusiasm and bump up the stock price. That would be valuable to the corporation and its stockholders, not just to its insiders. So it's not obviously a selfish act.

There are a number of possible responses here. If companies can't trade on inside information, as in the case of the corporate repurchase,[31] why should they be able to argue that it's in the best interests of the company to tip a friendly outsider? And note that if the official also owns company stock, or is more likely to get a promotion from what he did, there is an element of personal gain mixed in with the company-serving act. Whatever the merits of these arguments, the SEC came to believe that "selective disclosure" cases like these were not easily winnable.

At the same time, it was convinced that selective disclosure was bad for our markets. It benefited well-connected market players over the average investor, making the playing field more uneven. There was also the suspicion that companies used selective disclosure to reward boosters of its stock, and denied comparable access when analysts were more bearish. With this they could manipulate analysts into being more optimistic than they might be otherwise, because these contacts were seen as quite valuable.

The SEC's solution was ingenious. In 2000, it adopted Regulation FD ("Fair Disclosure"). The rule said nothing about insider trading or tipping. Instead, using its power to compel corporate disclosure, the SEC said that when any high-ranking company official made private disclosure of material nonpublic information to a market professional or large shareholder, the company would have to (subject to certain limited exceptions) make *simultaneous* public disclosure of that same information. Since that's impossible to do in the course of a private communication, the rule's desired effect was to ban such communications unless and until there was public disclosure.

The adoption of the rule was heralded as a promise of fair play in the markets for ordinary investors, and thus has a strong family resemblance to the prohibition against insider trading.

There are many curious angles to this highly political and symbolic rule. Critics have argued that it needlessly cuts off the kinds of discussions analysts need to have with company insiders to give credibility and texture to their recommendations. Company officials may just say nothing as to sensitive or hard-to-evaluate data, making the markets less informative. The empirical evidence as to these worries is mixed— some studies suggest that more skilled analysts do better in an FD world because the less skilled can't curry favor just to get an edge.[32]

Once the SEC insisted on public disclosure as the sole means of releasing sensitive information, it had to define public disclosure, which isn't easy. Precisely when is information publicly available? We've seen that for insider trading, the SEC has long said that the information must be accessible to a wide range of market participants, not just those paying very close attention. That would usually include a press release to the major financial media, though even there were always tough questions about precisely how long one would have to wait for that press release to make its way into the public domain. Questions also came up about company websites and social media. Clearly, the SEC's preferred form of public disclosure was an SEC filing, which would quickly be put up on the SEC's disclosure website, EDGAR. Then it was available to everyone through a government-sponsored disclosure channel.

As an endorsement of the promise of a level playing field, this was politically adept. In reality, it seems somewhat naive. In an efficient market, you'd have to be watching EDGAR constantly in order to expect to react to profitable news. As computers were replacing human in reacting to highly machine-readable news, even the fastest human wouldn't beat the market with respect to that kind of information. Recall the discussion of algorithmic trading from chapter 1. The point was simple. It's very costly to compete in an efficient market, and ordinary investors shouldn't bother to try. In the face of high search costs, the playing field will always tilt in favor the well resourced.

But the political rhetoric was otherwise, which ultimately created an embarrassing problem. This began with the well-publicized release of surveys of consumer confidence by a center located at the University of Michigan. Consumer confidence is a leading market indicator, and so this release was often market-moving. It turned out that the research center authorized the sale of a data feed that would give the subscriber a two-minute window of early access, before either the website posting or the press release. Not surprisingly, information about any survey surprise was being reflected in stock prices and market indices before the public could get hold of the news.

Under the federal securities laws, this would not be illegal—the information (which was costly to produce) presumably belonged to the university, which could give it to whomever it wanted, at whatever price. But this sale of access at a premium price offended the rhetoric of an even playing field, leading Eric Schneiderman, the New York attorney general (whose Martin Act authority is particularly far-reaching), to threaten to take action. He called it Insider Trading 2.0. Privileged access was quickly shut down.

Soon, however, it was discovered that the SEC was essentially doing the same thing with EDGAR. When filings come to the SEC, they are located, for a brief time, on a server in preparation of being uploaded to EDGAR itself. Anyone can get pre-EDGAR access to the server, but it takes sophisticated software to make timely use of this option. But the SEC also authorized a special private data feed to anyone wanting to subscribe to the premium service. Two academic studies found evidence that subscribers were getting a significant timing advantage (only minutes, but that's an eternity in a high-frequency trading environment) before nonsubscribers. This was particularly useful for the reports of trading by high-ranking officers and directors of public companies, given how investors covet that information.

When the *Wall Street Journal* broke this story in 2014, the SEC made no public comment, but the subscribers' advantage apparently soon disappeared.[33] But why then would they be willing to pay for the product? The Commission was caught by its own rhetoric. As a general matter, Americans are used to paying extra for faster delivery (think Amazon Prime), without resentment. As with Michigan, however, the optics of selling a service whose value was in the ability to confer a securities trading advantage were not good. This was especially so where the mechanism in question was supposed to even the playing field between the privileged and the ordinary.

My sense is that most investors don't care about discrimination that is nothing more than a matter of a minute or two. Very few retail investors try to keep up with market professionals on a real-time basis—that's the strange, overconfidence-driven world of day trading—and so this shouldn't be such a resonant political issue. Plus we all know that technology and data gathering are costly, so that public entities have a case for selling access in a transparent way that is open to all who are willing to pay, as opposed to insisting on taxpayer funding. We are back, yet again, to publicness: the growing sensitivity to the exercise of private economic power and the ability of those wielding such power to command more than their share of public resources. The expressive values associated with insider trading regulation are seeping into new domains, even if the law isn't quite in synch.

That seepage is noticeable on Wall Street. We've already noted investment analysts who do "sell side" research for the big securities firms. Analysts cover individual companies and industries, learning enough to make useful recommendations. This research is proprietary, but their estimates and recommendations are publicly available. Would it shock you to learn that these analysts have dinners with their firms' biggest and best clients, giving them a glimpse into the analysts' thinking and where changes might be forthcoming?[34] Again, the research (assuming it's not itself based on inside information) belongs to the securities firm, so favoring those who generate more revenue for the firm makes sense economically. Sharing research with elite clients confers an advantage, but isn't an unlawful tip under the law you've learned from this chapter. Nor does Reg FD apply. There *is* a problem if the analysts are telling these favored clients that they no longer believe in their recommendation at a time when the recommendation is still out in the public domain, which is the real concern with this form of "front-running." But both FINRA and state regulators have begun to attack the favoritism itself, as the level playing field imagery takes on more life of its own.[35]

THE POLITICAL ECONOMY OF INSIDER
TRADING REGULATION

The insider trading story is political, but much more nuanced than simply promoting some vacuous (and surely misleading) impression that all investors get to play on an even playing field. Insider trading enforcement is particularly resonant, tapping into deeply held feelings of envy, resentment, and a desire for respect among the public generally, not just retail investors. It is a particularly dramatic way of introducing at least a bit of accountability for the abuse of privilege, giving some legitimacy to the surfeit of private economic power and wealth that our system allows. To be sure, insider trading enforcement occasionally targets ordinary people who gain access to corporate secrets—secretaries, barbers, IT people, among many others—but that just democratizes the story. As noted earlier, the SEC and criminal prosecutors have found the insider trading script to be a powerful means of gaining favorable public attention to support their broader efforts, enough for all this to have become a brand symbol for the enterprise of securities regulation. The demonization is a crucial part of the script.

But one of the messages of research on the politics of regulation—public choice theory—is that organized special interests dominate, and we should look there for the real explanations for why regulation exists. At first glance, it might seem hard to fit insider trading into that account, but consider insider trading in terms of the relative interests of two powerful groups: business executives versus Wall Street traders.

As Jon Macey and David Haddock pointed out long ago,[36] executives possess the information (and thus trading advantages), which puts outsiders at risk of being exploited—an adverse selection problem. If a ban on trading on insiders is put in place, however, the advantage shifts to those outsiders with the best contacts and ability to trade quickly. In other words, Wall Street benefits from an insider trading rule that is directed at classical insiders, which just happens to be the way the law was articulated by Justice Powell in the *Chiarella* and *Dirks* cases. The business community wouldn't like this restriction, of course, but because, at the time, at least, insider trading opportunities were secondary to salaries and bonuses in terms of compensation, they didn't care about the issue as much as Wall Street did.[37]

The rise of the misappropriation theory didn't change this political equilibrium, even though it extended the scope of the insider trading prohibition. That theory protects the owner of the information against faithless fiduciaries—in other words, the only Wall Street traders who directly get in trouble are those who trade for their own personal accounts against their employers' best interests. Firms themselves could still exploit their informational advantages.

Today, however, Wall Street is in the crosshairs, largely because of how tipper-tippee liability expanded. If public choice theory is right, what happened? Todd Henderson cleverly points to two developments.[38] One is that corporate managers started to worry much more about insider trading enforcement as their pay packages came to be mainly about stock and options. The adoption of Rule 10b5-1—allowing trading plans adopted sufficiently in advance of possession of inside information—was a major accommodation to managerial political power in light of this marketplace change. The other development was the rise of shareholder activism threatening corporate managers without the need to resort to a takeover. Activist hedge funds were at the forefront here, making that category something of an anathema to corporate America. One could add—more powerfully perhaps—the rise of sophisticated short-selling strategies by hedge fund managers, whose activities were an effort to drive down stock prices of targeted companies. Corporate executives wanted them to be targets, thus shifting the political equilibrium.

Critics want to show from all this that insider trading enforcement is mere special-interest politics, mainly if not entirely driven by two very powerful interest groups. I'm not convinced that it's all so simple, or by their descriptions of how the emphasis in enforcement changed over time. But if we put aside the normative question, their insight is still helpful in an important way. Let's assume that the SEC genuinely believes in both the economic and political soundness of the insider trading prohibition. It will still be the case that political pushback will come from whoever feels most threatened, and assuming that the SEC is relatively indifferent as to which group is targeted as long as a continuous stream of cases can be brought, it will choose the path of least political resistance. This perspective also sheds light on one politically salient fact: that Congress has never chosen to define insider trading, instead leaving it to the SEC and the courts. Given how crazy-quilt the law can be, yet so severe the consequences of a violation, that seems (and probably is) inexcusable. In all other countries that regulate insider trading, they do so via statute, and many of these statutes are far more clear and expansive in their prohibitions than what we see in the United States. The European Union insists that all member countries have a prohibition that comes close to a total ban on the use of inside information (the aggressiveness of enforcement is a separate question, but it's growing).[39] Congress has been asked many times to enact legislation that would be better than the muddy body of law we now have, but has just tinkered around the edges, mainly with respect to sanctions.

This reluctance to clarify is more understandable, however, if we assume that the public expects and wants a prohibition. The SEC has long been wary of codification, not because it likes the law as it is but because it is horrified at the thought of congressional redesign. The main interest groups would go to war to reduce their own exposure and make life harder for those who threaten them, with unpredictable consequences. Members of Congress do not relish being caught in the middle, especially with the press and antibusiness constituencies watching closely to blow the whistle on threats to weaken the egalitarian message that regulation purportedly sends. The nerve is too sensitive to touch, which means most of the political maneuvering will continue to take place behind the curtains unless Congress is somehow forced to act.

4

The Partial Disinfectant of Sunlight

The last two chapters were about how securities law's messages can become distorted. In contrast to the economics orthodoxy that assumes clarity in both transmission and reception, my claim is that even legal messages as straightforward as "Tell the truth" or "Don't abuse inside information" are filtered through both individual minds and organizational cultures so as to lose both clarity and punch. This distortion is often self-serving, allowing both people and firms to complete more intensely and effectively, albeit at a heightened risk of unlawful dishonesty. Self-deception precedes the deception of others. All the more so when (as in the law of insider trading) there is no message clarity, or when (as under Rule 10b-5) the law is strongly intent-based and permissive in allowing concealment via puffery or bespeaking caution.

Such dissembling and concealment—whatever its motivation—is supposed to be made harder by mandatory disclosure. In the Securities Exchange Act of 1934, Congress imposed on all public companies an obligation of "periodic" disclosure of the truth about their financial performance and other facts—10-Ks, 10-Qs, and 8-Ks, now disseminated electronically. The idea was that the market price of the company's stock would be much harder to manipulate through deception if the truth about the company was readily available to investors. Insider trading opportunities would diminish as well, although we've just seen how the idea of equal access to information collapses of its own weight in a high-frequency trading world.

Of course mandatory disclosure means little if it is a lie. Today, the securities laws treat disclosure not simply as an event but a process. The legislative response to the Enron and WorldCom scandals, the Sarbanes-Oxley Act of 2002 (or "SOX"), has "better disclosure through better procedures" as its animating philosophy. SOX became extraordinarily controversial because of its intrusion into matters traditionally seen as corporate governance, a big reason to many managers and entrepreneurs to avoid the registered public offering and other paths to being a public company. At the time of its enactment, it was described by academic critics as corporate governance "quackery," a debacle for both companies and investors.[1] The name still provokes automatic managerial loathing. But the evidence on its performance is mixed, and quite a few empirical studies give it some credit for freshening the disclosure environment.[2] Whatever the benefits, its interventions have been costly in the aggregate, especially for smaller public companies, and so the controversy continues.

The SOX discipline demands that CEOs and CFOs of public companies certify in writing that, to the best of their knowledge (take special note of that loaded term), the company's disclosures are true and complete and fairly present its financial situation. There are severe criminal sanctions if this is untrue. Many CEOs and CFOs have reacted to this obligation by insisting that their key subordinates make a similar promise to them.

Congress did not trust that this ritual of attestation was enough. And so comes the march of the "gatekeepers": persons or institutions supposedly independent of corporate management but positioned to observe what is going on inside the company.[3] Some kinds of gatekeepers are present by requirement of law, others as a matter of practical necessity or good governance. By making these gatekeepers responsible if there was concealed misbehavior that they knew about or (perhaps) could have discovered, the law tries get them to refuse to tolerate deception or otherwise blow the whistle if management insists on concealing that which should be disclosed.

SOX pushes three categories of gatekeeper—independent directors, auditors, and lawyers—more deeply into the corporate disclosure process, in the hope that there are more pressure points at which any temptation to shade the truth will be frustrated. Although Congress had a more corrupt explanation in mind for why executives lied (and why their gatekeepers failed to blow the whistle), stepped-up gatekeeping can be a corrective to managerial bias, too, cleaning the perceptual filters and helping debias corporate disclosure. Outsiders might not have drunk the same Kool-Aid, or at least quite as much, and—if sufficiently empowered—can call management out if insider risk perceptions become unrealistic or self-serving enough.

This chapter takes on a number of different (but related) issues about the disclosure process. It begins with a look at the disclosure itself, and the surprising but necessary policy choice to make our system far less than a "full disclosure" regime. Then we turn to the gatekeepers and other people or mechanisms enlisted in the fight for better-quality disclosure. As we'll see, conflicts of interest are pervasive. Next we explore the behavioral effects of both disclosure and heavy gatekeeping, especially as the scope of disclosure grows to satisfy the increasingly voracious appetite of publicness. The chapter ends with the question of freedom: should companies have the choice to "go dark" (or stay dark) even though active in the capital markets, and thus avoid the bulk of the law's demands?

A reminder. Corporate dishonesty is the exception, not the rule. Conscience and prosocial norms play a role, even with all the filters and biases. The law has some deterrence bite, even with all its shortcomings. But mostly it's because sophisticated traders and marketplace institutions understand the temptations and can be pretty hostile in the face of doubts about credibility.[4] These are imperfect, too, subject to their own biases, but the system does generate considerable disclosure quality. For why this equilibrium might not be altogether satisfying, however, read on.

Over time, both the package of required disclosures and the governance rules relating to disclosure have grown hefty. Disclosure is extremely costly, which has led to a long-standing debate about standard-setting. The more academic part of this debate is about how much disclosure we would get if we left the decision entirely to the marketplace. Presumably there would still be a strong incentive to disclose, simply because investors wouldn't invest without some demonstration of candor, and shareholders anxious for liquidity would use the corporate governance power they have to insist that the truth-telling continue. They could demand contractual and other forms of precommitment to transparency, and drive down the stock price if they suspected that managers weren't following through. But many researchers doubt that these incentives are necessarily strong enough, particularly after the money is raised, investors dispersed, and entrenched managers ponder the trade-off of future access to capital against the alluring appeal of darkness. As we've seen, there are also numerous positive social externalities to quality disclosure—it's a public good in so many ways—for which the capital market itself might not provide adequate incentive.[5]

Hence the case for some mandatory disclosure for public companies is something of a given, even for efficient markets, though it might not be extensive (and limited mainly to "agency cost" matters that managers would be especially tempted to hide). That shifts the debate to content and process. The intuition that mandatory disclosure can be fairly limited is even greater today because technology and social media are changing the disclosure landscape, including how and to whom information goes first (as we saw in the last chapter) and how it's produced or filtered by various intermediaries.[6] We live in a rich, overabundant informational environment. Unfortunately, much of the mental model we invoke for how disclosure works comes from a time when filings were on paper, delivered by courier to an SEC office in Washington, and when other corporate news was scarce.[7]

Although the concern about too much disclosure is a real one—to which we'll turn later in the chapter—the hardest mandatory disclosure issues have to do with what *doesn't* have to be disclosed, even if it would be important to investors. Investors presumably make decisions to buy, sell, or hold based on a careful prediction of the forward-looking value of the company: how much is expected in dividends or capital appreciation, over the period of time the stock will be owned. That's a guesstimate based on the expected stream of earnings that company will generate, plus an assessment of the risk and uncertainty surrounding that prediction.

SEC-mandated public company disclosure will tell you mainly how the company has already done, however, not what it expects to do. The core is the set of financial results from the most recent fiscal period. While these historic performance data surely are useful information (especially to test whether management was being candid in what it had said previously about the company's financial condition), they are not entirely helpful when the company finds itself in turbulent times. The past is often a bad predictor of the future. What investors really want to know is management's internal view on what's coming up—risks, plans, strategies, projections, estimates, and the like, as the company faces its competitive challenges.

We've already touched on this. No company could possibly afford to reveal everything important that it privately knows, however, and not simply because of the risk of information overload. Giving away profitable plans and strategies makes them less likely to succeed—handing over the battle plan (and internal assessments of capacity) to the enemy.[8] For this reason, SEC disclosure requirements deliberately let companies keep many secrets. They do have to warn investors of known risks, but that is usually fairly useless boilerplate. There is also the Management's Discussion and Analysis ("MD&A"), which requires an assessment of known trends and uncertainties that are reasonably likely to occur in the future—to which sophisticated investors do pay a great deal of attention—but this is quite near-term in its focus and itself has a loophole for legitimate secrets. Informational asymmetry—things investors just don't have the ability to see—is inevitable, varying in degree depending on the nature of the company (most extreme among high-growth and innovation-oriented firms). This partial darkness is one reason insider trading is of such concern to regulators, and why securities analysts supposedly play such an important role in our markets.

DIRECTORS, LAWYERS, AND DISCLOSURE

Now let's turn to the gatekeepers and others who might be situated to dampen the temptations or blow the whistle on corporate dishonesty. We start at the top. As a matter of state corporate law, CEOs are not the ultimate authority in corporate governance: boards of directors are. Boards are elected by the company's shareholders to make key strategic decisions, advise management, and—most importantly—hire, compensate, and (if necessary) fire the executive team. But there is a long-standing academic and policy debate over the extent to which boards really do their jobs. Elections of directors are rarely contested, and most of the time it's safe to assume that the incumbents or their handpicked nominees will be the only ones seeking election. Thus, through much of the last century it was largely assumed that the CEO (who was probably also chairman of the board) was able to determine the makeup of the board as a combination of subordinate insiders and friendly outsiders, pretty much guaranteeing domination and control.

Over the last few decades, legal and economic pressures have pushed to require or empower "independent" directors (those not otherwise employed by the company, and thus hopefully more objective and prudent) to take on more responsibility in monitoring the CEO, to limit risk-taking, and ensure honest corporate disclosure. This is part of a much larger governance story. If the CEO is entrenched, powerful, and disdainful of shareholder pressure, such independent directors will mean little. The technical definition(s) of independence allow the appointment of outsiders who have close social ties to the CEO or others already in power, and are unlikely to be any more than sycophants. Psychology and economics bolster this tendency. Those selected to serve feel the pressure to reciprocate the kindness, and rarely does the outsider have so much skin in the game (i.e., shareholdings) to be motivated to push back in a crusade to enhance shareholder wealth. Outsiders also have relatively little familiarity with the deep inner workings of the corporation and thus are disabled from forming confident opinions about internal managerial quality or enterprise risks to allow them to have a robust debate with the CEO, even if so inclined. Enron had a famously independent board, to no avail.

That's the pessimistic account. But none of this is inevitable, and there is agreement among governance scholars that board independence and pressures on CEOs have actually increased in the last decade or two.[9] Most of this derives from the stock market itself, and the growing power and impatience of institutional shareholders, which as we'll see are something of a mixed blessing. SOX added additional board-level requirements as a matter of law, most notably that the board's audit committee—which is responsible for overseeing the financial disclosure—be more involved, entirely independent, and disclose the extent of its financial expertise (an obvious prod to *have* financial expertise). As a result of these shifts, some adjustment in our habitually skeptical attitude toward corporate boards is no doubt warranted.[10] Empirical evidence suggests that a combination of independence and expertise pays off in somewhat better-quality financial reporting, if not firm value.

That said, the success is at best partial. The informational asymmetry problem in the boardroom persists, as well as the subtle pressures of social ties, reciprocity, collegiality, and groupthink.[11] Research shows that when the CEO has the autonomy to choose other board members (and his or her own senior management team), fraud is more likely to occur at that company,[12] and such autonomy is still fairly common. Board members even sometimes bring temptation with them—options backdating (an accounting scandal from the last decade involving the manipulation of the value of stock option grants to senior managers and other key insiders) spread contagiously through interlocks on boards of directors, from one company to the next via some member who sat on both boards.[13]

Nor is it clear what the outcome would be were independent directors truly in control, ready to hold management's feet to the fire, because that tension itself sets in motion an interesting bargaining dynamic.[14] Think about it. Given the board's inevitable informational deficit—there is simply no way part-time outsiders can really know what's going on—there is a considerable risk of blaming the CEO unfairly for bad short-term outcomes, from which he or she would thus demand protection or compensation. In an environment where the CEO must constantly "bid" for his or her job, moreover, the resulting high expectations will not be easy to meet. A completely independent board will be tempted to look at the stock price on a real-time basis as a scorecard for how the (presumably efficient) market is judging management. If so, then over time the pressure builds for the CEO to both manage board impressions and deliver good news to the markets, precisely the temptations we saw earlier toward the slippery slope of financial misreporting and the doubling down of risk-taking. That effort can be depleting, ethically and otherwise.[15] A large body of research suggests that, while too little monitoring is surely dangerous, too much can be as well.

Finding the right balance is hard, especially in companies that are hard to comprehend from the outside (technology companies heavily dependent on complicated innovation and harvesting intellectual property are good examples). One intriguing study, however, suggests that with respect to the risk of fraud, independent directors can gain much by inserting high-quality lawyers as "executive gatekeepers." Indeed, the incidence of fraud drops considerably when the chief lawyer is properly motivated to push back against compliance risks.[16] Yet the same study notes that when inside lawyers are compensated with equity incentives (e.g., stock options like the top executives get, so that they covet a high stock price too), their fraud-prevention drops considerably. Sadly, such incentive compensation is commonplace.

Why? Perhaps it is a matter of excessive executive power. Managers usually seem quite insistent that the company's lawyers be in synch with the executives' mission. Directors rarely get into a tug of war about attorney loyalty. For this and other reasons, they will often be the last to know. And if any appreciation of fraud tends to come late, as we've seen, the board is likely to be caught in the same optimism-commitment trap as anyone else. By the time there is evidence of dishonesty strong enough to penetrate the denial, revealing it publicly will be disastrous not only for the CEO and the board, but for shareholders, employees, and other stakeholders. It's not likely to happen unless and until the lawyers and accountants insist, after the damage is largely done. In sum, although independent boards have some capacity to prompt more accurate disclosure, they are not entirely dependable as gatekeepers.

Bringing lawyers into the gatekeeping story is important. After all, if lawyers understand their role as avoiding (or at least managing) legal risk for their clients, they should be a strong force for compliance with the law, as the study suggests. Often they will be. But there are limitations here, too, besides their compensation packages. One is that lawyers often don't have direct knowledge of what is happening on the ground inside the firm, and have to depend on management for a depiction, especially subjective, risk-based impressions that form a big part of disclosure judgments. Managerial biases thus indirectly affect what the lawyers think. There is a risk of self-serving inference as well. Lawyers prize loyalty to their clients and operate under norms that stress discretion and secret-keeping. They can get caught up in slippery slopes like anyone else, losing objectivity if some innocent-seeming decision turns out to be poor judgment. And although the SEC very occasionally goes after lawyers for complicity with client fraud, they face relatively little legal risk when their conduct or advice is arguably within the bounds of the law. In the aftermath of SOX, Congress empowered the SEC to demand more of lawyers who suspect internal corporate wrongdoing, but the SEC—under heavy pressure from the legal profession (and remember that the SEC is a lawyer-dominated agency)—limits the lawyers' obligation to report their unresolved suspicions to the board of directors, not blow the whistle publicly.

AUDITORS

Of all the gatekeepers in securities regulation, probably the most important is the independent auditor. Since the 1930s, the securities laws have required that public companies be audited annually by an independent accounting firm, with an expression of opinion by the auditor as to whether the required financial statements have been prepared in accordance with generally accepted accounting principles and fairly present the company's financial condition. As a result of more recent regulatory reforms, auditors (unlike lawyers) do under certain circumstances have a whistle-blowing obligation to report illegality that they spot in the course of their engagement to the SEC.

Sustained securities fraud usually distorts the financial performance of the company, and so—given these rules—the perpetrators must also either deceive the auditor or make the auditor complicit in the conspiracy. Successful instances of fraud, therefore, have long raised the question of why the supposedly independent auditors failed to detect the problem—where they asleep, or bought off? To be sure, it's unfair to draw conclusions simply from a handful of dramatic failures, but when Enron and WorldCom went down, it was readily noticed that both had the same outside audit firm, Arthur Andersen, which later disappeared in the face of an indictment for allegedly destroying suspicious records. In fact, however, all the major audit firms have had their share of troubles.[17]

Corporate fraudsters are sometimes clever enough to deceive even the auditors. Sadly, however, there has been ample evidence of willing complicity. Litigation has identified instances of auditors seemingly born without backbone, readily bullied, or cajoled into acquiescence. By the mid-1990s (a few years before Enron) the SEC began asking where the breakdown was, and why. The Commission soon focused on a likely possibility. Audit firms had rapidly expanded into multiservice enterprises, offering tax, consulting, and information technology services in addition to their audit work. The business became more remunerative as a result, and regulators feared that the hunger for nonaudit income (cross-sold to audit clients, among others) was compromising both objectivity and courage.

Psychologists' Warnings

At this point, some well-known psychologists with an interest in behavioral ethics, led by Harvard's Max Bazerman, became interested in the subject and presented their research to the SEC—one of the first efforts to apply this sort of behavioral science to regulatory policymaking.[18] They concurred that the nonaudit income conflict was a problem and should be curtailed. But they also expressed doubt that that change alone would be enough to solve the problem. We'll look at their evidence in a bit, but it's worth fast-forwarding to the political response: a massive lobbying effort in Congress soon squelched the Commission's initiative.

Accounting is an art as much as a science. Financial reports are supposed to fairly reflect economic reality, a reality that is both complex and highly variable from industry to industry and company to company. They're supposed to be prepared with a bias toward conservatism, being cautious about valuing income and assets, stringent with respect to costs and liabilities. But like any bias, conservatism ensures a departure from economic reality, which has led to a lively professional debate about which is more important, especially in companies engaged in sophisticated and complex lines of business. Advocates of "fair value" accounting had much success in creating more judgmental discretion for accountants (and corporate managers); thus, accounting judgments became more subjective. Some of these battles were also quite political, because greater discretion (in good times, at least) enabled higher reported earnings and stronger balance sheets, which corporate managers coveted.

That ever-growing subjectivity was the heart of the problem. In a notable experiment, for example, Bazerman and his colleagues took various financial professionals and assigned them a task of valuing a hypothetical company that was being acquired, with the sole objective being accuracy. But some of the subjects were told that they were working for the buyer, others for the seller, while still others were in the role of auditors. Even though there was no possible reward for bias (the only objective was accuracy), simply being placed in one or another role had an immense impact on the valuations, which were more than 30% higher on the seller's side than on the buyer's side.[19]

This is the product of motivated inference, of which we've seen examples throughout this book, in the face a potent mix of significant ambiguity and judgmental discretion. The problem starts simply from knowing who's paying the bills (companies pay for their audits), without any additional pressure. Once a bit of discretion is exercised in a client-serving way, going one little step more is easy the next time. Cognitively, auditors become captured fairly quickly, rationalizing until it is too late and they are stuck in a bigger and bigger deception. (A more recent experimental study shows how deep the problem might be: notwithstanding supposed norms of professional skepticism, auditors seem to react positively to management's assessments simply because of the confidence with which they are expressed.)[20]

Bazerman and colleagues predicted, and told the SEC at the time, that it could expect continuing auditor complicity unless there was far more vigorous reform than the Commission was contemplating. They suggested that in addition to cutting back radically on nonaudit services, there also be required periodic rotation of audit firms so that the slippery slope could be leveled somewhat, and also a ban on auditors leaving their firms and going to work at their clients (for higher pay, normally), closing a revolving door. And even all this might not be enough if auditors kept thinking of themselves as on their client's side, willingly taking advantage of accounting's soft spots.

Reform

The regulatory effort didn't succeed immediately because of the political blowback, but after Enron and WorldCom raised the profile of auditor conflicts, Congress finally did strengthen the independence requirements. There were also a handful of process reforms, including a direction that the SEC adopt an antibullying rule when the victims are accountants and auditors and mandatory rotation of audit engagement partners. But the big change was structural—the creation of a new quasi-governmental entity, the Public Company Accounting Oversight Board (PCAOB) with the power to set audit standards and inspect and discipline auditors. The professional autonomy of the audit profession was diminished considerably.

As noted earlier, considerable research indicates that financial reporting and audit quality have improved since the Sarbanes-Oxley reforms.[21] We can't say that that improvement is *because* of the audit reforms in the act, because a number of other regulatory and marketplace reactions to the scandals also demanded improvements in the quality of corporate disclosure and increased the likelihood that cheaters would be caught and punished more severely. Anecdotally, the common perception is that auditors do have more power vis-à-vis managers when there is a dispute, and post-SOX, auditors have become relatively more likely to help reveal financial wrongdoing.[22]

The reforms have limitations, however. Auditors—now down to only four national firms after the demise of Arthur Andersen—are still able to deliver tax services if approved by the audit committee, and a number of senior accountants (and lawyers) pled guilty to tax fraud in a new scandal involving illicit shelters that unfolded in the early 2000s.[23] The tax angle illustrates difficulty of redirecting the loyalties of audit firms, because so much money can be made by aggressively helping business clients avoid taxes, and dishonesty in tax planning relates to dishonesty with investors.[24] Nor has the PCAOB been unscathed when pursuing aggressive reform, like the audit firm rotation rule that Bazerman urged. In the deregulatory JOBS Act of 2012, Congress took the unusual step of offering most newly public companies freedom from changes in public company audit standards that were yet to be adopted by the PCAOB, just in case they might be a bother.

Auditors surely got the message about political vulnerability, which no doubt further diminished the perceived legitimacy of the new regulatory regime. Nor is increased monitoring by a new bureaucracy necessarily a good way of redirecting auditors' loyalty toward the public good. More intense oversight may force obedience, but it also produces reactance. The overall message is one of distrust, which as psychologists frequently point out, does not inspire a willing embrace of the regulators' goals. Instead, it feeds an oppositional culture, cynically doing no more than what regulators insist on and are able to enforce. Heavily regulated gatekeepers can become more passive-aggressive, and identify more closely with other victims of what they see as government overreach.

So even here, motivating good behavior is hard.[25] Company managers, with the acquiescence of the audit committees of their boards of directors, still choose their audit firms and have the ability to fire them. As Bazerman and his colleagues pointed out, the gatekeeper failures start there, with the desire to please. (We also let the threat of private securities litigation against auditors soften quite a bit in the 1990s, making fraud-on-the-market litigation somewhat less of a deterrent to complicity.)[26] Once more, the gatekeeping strategy has a mixed payoff.

Of course, all disappointment is relative—the accounting profession likes to speak of the "expectations gap," the idea that the public has an unreasonably high expectation of how surely auditors can prevent fraud at reasonable cost. There is some truth to this, even if it's a bit self-serving. Costs do matter. The issue of audit firm rotation, for example, makes a great deal of sense from a slippery slope perspective, but at the same time would mean that new auditors come on every so often low on the learning curve, which means they have to come to know the company. As this is happening, which is costly in and of itself, they may be more likely to miss a great deal of cleverly disguised book-cooking.

INTERNAL SURVEILLANCE

Managerial blind spots are the product of both biases and lack of good information, which feed on each other. In any large organization, information is likely to be widely diffused among many individuals. In theory, they are all supposed to report what is important to their superiors, so that there is a constant flow upward from which the big picture of the firm's financial condition and riskiness can be drawn by those at the top. But if everyone is subject to bias—not wanting to see or report up information that makes them look bad—the whole process is subject to both deliberate and unconscious distortion.[27] This facilitates the plausible deniability we saw in chapter 2, where top executives defend themselves by saying they were misled by their subordinates or just didn't know what was going on, and thus are innocent.

Internal Controls: From Watergate to Enron

The law (not just securities regulation) has spent decades trying to fix this information gap, making those at the top more aware of—and thus more accountable for—bad things that might be happening down below that might be significant in terms of the company's future performance and prospects. Part of this relates to the quality of the company's financial reporting, but it extends to corporate governance, risk management, and legal compliance. We needn't detail this history, except to note it first became of special interest to the SEC in the aftermath of the Watergate scandal in the mid-1970s. (The Watergate connection? Some of the money paid to those who broke into Democratic National Committee headquarters in the Watergate came from corporate slush funds, which were hidden from normal accounting controls.) Congress passed a statute, the Foreign Corrupt Practices Act, designed, among other things, to force better internal controls.

Twenty years later, after Enron, WorldCom, and other corporate catastrophes demonstrated the inadequacy of the existing rules, Congress stepped up the regulation considerably by insisting that (1) management take responsibility for assessing the quality of its control system on a regular basis, and publicly disclose material weaknesses that it finds; and (2) the company's auditors review and assess the control system as well. The latter proved to be an expensive redundancy, as auditors—uncertain of how deep to dig but paid well for their time—made these reviews quite intrusive. To an extent, this is a success story. We now have plenty of empirical evidence to show that investors have come to value these internal controls assessments, because stock prices react strongly to unexpected deficiency disclosures. In a survey of financial executives—SOX loathers, often enough—they grudgingly acknowledged that the new regime produces better financial reporting than the old days.[28]

But because of the rapid increase in audit expenses (and maybe management's loss of privacy), this reform set off a cry to Congress that echoed for a decade. The internal controls audit soon became a potent symbol for regulatory overreach. Even though the SEC later relaxed the requirement and costs did go down, the business community—especially smaller companies—remained obsessed with seeking repeal.[29] Congress eventually responded to the continuing political clamor by eliminating the internal controls audit entirely for smaller public companies in 2010, and giving newly public companies a grace period exemption from it in 2012.

The technical implementation story is beyond what we need to be concerned with here. What is fascinating is a fundamental question embedded in this history: how do we balance the costs and benefits of internal surveillance? Intuitively, the external audit of internal controls can guard against management (strategically, to cut costs, or from overconfidence) leaving too many places in the dark, where wrongdoing can fester. The costs, on the other hand, are also considerable. We've already seen two kinds: the out-of-pocket expenses of hiring forensic experts both inside and outside the company, accountants and lawyers in particular, and the distraction of having to deal with reporting issues, which can be very time consuming, rather than a focus on driving the business. These are both fixed and contingent—both lawyers and accountants can come across suspicious activity that demands a new round of expenditures to investigate and, if necessary, fix. Stories abound of millions of dollars spent on internal investigations that ultimately determine that the problem was not that serious after all.

See All, Know All?

Especially as technology evolves, the potential for internal surveillance has almost no stopping point. Imagine that we could build a "panopticon"—the Orwellian kind of system (envisioned long ago in prison form by Jeremy Bentham) that could see and tell *all* inside the company. Consider, for example, tracking systems that are programmed to spot the use of key words and phrases in all the email traffic involving company employees. The field of using psychology of the sort we're invoking to help predict noncompliance and unethical behavior is a new one, behavioral compliance.[30] Given the rapidly growing body of research on the correlates with fraud and other forms of wrongdoing, one can readily imagine a behaviorally attuned program that seeks to identify markers as they point toward more intense motive and opportunity. MIT behavioral economist Andrew Lo has suggested that a linear factor model could eventually be constructed for each executive that estimates risk appetite at any given time, and which in the aggregate might depict the taste for risk in the firm as a whole, or in individual subunits.[31] A news report about J.P. Morgan (which has had more than its share of recent compliance troubles) describes an effort there to design algorithms that know you're a rogue employee before even you do.[32]

Putting aside the out-of-pocket costs, the mind-numbing mass of data, and the interpretive problems as a result, what would the behavioral effects be? Chances are that this system would adversely affect productivity because of the signal of distrust that it sends. When people feel that they are being watched closely, they act self-protectively, and motivation drops. Research on internal compliance suggests that the routines come to dominate, crowding out whatever sense of personal or group ethical responsibility might otherwise be brought to work each day.[33] (One of the most famous psychological research studies in this area involved Israeli day care centers, which tried to solve the problem of parents coming a little bit late to pick up their children by charging a small fee based on the length of the delay. The result was much more lateness, as parents came to think about when to pick up their kids as a simple question of price rather than a responsibility to think about the inconvenience they were causing for the school's staff.)[34] Those who study organizational behavior take this as a lesson that applies directly to all compliance monitoring: trust and autonomy have their place. Intense surveillance can backfire.

If so, the organizational consequences of intrusive surveillance could be considerable. Even within conventional financial reporting, managers might be more reluctant to invest in riskier projects if they would create greater accounting difficulties.[35] The effect is amplified by SOX: with the ramp-up of internal controls and other structural reforms, there is more and more process that diminishes managers' enthusiasm to push the envelope in terms of risky innovation. There is research to suggest that this is one of SOX's stronger effects.[36] Compliance norms threaten beliefs, behaviors, and cultural tropes that are instinctively success-producing.

So in the end, exactly how much internal surveillance is required, and who chooses? There is no better illustration of the dilemmas of modern securities regulation than this question. Leaving this to management's discretion seems foolish if we want greater accountability, unless we somehow believe that market forces (i.e., shareholder pressure) will suffice to find an optimal balance. (This mimics the optimal disclosure question discussed earlier.) That said, one can see how investors would be ambivalent about the costs and benefits, not wanting to unduly dampen morale or risk-taking simply in the name of transparency. Presumably the right answer, from shareholders' perspective, varies considerably from company to company.

But when we're talking about hidden corporate wrongdoing that has potentially harmful *social* consequences, maybe it shouldn't matter what's most efficient for investors. Society can demand more caution than that. (Where what is uncovered is illegal, the company is put in the difficult position of deciding whether it has to self-report to regulators or the Justice Department, increasing the likelihood of something bad as a result.)[37] In the end, the thumb on the scales comes increasingly from regulators and prosecutors, who not only invoke the SOX rules but use their subjective assessment of the strength of internal compliance and controls in deciding whether the corporation itself was at fault, deserving of more severe punishment, when there was a breakdown.[38] The government is plainly asking whether the system, viewed in hindsight, was controlling the risk of bad behavior, of which financial misreporting is just one example—publicness, yet again. Surveillance-creep is destined to continue, whatever its murky mix of costs and benefits.

From a regulatory perspective, whistle-blowers—people inside companies who report suspected wrongdoing either internally or to governmental authorities—can be a godsend. To encourage internal whistle-blowing, SOX created a new, if not artfully drafted, federal protection from retaliation, and required the audit committee of the board of directors made up of independent directors to take responsibility for encouraging the upward reporting of danger signs. When company employees see something, they should feel comfortable saying something.

The social psychology of whistle-blowing is very well studied.[39] The strongest norms in a tight-knit organization are of loyalty, particularly to peers. "Ratting" usually violates that norm, even where there is real evidence of wrongdoing. When the suspected wrongdoer is a higher-up, the fear grows that the whistle-blower will be the loser in any power struggle, or the messenger who is shot. Higher-ups may well be motivated to construe the evidence differently from the whistle-blower. Not surprisingly, the most likely whistle-blower—least deterred by these fears—is one who has already left the company. But at that point, the whistle-blower can be portrayed as a disgruntled ex-employee whose credibility is open to doubt because of anger and frustration.

The reluctance to blow the whistle is compounded by cognitive constraints and the diffusion of information. People are less inclined to notice and act on wrongdoing by others when that behavior evolves slowly over time.[40] Or an employee may see evidence of wrongdoing but not have the whole picture. If there is room for doubt, the mind can find ample justification for construing the situation in a way that extinguishes the guilt for doing nothing. You certainly don't want to hurt someone else's career by bringing an accusation that might be unfounded. The can of worms is best left unopened. There is also a timing issue—by the time the evidence of wrongdoing is clear enough, public disclosure may be devastating for the company and many innocent stakeholders, and hence a difficult step to take.

So the hoped-for ex ante effects of whistle-blower encouragement and protection are debatable. SOX offered a means of corrective justice for some wrongfully terminated employees who tried to do the right thing but were punished instead. But, partly because the statute was poorly drafted in a number of key respects, courts have made this action hard even for them. Among other things, there had to be a "reasonable basis" for believing a securities law violation, which is not an easy impression for a nonlawyer to form. There are the inevitable fact battles as the employer-defendant brings forth every possible deficiency in the employee's work history to show that the cause of the termination was unrelated to any alleged whistle-blowing. Justice was by no means certain, or even particularly likely, a message that further undercuts any encouragement to future whistle-blowers.

In 2010, Congress shifted its strategy with respect to whistle-blowers from protection to incentive. The headline reform was that whistle-blowers were now encouraged to go directly to the SEC with evidence of a possible securities law violation, and could get paid for doing so. This provision, part of the Dodd-Frank Act, gives a whistle-blower who provides original information leading to an SEC enforcement action or criminal prosecution that produces a penalty of more than $1 million a right to a bounty of between 10% and 30% of that amount. There are plenty of corporate fraud cases where the penalties are in the hundreds of millions of dollars. Where a whistle-blower was a sufficient factor in a $100 million case, he or she would have a right to at least $10 million, and might get much more. To make its new approach work, the SEC created an Office of the Whistleblower to handle the expected volume of tips, and tries (somewhat) to be user friendly by allowing for anonymous tips and lawyer representation.

How well this now works is hard to evaluate; it's still early. There is research to suggest that rewarding whistle-blowing with money "prices" the decision rather than stressing its moral nature, thus making it less likely except when the cost-benefit differential is large.[41] Moreover, to be motivated by the rule to overcome all the reasons not to report, internally or to the SEC, an employee has to be fairly confident that he or she will be delivering original, high-quality information and first in line to do so, and that it will result in a big-enough penalty. There are lots of contingencies there that could still be demotivating. There is a robust fear in the business community that compliance officials inside companies will use their access to sensitive issues to bypass the chain of command and tip off the SEC. To date, there have been a handful of large bounties announced by the SEC, including one of $13 million. In 2013 the SEC got over three thousand tips, around 17% of which were related to disclosure and financial reporting. We can't tell the balance between tips from current employees and those from outsiders; anecdotally, SEC staff has mentioned that ex-girlfriends and ex-spouses seem especially motivated to share their stories.

ANALYSTS: CREDIBILITY, BIAS, AND OPPORTUNISM

Securities analysts play an important role in our financial markets, akin to the more conventional gatekeepers even though they aren't insiders. Our focus here is on the sell side, analysts who work for brokerage firms and investment banks, providing commentary, forecasts, and recommendations for buying and selling securities to aid clients and customers of these firms. These analysts typically make their recommendations and estimates public, so that they potentially influence a large population of investors. Precisely because our mandatory disclosure system doesn't compel much in the way of forward-looking information, analysts do their own projections and estimates: disclosure's gap-fillers. Though mainly fixated on the task of valuation (which should enhance market efficiency), they are also in a position to assess whether what management is saying about the companies they cover is untrue, and hopefully blow the whistle by withdrawing positive recommendations and estimates that they've previously made if they come to doubt management's credibility.

Decades ago, research was profitable for brokerage firms because it brought in customers—in an era of commission rates that were fixed by regulation, firms competed for customers by offering them proprietary research in return for the inflated commission revenue. But when commissions were unfixed in the late 1970s, they dropped, ushering in an era of intense competition on price. And because a large brokerage firm couldn't really make research available to thousands of retail customers but keep it secret from the public at large, the incentive structure broke down. Investors could take advantage of the public research without routing trades through that firm at high cost, a classic free-rider problem.

Spitzer's Crusade

So if sell-side research was to continue, there needed to be some alternative source of profit from the firm's perspective. To put it bluntly, that added value for a time was as cheerleader for companies with which the firm (and by this time the largest brokerage firms were often part of financial conglomerates) had a profitable relationship, which depended on the goodwill of company management. Investment banking in the 1990s was in a time of bountiful opportunity because of a booming tech-driven stock market (meaning lots of public offerings of securities) and a cresting wave of mergers and acquisitions. Managers of those companies wanted a high stock price, a hungry market for their shares. They were willing to select their bankers based at least in part on how enthusiastic that firm's analysts were willing to be.

The conflict of interest was fairly obvious, and exposed as soon as the tech stock bubble burst (actually, academic researchers had been onto this well before). Investors were losing money, and it was easy to look back to see how strongly analysts had promoted stocks in companies that were now sick or dead. Most still had buy recommendations in place on the eve of the crash. New York attorney general Eliot Spitzer, invoking his state's capacious Martin Act, took aim at these scandals and maneuvered a massive global settlement, which the SEC joined as a late-comer, mixing big financial penalties with internal reforms. His weapon was the then relatively new phenomenon of searchable email files. From among a massive number he had demanded, he found some smoking guns—well-known analysts with buy recommendations out privately referring to the companies in question as dogs and "P.O.S." (pieces of shit).[42]

Because analyst recommendations are public and can be tracked, it's actually fairly easy to test for bias driven by investment-banking interests, making this an ideal research subject. There is a confounding factor, however. Recall that investment analysts have a strong incentive to curry favor with corporate management, even if they have no investment banking prospects in mind, simply because access to the best information (material or not) depends on the willingness of company insiders to share. Managers are likely to be much more open with an enthusiast for the company than one persistently critical, which creates an incentive for the analyst to be favorable at least in the publicly available research. The more pressure there is to deliver an edge to well-heeled clients, the greater the incentive. As a result, we might expect to observe a bias even without investment banking connections. Regulation FD was adopted, as we saw in the last chapter, to deal with the worst of these selective disclosure problems, but it may be fairly porous, especially with respect to marginally material information, which still may be coveted by sophisticated investors.

To complicate things even further, consider the situation of an analyst whose best clients are mutual funds or hedge funds that take big positions in a company. Even if that analyst overcomes the investment banking and inside information temptations, those buy-side clients are likely to be very angry if the analyst downgrades the stock in a way that leads to a sell-off and downward pressure on the stock price, unless first given ample time to bail out.[43] For many reasons, then, the lot of an optimistic analyst is much happier.

So what does the research tell us about sell-side analysts? As you might imagine, the volume of work in this area is such that there are studies supporting (and refuting) nearly any conjecture. On average, sell-side analysts are valuable, contributing to pricing efficiency. There is support for the somewhat heartening idea that even in the face of these conflicts, the best (i.e., most highly rated) sell-side analysts act as if reputation matters, and even investment banking mandates can be sensitive to analyst skill as well as analyst enthusiasm. As to those conflicts of interest, there are two themes. Not surprisingly, analysts overall do mirror their employers' self-interest, whether from driving more trading, and thus commission revenue, within brokerage firms, satisfying hedge fund and mutual fund clients, or the long-suspected investment banking connection. Even today, analysts acknowledge heavy pressures to please.[44] These especially affect the likelihood of a downgrade of a previously positive recommendation or forecast. Whether this is conscious or the product of cognitive bias is hard to say[45]—most economists don't inquire into state of mind, just outcomes. Some researchers have made a case for some degree of unconscious bias, potentially putting analysts in the Kool-Aid-drinking category. But maybe they're hired for their innate optimism and come to enthusiasm naturally, widening the advantage over more downbeat types over time because of the advantages a positive attitude brings. When a very positive analyst catches a wave of equally positive investor sentiment, the two work in synch and the analyst looks positively brilliant as the market follows prediction as if by direction.

On the other hand, market forces may push back against bias, moderating its impact.[46] Even if recommendations are skewed, the smart money in the market may discount the advice. The more institutional investors there are invested in a company's stock (which tends to correlate with the size of the issuer), the more robust this check is. The latter point is important, because buy-side analysts have a somewhat jaundiced view of the value of the sell side, and they make the bulk of the trading decisions.

Reform

This conflicting evidence poses a regulatory dilemma, made somewhat more challenging because analyst bias is hard to address directly via enforcement. What analysts say about a company's future is a matter of opinion, and courts say proof of a false opinion ordinarily involves showing that the speaker actually disbelieved what he or she was saying. That's where the conscious versus unconscious bias debate has bite. (We're also heading into treacherous First Amendment territory here, because this is very public commercial speech.) Private securities litigation hasn't been particularly effective either, with a number of well-publicized class action lawsuits faltering because courts said that even if the analysts were biased, it's nearly impossible to identify what if any portion of the market-wide stock price drop was their responsibility.[47]

Thus the Spitzer-driven global settlement with major investment banking firms was highly prophylactic. The resulting reforms require more disclosure of conflicts. They also try to ensure that analyst compensation is not influenced by investment bankers, and limit the ability of analysts to take part in "pitch meetings" where bankers compete for underwriting and other corporate financing mandates. These requirements seem a bit naive, because analysts don't need close involvement by or with the bankers to understand that their employer prefers positive to negative. They know what's good for their careers and act accordingly, if not necessarily consciously.[48] Equally doubtful was the SEC's main contribution, called Regulation AC (for "Analyst Conflicts"), which requires the analyst to pledge that an opinion is his or her own, not the product of anyone else's influence. In the first place, it's foolish to ask for such a promise when analysts act as part of teams (no one has autonomy as a result) and are subject to supervision by superiors. Second, psychologists point out that having someone certify *after* some action has been taken tends to produce defensive bolstering, simply justifying whatever the prior action was.[49]

What happened in response to all of this should come as no shock. Most importantly, securities firms pulled back on their research coverage, spending less on what was becoming a less and less profitable exercise. This led to fears among smaller companies that their stock prices were depressed because, with the loss of coverage, fewer investors were familiar with or had confidence in them (other factors, like lowered spreads for market-makers and Regulation FD, barring private conveyances of material nonpublic information, also played a role here). What was left of sell-side research became much more focused on gaining private edges for buy-side clients, as we saw in chapter 3.

Average investors can't assume that the advice given to them for free is always in their best interest to follow. As a result, sell-side analysts aren't perfect gatekeepers either, even if they also aren't the demons they're sometimes made out to be. When conditions are right, sell-side analysts can add substantial interpretive value and bring promising companies to greater public attention. It's just that conditions aren't always so right, and regulators have their hands tied—economically, legally, and politically— in how much more they can do without threatening the long-term viability of that part of the research function that is socially valuable.

SUNLIGHT, EXECUTIVE PAY, AND SHORT-TERMISM

To this point in the chapter, we've surveyed a set of mechanisms designed to make corporate disclosure more credible in the face of high informational asymmetry. We've found plenty of conflicts of interest that diminish the power of these mechanisms, even though—collectively—independent directors, auditors, and analysts probably do contribute to better disclosure quality than we'd have without them.

We now turn to the behavioral effects of disclosure, keeping in mind Louis Brandeis's famous thought that disclosure works not simply to deliver useful information but through the cleansing power of sunlight. People supposedly act better when they others are watching. There is much to be said for that idea, but as we're about to see, the situation is once again more complicated.

Self-Dealing

The place where the Brandeisian disinfectant seems to work best has to do with conflict-of-interest transactions, where a company insider enters into some kind of deal with the corporation and so will be tempted to use power or influence to make it unduly favorable to him, at the expense of the company. SEC rules make public companies disclose all transactions involving more than $125,000 when an officer or director has a conflicting interest.

We saw earlier that the psychology of disclosing conflicts is surprising. Disclosure sometimes enables opportunism. But it all depends on context, and likely adverse consequences beyond the mere possibility of alerting the receiver of the message. In the securities context, disclosure that creates even the appearance of overreaching can put your reputation at risk, and invites further inquiry and fiduciary-duty litigation if it smacks of unfairness.[50] The SEC has shown a strong willingness to bring cases where there is concealed managerial self-dealing. In countries that have less effective disclosure regimes, such transactions—which go under the label of "tunneling" because of how easily corporate assets disappear underground into the hands of managers or controlling shareholders—are sadly much too common. In the United States, disclosure related to managerial agency costs seems to be one of securities law's success stories,[51] a helpful (probably necessary) supplement to state law norms of fiduciary loyalty.

But it takes both clarity and enforcement effort for this to work. One of SOX's other reforms was to have all public companies adopt codes of ethics for senior financial executives, dealing with a wider variety of conflicts of interest than the specific self-dealing disclosure rule. Codes would have to be publicized, as would waivers or exceptions. But here research has shown almost no positive effect, and a simple check-the-box practice in most companies. Partly this has to do with how vacuous codes can be. But just as important, the SEC signaled no real interest in this task among all the other disclosures it has to police, allowing weak compliance norms to fester.[52]

Executive Pay

Disclosure only cleanses if the obligation is well policed (because those tempted toward abuse will lie or conceal anyway) and insiders feel some shame or threat from what is revealed. A familiar but less inspiring example of disclosure's behavioral effects has to do with executive pay. A quintessential fear in corporate governance is that managerial power and weak boards of directors lead to inflated salaries and other remuneration.

The SEC has long insisted that companies disclose what their highest-ranking officers and directors are paid. Over time, compensation packages have become more complex (lots of deferred or contingent compensation, for example), meaning that the rules keep changing. Under pressure to use moral suasion as a tool to keep such pay in line with reasonable expectations of good performance, the SEC has gradually increased the disclosure intensity in a variety of ways besides the volume of information (which itself is considerable). Thus, in the 1990s as exorbitant pay packages gained traction as a public issue, the SEC insisted on the addition of a performance graph showing the stock price movement of the company vis-à-vis its peers, so that highly paid laggards could be identified. It also forced the company directors to provide a narrative explaining how and why they arrived at the decision to pay the top managers what they did. In other words, much more sunlight, and hope for shaming.

But there was no downward effect on executive pay; if anything, the rate of compensation inflation increased.[53] To be sure, maybe this had to do with an efficient market for executive talent—the challenges to running a company are ever-increasing and the demand for top talent strong, so that disclosure may have been a nonfactor. Numerous academics, on the other hand, invoke the "Lake Wobegon effect"—Garrison Keillor's reference to a place where everyone is above average. If you think of your skills in an inflated fashion (or the board of directors thinks of you that way), you *deserve* more. One effect of executive pay disclosure is that everyone knows what everyone else is being paid. Thus pay ratchets up faster, because few executives accept a below-average wage as fair, and no board of directors wants to explain that they have chosen a CEO to run the company who isn't at least somewhere in the top half talent-wise. Sensing this, it appears that companies engage in impression management by strategically selecting high-paying peers for comparison in order to justify increased pay.[54]

The point is that what has the potential to shame someone with disclosure depends on that person's point of view and the milieu he or she inhabits, and these can be thoroughly self-serving. The Dodd-Frank Act introduces a concept called "say on pay," giving shareholders a nonbinding referendum vote on the company's top executive pay package. It is much too early to tell, but there is some evidence that this could be having a bit more of an impact than the pure disclosure solutions. Perhaps executives, or the directors who set the pay, are uncomfortable about the risk of losing the referendum and being told by the shareholders that pay is way too high in light of the company's recent performance. We'll see. The most recent round of disclosure changes—requiring disclosure of the ratio between the CEO's pay and that of the median worker at the company, making more salient the issue of income inequality—injects a bit more publicness into the vote. One shouldn't bet that any more shame will follow at this point in American culture.

Short-Termism

Of all the debates about the behavioral effects of disclosure, the most consequential is whether managers are pressured to focus overly on short-term results, to the exclusion of longer-term investment, growth, and sustainability. Frequent disclosure is one of the named culprits here, because—almost uniquely around the world—the United States requires domestic public companies to state their financial results every ninety days, and the financial markets seem to obsess on whether these results meet, beat, or fall short of expectations. If the market demands that near-term targets always be hit, there may not be much room to plan for the longer term.

Of course, disclosure requirements themselves are not what make stock prices so important—that's a matter of corporate governance. Scholars disagree about the connection between stock prices and short-term pressures.[55] Some point out that rational investors and efficient markets place considerable value on the long-term future, so that the pressure is just a myth. Think about Google or Facebook, neither of which has a valuation based mainly on near-term results.

The problem is that knowing whether the long run to which management seems committed is a solid vision or a self-serving rationalization is hard for anyone on the outside. It involves an assessment of an immense amount of confidential strategic information, and is speculative in any event. Investors can become overly committed to a belief in the company's long-term future, so that the market becomes insufficiently critical in judging that vision. That kind of exuberance aside, however, the rational response to opacity is skepticism. Thus, in relatively efficient market conditions, stock prices may overweight the near-term simply because that information is more transparent and credible. "Market myopia" is not necessarily a behavioral bias (though it certainly can be), but rather a natural response to informational asymmetry.

Corporate insiders find this frustrating, of course. Complaints about having to manage to the market—short-termism—start here. The evidence is fairly substantial that most managers *do* focus heavily on short-term results. There are numerous surveys of financial executives that suggest that these managers believe that the market must be obeyed, and that certain projects that might be intrinsically valuable are rejected out of fear of adverse market reaction. Indeed, in recent years there is a perception that there is less cooking the books than there used to be, but more of "real" earnings management—financial choices made simply because of anticipated market consequences.[56] As more firms act out this belief, others feel pressure to conform. One common manifestation of short-termism and investor impatience, supposedly, is less corporate investment in innovation and sustainability. If reducing valuable research and development means more dollars in quarterly earnings, they say, foolishly impatient investors are for it.[57] One group of researchers has demonstrated a significant decline in real investment activity associated with frequent (i.e., quarterly) reporting,[58] and less frequent reporting is a common recommendation of those convinced that management's frustrations are legitimate.

Note the political intervention here, putting innovation (and presumably job creation) on the side of the incumbents. But the other side of the argument isn't hard to see. Let's divide managers into groupings. We'll put aside the group that, based on their inside view, believe that their stock is overpriced because of market euphoria. Such fortunate insiders gain all the advantages in terms of compensation, acquisitions, and goodwill, at the psychic expense of have constantly to meet inflated expectations. For reasons we saw in chapter 2, fraud becomes very tempting, if they are not already in the muck of deceit. That's worth keeping in mind as a regulator, but not what we're after here. We'll also put aside those lucky companies that have persuaded the market to accept their long-term vision, so that their stock price accommodates some degree of managerial freedom to do what has generated success in the past. (Those companies are favorites of patient long-term institutional investors.)

The next group is made up of those who genuinely believe that the market under-values the company's long-term prospects. They may be right, of course, given their informational advantage. Many companies go through a rough patch, disappointing investors, but then invent their way out of the problem so that they truly back on track. But the market, already once burned, remains doubtful. These companies face the dilemma that critics of short-termism stress: keep investing in the plan and risk the wrath of impatient shareholders, or manage to the market by doing things more likely to please the impatient. We're all worse off when the latter happens.

Anyone who has gotten this far in the book, however, will see that some portion (I would say significant) of that genuine belief is driven by some degree of self-deception. For a host of psychological and cultural reasons, management's commitment to that long-term strategy exceeds any objective valuation. What investors fear, then, is that managers are wasting shareholder money by empire-building, sloth, or foolish proj-ects in the name of the long run. But it's a Kool-Aid-laced rationalization. Here, of course, the market skepticism is amply warranted, and shareholders would prefer the shorter leash of short-termism.

Finally, there some managers who realize that the market's jaundiced view is correct—there isn't untapped value out there in the long run. They want to hold onto the private benefits of control for as long as they can, taking advantage of whatever free cash flow the company can continue to generate. This is a dead-weight social loss, simply because control can be sticky.

How you feel about the pressures of short-termism probably depends on your per-ception of the relative size of the latter three categories. The argument that managers deserve insulation from myopic shareholder and market pressure wants you to assume that most companies are in the first of these categories, genuinely sensing a long-term route to value and sustainability but encountering too much investor resistance. The argument for the short leash wants you to concentrate on the second and third of those categories. If you believe strongly in efficient markets, you have all the more reason to trust the discipline, even if it has some unfortunate consequences for com-panies in the first. The rhetorical trump card for those opposing managerial autonomy is that so much of our collective wealth—especially retirement savings—is invested in corporate stock, and shouldn't be sacrificed to managerial selfishness or self-serving illusions when there are near-term ways to enhance that wealth.

Shareholder Activism

This contentious debate plays out dramatically with respect to evidence of growing shareholder activism, a hedge fund-driven phenomenon. Activist hedge funds take a significant equity stake in a company, then demand that management engage in some immediate action (anything from distributing cash to selling the company) that would deliver tangible shareholder value as reflected in a higher market price.[59] There are two parts to the threat: first, the possibility that shareholder at the next annual meeting will punish incumbents who resist (for which the activist would need many more shareholder votes than it has); second, that the market will be disappointed by the incumbents' intransigence and drive the stock price down further. Activism is self-defeating if the stock price does not rise, and so the key to success is the credibility of the governance threat. Hence the debate about the extent—via greater voting rights, ability to nominate directors, or hold referendums—that we should further empower investors to threaten managers if shareholders lose faith in management's long-term plans.

You can pick which side you're on in this debate—whichever you choose, you have the company of many thoughtful people. On the managerialist side, some attack the motives of shareholder activists. But while there may be some governance battles where the activist is pursuing a selfish interest not shared with other investors in the firm, these instances appear to be unusual. As a result, the business community has gravitated strongly toward the market myopia view, that financial markets mindlessly value the here and now over the future in supporting the activists. In doubting the motivations or good sense of the markets, however, the business community gives away a political prop that it has long happily put to use in all sorts of settings where the effort was to avoid regulatory intrusion—that markets are wise and can be trusted.

The SEC has gotten pulled into these debates in a number of ways beside the frequency of financial reporting. The securities laws require disclosure of plans and intentions by activist shareholders within ten days after acquiring a 5% equity stake in the company, which the activists are pressuring the Commission to relax to give their campaigns more secrecy and thus potency, while managers want the current rule enforced more aggressively to smoke out forthcoming attacks. At one point, the SEC sought to facilitate the ability of large investors to nominate corporate directors to stand for election against the slate endorsed by the incumbent board—a rule promptly struck down by conservative judges on the DC Circuit Court of Appeals for failing to do a rigorous cost-benefit analysis of the change.[60] A not-so-subtle message was that the Commission should be wary of claiming expertise in an area traditionally left to the states. These battles are intensely political, as you might imagine, and the SEC has seemed for the moment to lose its appetite for any more big corporate governance fights.

SOCIAL RESPONSIBILITY

Matters of risk-taking, corporate research, innovation, and employment opportunities—the stuff of the short-term, long-term debate—are not simply of interest to investors. They are matters of social importance, as are sustainability issues relating to climate change, human rights, cybersecurity, public health, and the like. The internecine debate between investors and managers about shareholder primacy obscures the question of what is best for the rest of us, and whether the disclosure responsibilities of public companies should be extended to a wider variety of social issues regardless of how investors and managers feel about the cost-benefit trade-offs.

This is one of the most noteworthy trends in securities laws over the last decade or two, though its history goes back much further.[61] In 2010, for example, Congress directed that SEC-registered public companies investigate and disclose the extent to which their products use so-called conflict minerals coming from the Congo region of Africa. The reason had to do with human rights. Money from the mining of such minerals supports violence and repression, and we know that such minerals make their way globally, through convoluted supply chains, into many different products, especially technology-based ones.[62] Public companies were furious; the cost of investigation into supply chains is considerable. (By the way, while this seems like a thoroughly left-leaning requirement, its chief proponent was Senator Sam Brownback, a conservative Republican from Kansas.)

While disconnected from mainstream investor interests (though there are significant socially responsible investors who do have an interest), can this be ruled inappropriate if it's what Congress or the public wants? As we've seen, big corporations have large footprints on the global economy and in society generally—their actions have massive consequences. What's wrong with using public company disclosure as a means to enhance the transparency and accountability of the economically powerful? In recent years, public company disclosure has taken on board-level diversity, income inequality, doing business with Iran, mine safety, natural resource "extraction," and a host of initiatives relating to global warming and the environment. They are efforts to open up powerful companies to greater public scrutiny and pressure, pouring on disinfectant in the hope of something better, or at least to make them more uncomfortable: publicness requirements, in other words. In sociology, there is much attention to perceived legitimacy ("social license") as something very important to the attraction of the economic and social resources needed for an organization to succeed.

Try this to see where you stand. Should public companies be required to disclose how much they spend on political action, broken down so that outsiders can see what issues or candidates management is favoring? To make this economically material, you have to believe that management often enough misuses company money by supporting positions and candidates contrary to the company's best interests.[63] This is possible, but not all that likely and not what most of us imagine when thinking about the issue. If disclosure is appropriate here, it comes out of the publicness impulse: unease at making such potent political action a matter of private managerial choice. (The famous Supreme Court case endorsing corporate First Amendment rights as to political spending, *Citizens United*,[64] partly justified its logic by noting that shareholders can remove managers who misuse company money—something hard to do if there is no good disclosure about the expenditures.)[65]

The sunlight conundrum affects many different public company disclosures. Conflict mineral disclosure, noted earlier, is likely to affect public company behavior only if investors, consumers, or other stakeholders punish companies that use conflict minerals. Given the attenuation of supply chains, we'll have to wait and see. Hopefully something good will come of this; maybe the disclosure due diligence will lead to greater use of supply chains found to be untainted. I do have some unease that these kinds of disinfectant disclosures are based on the false consensus belief of the proponents that *they* would certainly stop acting in such a socially irresponsible way if subject to public scrutiny, rather than considering the very different belief systems of corporations and their managers. This is reminiscent of a scene in the old Woody Allen movie *Manhattan*, making fun of a New York partygoer who imagines that pro-Nazi demonstrators would be so devastated by a critical op-ed piece in the *New York Times* that they'd call off the rally. Maybe the disclosure is meant to be a small "feel better" tax on the activity in question (and finds its political motivation there), whether or not it does much good. And of course it may generate information that can be used by noninvestor interests for their advocacy and protest efforts, something managers particularly loathe and consider out of bounds for securities regulation.

Many critics of social disclosure argue that social responsibility comes at the expense of corporate and shareholder value—that there is a stark difference between doing good and focusing on the bottom line, and that managers who commit to doing good are just seeking cover for their own selfish interests (though perhaps rationalized in more noble terms). Some studies support this agency-cost view. But there is actually quite a bit of support for a positive correlation between paying close attention to social license and financial value. For example, Allen Ferrell of Harvard and two European colleagues found that higher-rated companies in terms of corporate social responsibility have better corporate governance and their activities are associated with higher firm value.[66] Another study shows that companies with a high corporate social responsibility index rating get more lenient treatment when accused of wrongdoing, which is tangibly valuable.[67]

If they're right, it can't be said that social disclosures are necessarily irrelevant to financial investors. Indeed, an increasing number of influential people think that required corporate disclosure should move beyond backward-looking financial performance data to a more diverse set of metrics that are associated with long-term value, like human capital, innovation, and sustainability (environmental and otherwise). Auditors would be happy to oblige in assessing compliance, for an extra fee.[68] One of the big questions for the future of securities regulation is whether this project will take hold, creating a truly public form of accounting, over which managers, investors, and political actors would fight endlessly given the lack of solid data about costs, investor benefits, and societal benefits.

The SEC has thus far shown relatively little interest in social disclosure, acting only when required (as with conflict minerals) or pressured. It seems to understand the treacherous political waters it's being asked to swim in when securities regulation loses touch with a more focused form of investor protection and the organizational benefits of preserving a distinctive investor-focused mission. But the SEC doesn't always get the choice, and we can expect the publicness disclosure and governance agenda to continue to grow unless the conservative vision of the corporation as a free economic actor with a strong right of privacy somehow triumphs. So let's finish this chapter by turning to the critics' freedom train.

GOING (OR STAYING) DARK

A few years ago, before it made its celebrated initial public offering, Facebook was in a quandary. It had grown massively large and celebrated, and many of its shareholders—particularly early-stage investors and employees who held options and stock—wanted to be able to cash in on their now immensely valuable holdings. But to go public meant incurring the costs that we have been examining, especially the transparency that would allow the public (and its potential competitors) to see more deeply inside the company than its owners wanted. Facebook was unwilling to go public until the balance of benefits and costs tipped in the right way, and it wasn't yet ready. In the meantime, however, it needed capital to grow as a still-private company.

The catch is that under the Securities Exchange Act, private status is forfeited as soon as a sizable corporation has more than a certain number of "shareholders of record," at the time, five hundred. Facebook wanted to avoid that trigger, of course, and reportedly worked with Goldman Sachs to structure a private offering that would bring in a large amount of money from a large number of Goldman clients, but structured legally in such a way that that the number of record shareholders would only increase by one.

That plan ultimately caught the attention of the press, and the deal reportedly was called off, which set in motion the political process leading to the JOBS Act in 2012, which I mentioned in the introduction and will come back to repeatedly in chapter 5.[69] Conservative members of Congress thought that emerging companies like Facebook deserve more choice over whether or when they are public or private. The animating idea behind the legislation is to make it less burdensome to become public, but also easier to stay private. That included raising the trigger from five hundred record shareholders to two thousand (not counting employee-shareholders), no more than five hundred of which could be nonaccredited (i.e., nonwealthy) investors. Congress said nothing about what "record" means or whether the kind of deal Goldman designed was legitimate—if it is, counting means little, and there is an easy way to stay private.

While all this may sound very technical, in the deep weeds of securities law, it takes us to an inflection point in our regulatory future. We've seen the weighty demands of publicness, in terms of both regulatory burdens and the short-term pressures emanating from the stock market and shortsighted investors. Managers increasingly despise both. And we're seeing more clearly the benefits of privateness in terms of creativity and innovation. There is evidence, for example, that innovation inside a firm *drops* after it goes public.[70] In addition to the risk of investor impatience, there is an issue of entrepreneurial motivation—the most highly skilled innovators benefit more by inventing when they have a relatively large stake in a yet-private company than when they've been diluted and are sharing ownership with a vast number of public shareholders. Some scholars believe that the twenty-first-century innovative firm is more likely to prefer private equity-type financing arrangements, precisely because the challenges of informational asymmetry are so hard to manage with dispersed shareholders when intellectual capital is the firm's dominant asset.[71] Exceptions readily come to mind—Apple would be the favorite of many—and evidence does show that some companies do attract a patient institutional shareholder clientele that supports longer-term investments.[72] But one can see how firms might well come to see the appeal in delaying public status much longer, or not go public ever. Global companies like Cargill and Koch Industries are happily and successfully private (the latter, given the Koch brothers' conspicuously conservative politics, especially so). There is a temptation for public companies as well to go dark through private equity buyouts that bring the number of shareholders to a minimum, a phenomenon that boomed during the first decade of this century. In fact, the number of public companies in the United States has dropped by more than half in the last twenty years, albeit for a number of reasons beyond the mere preference to be private.[73]

Historically, the reasons for going and being public had to do with liquidity and cost of capital. Founders, employee-stockholders, and venture capitalists all wanted some ability to exit their investments once the business was thriving. And especially if investors were exuberant, the public markets offered rich valuations at the time of their public offering (a subject we'll also explore in the next chapter). Those two reasons still exist, though the former is lessening as a result of the growth of private secondary markets—SecondMarket and Sharespost have gotten lots of attention[74]—that allow restricted resales to well-off investors. There are technical legal complications here, but conceptually it seems hard to explain why affluent investors who are deemed able to fend for themselves when buying in a private offering (a subject we take up in the next chapter) cannot freely sell among themselves on a private stock exchange or trading platform. There is much interest in another round of deregulation to enable this, which would make privateness even more attractive. Successful private companies could enable exit by early-round investors (the venture capital firms) by passing the equity on to other institutional investors, with increasing external investor participation. That's the question: if a company limits its investor base solely to the sophisticated and well-off, no matter how many, should we take away all the legal requirements we've surveyed in this chapter?

Such private market flourishing would be a massive threat to the public markets as we know them, and could easily become contagious. The temptation to go public during frothy economic times would still be there, but the private option might well come to dominate as the frustrations of publicness mount. And there is much to be said for this outcome.[75] A deep and liquid market that excludes retail investors would probably be less susceptible to noise trading and sentiment. Corporate governance might improve, with the exit of the more apathetic end of the shareholder base. As to disclosure, some would be produced—even if voluntary—to attract the necessary institutional capital, and one could expect the trading markets to pressure for ongoing disclosure commitments by issuers long after the capital-raising was done. Maybe there would be a role for the SEC to enforce these commitments (and presumably the antifraud prohibitions), but it would not set the rules. And although this shift from public to private seems patently antidemocratic, public investors would still have indirect access to these restricted markets via their mutual fund, exchange-traded funds, and pension holdings, which are the dominant forms of public investing anyway.

To many, this would be a deregulatory economic nirvana, even if it causes public markets to wither. Companies would control the extent of their external financing over a very wide range before hitting full public status, with the ability to choose from a menu of options to stay entirely or partially in the dark. The SEC's bureaucratic power over corporate disclosure and governance would disappear, in favor of negotiated solutions between managers and sources of capital. In many ways, this resembles the Delaware solution in corporate law, of which we took note in chapter 1: largely enabling, and deliberately walled off from distracting public and stakeholder interests. The SEC could turn its attention to where its heavy-handedness is better justified: antifraud enforcement, mutual fund and broker-dealer regulation, and the like.[76]

This would also be a profound rejection of publicness as an interest that competes with efficiency and capital formation in formulating corporate disclosure and governance obligations. The considerable political effort that is currently going into the architecture and design of the private financing and liquidity option shows just how much some see this as a deregulatory holy land that embraces economic freedom and privacy. But if this shift to darkness happens, is it politically stable? This is a coming political test for the future of securities regulation, of which I'll say more at the end of the book.

5

Selling and Swindling

To this point in the book, we've been focused mainly on investor protection issues involving securities traded in the public stock markets. The relative efficiency of such markets allows us to pay less attention to individual-level investor behavior except to the extent that it aggregates into something powerful, because the integrity of the market is what is important. If we can ensure that, all investors will pay or get a fair price, which should be enough to protect and inspire confidence.

But there are many personalized or less-than-efficient investment settings where this is not so: granular decisions are important, and old-fashioned salesmanship takes place. One of the old aphorisms in the investment world is that securities are sold, not bought. To be sure, many investors today are do-it-yourselfers, using lower-cost brokerage firms like E-trade in a way that bypasses the human stockbroker, the quintessential securities salesperson. Even full-service brokers nowadays are shifting to more fee-based income from managing assets than generating commissions. Influence and persuasion of some sort are still usually lurking somewhere, however. We just have to widen our scope to advertising, investor relations, analysts, traders, spammers, "money doctors," and the like. This chapter looks at various places where sales pressure and hype get personal.

INTERNET FRAUDS AND PONZI SCHEMES

New Age Scams

Nearly everyone has gotten an email or happened upon some blog or chat on the Internet, touting a stock poised to rise quickly and dramatically in value. We usually don't know much or anything about either the source of the tip or the company involved. Most people's reaction is—consistent with economic theory—that it would be foolish to pay any attention to such hype.

In 2000, the SEC brought a well-publicized case against Jonathan Lebed, a New Jersey teenager who ran an Internet-based tout scheme, apparently preferring that to schoolwork.[1] He would buy shares, post testimonials and touts (like "the next stock to gain 1000%," or "the most undervalued stock ever") and, if the stock price took off, quickly dump the shares at a profit. Doing so, he made hundreds of thousands of dollars (and his teachers were starting to ask for his investment advice). He defended himself by saying that he was doing research and picking good stocks, but the SEC was doubtful. He ended up settling and agreed to disgorge $272,826, though the press speculated that he had made much more than that.

The case, just one of a number of Internet fraud actions the Commission has brought, is fascinating in a number of respects. To win such a case, which essentially alleges stock market manipulation or fraud, it would have to show that Jonathan said or did something "materially" false or misleading. If the SEC was right that this was just pump and dump, the falsity would be easy to spot—all the touts lacking a serious basis. But the courts usually demand a showing that the deception would be material in the sense of being likely to affect the judgment of a *reasonable* investor.

Could the SEC have won had the case gone to trial? This takes us to a perplexing question of how we define reasonableness in a world of human frailty. One approach would be to ask whether enough investors would in fact be taken in—an empirical question. Alternatively, a judge or jury could pass judgment, bringing to bear their own assessments of whether a person *should* rely. Many judges, especially conservative ones, favor the latter and can be pretty harsh in assessing how reasonable investors behave. Fools lose. One illustration of this, which we saw earlier, involves "puffery," which is loose sales talk or general expressions of optimism to which no reasonable investor supposedly would attach importance. If we take this tack, Jonathan Lebed may have not been engaging in any fraud at all.

Yet spam works. Harvard's Jonathan Zittrain and a colleague studied a large number of spam messages relating to penny stocks (very low-priced stocks not traded on an exchange). On average, spammers could gain nearly 5% buying and then quickly selling shortly after the impact of the messages; conversely, a person buying on the tout day would lose almost as much.[2] Another study showed that investors discriminate somewhat based on the content of the spam message—those that have the biggest impact had information about the company, referenced press releases, and so on, rather than just naked touting—but still fall for the blandishments to a surprising extent.[3]

This is a fairly vivid illustration of a clash between the two visions of materiality, with significant legal ramifications. But are we sure that gullibility is the whole story here? Consider this possibility. Imagine that you see some kind of tout that suggests pump and dump. If you feel quick and nimble enough, you might try to buy quickly and sell before others in the market. If enough others do the same, the result is a run-up of the price and then a collapse—precisely what we observed in the data. In essence, the original touter is just firing the starting gun in a drag race, with "players" competing with each other to see who has the best timing.

This seems like a fool's game, but a game nonetheless—not a fraud that tricks other investors. One can readily imagine people who get a thrill out of the game even though the odds are against them; one can just as easily imagine people who are habitually overconfident in their nimbleness (day traders exhibit this, especially younger males) being inclined to play with excess optimism. Here we come back to the lottery ticket analogy—there is a visceral "play value" to certain kinds of investing that may offset the perceived (and maybe underestimated) risks. Many researchers have pointed out that gambling and investing are kindred phenomena.[4]

If this is closer to an apt description, the law might have some difficulty proscribing it—in my account, no one is being fooled (or at least any more than when visiting a casino). Yet what the players are doing, at the instruction of the touter, are hijacking the market from legitimate buyers and sellers who expect the normal interaction of supply and demand. They threaten the "safety" of these thinly traded markets the way drag racers threaten the streets. The SEC seems to concur, but has not yet had to convince a court that the kinds of activities Jonathan Lebed was engaged in were actually fraudulent or manipulative, not just a safety threat.

Internet fraud illustrates a number of important points. First is the role of hope— or greed, desire, or whatever other name you want to give it. Psychological research has demonstrated what common experience and observation amply suggest: desire clouds judgment. To put the point more precisely, once the mind wants something, it becomes selective in evaluating information, biasing judgment in favor of the desired goal. Research in neuroscience is beginning to show how the parts of the brain that covet rewards light up when faced with a tantalizing opportunity in ways that run ahead of deliberative processing—that is, good judgment. Jon Haidt memorably invokes the image of an elephant (wants and desires) and its rider (deliberative decision-making)—the rider may think he's in charge, but if the elephant really wants to go in a particular direction, it can and it will.

Prompting that desire is a crucial part of good salesmanship; getting the "close" is just as important. There was no conventional salesperson (i.e., stockbroker or financial adviser) in Jonathan Lebed's situation—he was using a contained informational environment to stimulate interest through his many posts. That is often the case. An infamous investment scam a few years ago was the answering machine game: the schemer would call home phone numbers, hoping no one is at home and that the answering machine would turn on. She ("Debbie") would then leave a message for a friend, saying that she had gotten a hot tip about a particular stock that should send it skyrocketing. Buy now. When the homeowner hears the recorded message, he thinks that it was a wrong number but that he has stumbled on a big stock tip as a result. Lots of people, it turns out, then call their own brokers and buy the stock. The information is bogus, of course—the scammer is just playing the pump-and-dump game, watching the stock price rise not because of any real information but simply because of all the buying activity, selling out before the effects dissipate.[5]

Ponzi Schemes

There is often more sales pressure than this, however—someone who knows how to close a sale before doubts set in. Consider the Ponzi scheme, the most notorious of all kinds of investment scams.[6] A classic Ponzi scheme is one where the scammer approaches a small number of investors with an attractive opportunity, usually promising greater than average returns, with some explanation for how and why that is possible (accessing emerging foreign markets is popular, hoping that the targets can be led to believe that the general rule that risk and return go together somehow loses applicability abroad). As noted earlier, Bernie Madoff's was different, promising returns based on a complicated split-strike options strategy that was characterized more by steadiness over time than any outsized payoffs.

Most people are immediately a bit skeptical of a stranger's pitch, so the next step is gaining credibility. Madoff had a stellar reputation for his other securities activities—he had a close working relationship with the stock exchanges, and even securities regulators—as well as for his involvement with charitable causes. Other schemers use friends, family, clubs, churches, organizations, and other forms of "affinity" to pump up their credibility.[7] The most aggressive fake it—approach X on the "suggestion" of X's friend Y, and then approach Y on the "suggestion" of X (and so on), predicting that no one will immediately figure out the setup. Remember motivated inference—much as you think X, Y, and the others should be on their guard, the prompting of desire leads many people to construe bits of information in ways that bolster the desired choice, not fight against it.

It just takes a couple of investments (which need not be large) for everything then to fall into place for the Ponzi schemer. The key to the Ponzi scheme is to find the money to make sure that the first investors get paid the desired returns quickly and in full. Of course the easiest way to do this is to take investments from later investors and use those funds to pay the earlier ones. Whatever the source, the early investors are now thrilled that any worries or doubts were for nothing—and are now credible sources of testimonials for the legitimacy of the investments. Now the schemer goes to work on friends, acquaintances, and anyone else who might be impressed. And so the network expands, with more and more money available to bolster the illusions, turning at least for a time into a classic self-fulfilling prophecy. The schemer can start pocketing some of the money for himself, more and more as the network of potential victims starts declining—at which point an exit strategy, often involving a new identity in a remote foreign country, becomes a necessity. (When there is no exit strategy, as was the case with Madoff, something else is probably going on—typically an investment arrangement that started out as bona fide but which fails to provide the hoped-for returns. Rather than admit failure, the promoter uses other money to cover up the shortfalls, which gradually turns the effort into a classic Ponzi scheme as he gets deeper and deeper into the muck.)

So greed and desire set all this in motion, making the trappings for fraud more believable. But note that the motivations can be more subtle. Schemers take advantage of their victims' egos, making it seem that their particular investment is a special privilege available to only a select few. "X" invested—now you can be just like X. Madoff's scheme was highly dependent on the impression that you had to be special, to know the right people, to get in on the arrangement. There was an affinity element here as well, with a global network of investors using the upper-class Jewish community in the New York and beyond as a base. The trappings of exclusivity and legitimacy were exquisite, which allowed Madoff to demand a hush-hush secrecy to the arrangement, discouraging too many questions or demands for authentication, and thus aided the concealment.

Boiler Rooms

By now you should see the common elements to these kinds of investment scams in terms of investor psychology. And it's now just a small step to another infamous source of abuse: the boiler room. Most of us have also received a cold call (at dinner time, often enough) from a salesman with a hot stock to sell. There isn't anything short of hanging up immediately that isn't met with a conversation extender, usually some sort of easily answerable question (would you like greater returns on your investments?) that allows the salesperson to push the desire buttons and, like the Ponzi schemer, deflect doubts as to credibility. Readers familiar with the sex and drugs-filled 2013 movie *The Wolf of Wall Street*, or the books by Jordan Belfort on which it was based, saw a sensationalized version of the boiler room and the visceral excitement it generates as big sales are celebrated around the room. Belfort was the founder of Stratton Oakmont, a bane of the SEC's existence for a good while in the 1990s. You can now guess how it works: the firm takes a large position in some new or relatively unknown stock (Steve Madden Shoes was one of Stratton Oakmont's big positions) and then sell big time to push the stock price up. The cold calls anticipate skepticism and invite very small purchases at first, with little at risk. These are contrived to pay off—the salesperson ensures that a sale (sometimes real, sometimes fake) takes place before the bubble pops so that the proceeds are real. The salesperson reminds listeners how much more they would have made had they put up real money (desire) and steps into the role of the customer's new best friend (credibility). The road to big forthcoming purchases is now straight and short. So this might also be a good time to ask the customer for names and numbers of friends who might like the same opportunity at good fortune.

The cold-call scripts are fascinating, as the SEC discovered after breaking some of these cases.[8] Every objection is anticipated, and every likely hot button pushed. For a man to try saying that he needs to talk to his wife before purchasing (and she's not home right now) there is a prompt, subtle challenge to his manhood, his role in his own home, and his self-confidence. (And, they quickly add, your wife would certainly appreciate the extra money, right?) The market is hot right now, and you know your friends and neighbors are profiting—you don't want to be left behind, do you? One of the best lines about investor behavior is from MIT's Charles Kindleberger, who observed in his classic study of investment manias that "nothing disturbs a man's judgment so much as watching his neighbor get rich."[9] Ego, status, pride all get put to work. Although both genders are susceptible to investment scams, men are often the more exploitable targets.

Pump-and-dump schemes get some help behind the scenes as well. Market manipulation often goes beyond heavy sales pressure to include fictitious sales (in other words, sales between the same or related persons who are indifferent as to price but falsely report their trades as bona fide); a series of these "wash sales" at ever ascending prices can pull in buyers who think the momentum is real and try to ride it. Rumors and touts get planted. In other words, some of the demand is real, some of it contrived.

What I have done here is simply to describe investor behavior in certain settings involving some form of exploitation. You may rightly object that this may all be fairly aberrant. Most people are not the victims of scams such as these, so maybe we're just looking at the extremely gullible end of the investing spectrum, who ought to be left to their own folly. But that doesn't quite work with the Madoff victims, for example, who were in many cases quite sophisticated. And the evidence on the extent and likelihood of being scammed suggests that the numbers of victims is greater than you might think. Though the examples we have used may be unusual, the idea of investing as a struggle between unconscious wants and deliberative thought, with the former having a bit of a structural advantage inside the brain, is useful generally. So is the idea of investing as a social act, heavily influenced by perceptions of what others are doing. Active investing by some begets more active investing by more.[10]

As to what lessons for regulation there are here, we have to travel much further down the road we're on to find them. With respect to deliberate scams, required disclosures will probably turn out to be lies, so disclosure by itself won't be much of a solution. Only heavy policing will do. For now the most important observation is that the spaces where investment activity takes place vary considerably in terms of light and darkness, that is, how much enforcers of various sorts can monitor what is going on and step in to prevent harm (or at least catch the bad guys soon enough). My sense is that victims of investment abuse are characterized less by unusual gullibility vis-à-vis the rest of the adult population than an inclination—or simply the misfortune—to wander into those dark places, alone and without protection.

THE IPO LOTTERY

As we saw in chapter 1, the first of the federal securities statutes—the Securities Act of 1933—was designed to bring honesty to the public offering of securities. At the risk of great oversimplification, it has the following basic structure:

1. A business wanting to raise capital by offering its securities "to the public" must file a lengthy disclosure document with the SEC, telling a great deal about the business and the offering.
2. Securities can't be sold unless and until SEC staff is satisfied with the disclosure.
3. There are limits on the manner of the securities marketed so that sales hype doesn't overwhelm the truth-telling in the disclosure.
4. The business, its insiders, and investment bankers all suffer potentially devastating liability in a lawsuit if anything important in the required disclosure is misstated or omitted as of the time the selling begins.

Wall Street was horribly incensed at the time, predicting that sales of securities would grind to a halt, and angrily put its lobbyists to work from the beginning to soften the punch in the name of capital formation.[11] They succeeded only slightly, making the Securities Act a long-lived exemplar for the supposed triumph of investor protection over the forces of greed. (A backstory: they gained something as well—restraints on communications and competition among firms that worked to the benefit of the larger and more established.)[12]

The initial public offering (IPO) is the quintessential investment opportunity, and the transaction that originally motivated the Securities Act. A company whose shares are not already publicly traded issues a large number of new shares for sale, raising hundreds of million (if not billions) of dollars in a single transaction. We all recall the winning lottery tickets—Intel, Dell, Amazon, Google, and so many more household names, where any investor who got in early and big made a fortune. On the first day of trading alone, market prices tend to "pop," which itself makes news. However, even with all this dense regulation, the IPO story is not always such a happy one. Smaller IPOs have a decidedly poor track record,[13] and even among larger ones, there are lots of losers in terms of long-run returns, making this a risky place for bargain hunters.

As we saw at the end of the last chapter, emerging companies are confronted with a choice as to whether to go public and when, and increasingly have the ability to delay publicness or not go public at all. The rate of IPOs dropped steadily during the first decade of the 2000s, even before the financial crisis hit. One diagnosis was that the Securities Act overregulates, justifying some pullback.

Even a cursory look at the mechanics of an IPO makes a strong case for deregulation. Today (putting aside the increasingly rare small IPO) the typical public offering involves sales made by the company through an investment-banking syndicate mainly to large institutional investors.[14] They have the opportunity to meet privately in road shows with company officials and the underwriters to discuss confidential forecasts and estimates, and are repeat players—if they feel burned by being sold securities they later regret, the salespeople will have a harder time earning their business in the future. Reflecting this "book-building" dynamic,[15] the initial distribution is typically underpriced, such that over the first days and weeks of trading the price of the securities usually goes up, often dramatically. So intense, costly regulation seems unnecessary—the big investors who bargain for the allocations demand a favorable price, which then becomes the public offering price for all purchasers. Where is the need to worry about the "mesmerizing" dark arts of the salesman that Felix Frankfurter was so worried about? Of course, even big investors need information, which registration provides. But given the costs and delays associated with going public, the regulatory straitjacket might be a bit much—the institutions can bargain for what they need, and issuers have little choice but to give it to them.

Hyping the Aftermarket

But a more serious investor protection issue lurks one step down the road. Once the securities are sold, market trading begins. If there are lots of investors who covet the stock but didn't get the privileged allocations, they will be buyers in the aftermarket and quickly push the stock price up. That's the source of the pop. Some, if not most, of these will be retail investors without access to those private discussions about the company's future. So now you can see the game. If the aftermarket is frothy and exuberant, those who sell into it can make considerable money. This would include the initial round of buyers (although underwriters try to limit "flipping" so that sell orders don't overwhelm the market too quickly) and insiders at the company, who usually face a relatively short lockup period before they can sell. There is little doubt that the pressure to move the aftermarket stock price up remains a big part of a successful offering, to the detriment of those who buy as the bubble begins to deflate. A recent study found that those IPOs that attract especially high retail investor attention (as measured by Google hits on the issuer's name) had bigger pops and longer-run underperformance when the exuberance faded.[16]

A decade and a half ago, during the high-tech stock price boom, evidence surfaced that some underwriters were doing more than this to pump the stock price.[17] Precisely because underpriced allotments were so valuable, they were coveted, and underwriters chose who received them. There were many ways for the bankers to extract value, one of which was to condition the allotment on an agreement by the buyer to also purchase (perhaps heavily) in the aftermarket. Practices like these were exposed and outlawed, but as we'll see, the problem is not entirely solved.

Because the Securities Act is so focused on the first round of sales (the allotments), it does less to help aftermarket purchasers. For a while, the act had a heavy-handed restriction on marketing prior to the date the selling could begin, which restricted publicity efforts that might whet the appetite of investors for the stock. (Google got in some trouble for this when it authorized a story in Playboy magazine when it was supposed to be in the "quiet period" pending its IPO.) But in 2005, the SEC deregulated in ways that made hyping publicity easier.[18] And brokers have always been able to work the phones and do face-to-face meetings to push the stock in the month or so before sales begin, a freedom that now (within some technical limitations) extends to email and social media. Academic research shows fairly convincingly a link between hype and underpricing, including some subtle means. Earnings management (the self-serving use of accounting discretion) increases. Companies also engage in greater product advertising in anticipation of an IPO, suggesting that the brand message is directed at potential investors as well as potential customers. And it seems to work.[19]

Whether this bothers you or not is a good test of your gut feelings about investor protection. Hype and earnings management are not necessarily fraudulent, even if they play on emotions and trust—maybe we should insist on a showing that what we said was actually false or misleading before regulators interfere with the market. (While it goes beyond our focus here, new-age constitutional lawyers might invoke the First Amendment for a "freedom to hype" in commercial speech like this.) On the other hand, the marketing effort is designed to stimulate in the brain the image of a winning lottery ticket in the investor's hands, burying the reality that if those inside the company believed the shares were worth so much, they probably wouldn't be selling at the chosen offering price. Which is worse, opportunism or gullibility? When you choose gullibility, or even just sigh and say there is nothing to be done to help the gullible except make them learn from experience, Wall Street smiles. Hope often triumphs over experience in the waves of sentiment when IPO windows are wide open.

JOBS Act Reform

In the JOBS Act of 2012, a rare recent display of bipartisanship, Congress made clear its belief that there are not enough IPOs—and thus not enough entrepreneurial capital-raising of the sort that might produce what our contemporary society most seems to covet, good jobs. And it decided that there was too much IPO regulation, which is what was making entrepreneurs wary of going public.

The IPO deregulation for the benefit of "emerging growth companies" took a number of forms, including the ability of insiders to say less about their own compensation, always a touchy subject. There was some relaxation on accounting, the ability to file confidentially so that preliminary discussions with the SEC would be private, and encouragement of more analyst research, even though infected by conflict of interest. None of this deregulation was radical, but the cumulative effect is hard to predict. Early academic research is at best mixed on whether it has had much effect on the number of IPOs; it has increased informational asymmetry as measured by the extent of underpricing.[20] In other words, the truth is now a bit harder to see.

The most perplexing JOBS Act on-ramp reform has to do with securities analysts. As we saw in the last chapter, conflicts of interest abound on the sell side because the analysts' employers—investment banks and brokerage firms—are in the sales business, usually on the issuer side. Even before the analyst scandals of the early 2000s, the SEC was wary enough of these conflicts of interest to prohibit analysts affiliated with the bankers underwriting a company's IPO from issuing research at the time of the offering. Later on, the securities industry self-regulatory organization, now called FINRA, used its authority to extend the ban on conflicted research for a few months after the IPO, fearing that the temptation to hype continued into the aftermarket for at least as long as it took for insiders' lockups to expire, to facilitate those sales. This collection of rules had a noticeable effect, although a 2014 FINRA enforcement proceeding charging violations of these rules involving a planned IPO for Toys "R" Us demonstrates how strongly analysts still feel the pressure to shill. One analyst from Needham & Co. said in an email, "I would crawl on broken glass dragging my exposed junk to get this deal." He added in another: "My whole life is about posturing for the Toys R Us IPO."[21]

Yet in the JOBS Act, Congress *removed* some of those anticonflict rules. Indeed, it removed Securities Act restrictions and threats of liability for any communication or publicity by a brokerage employee in the typical IPO that "includes information, opinions or recommendations" with respect to the securities in question. It doesn't take a trained lawyer's eye to see that there is very little a broker might want to do to hype the aftermarket that wouldn't be protected by that exclusion.

Congress was not necessarily being disingenuous. Small companies, especially, do suffer from a lack of research coverage, and some of the loss of coverage can be traced back to the severe regulatory reaction to the scandals of a decade ago. Research became significantly more costly, and so less available. Given the concentrated nature of the investment-banking business, finding unconflicted sell-side analysts isn't easy. Conflicted advice might be biased but not entirely bogus, so this might be a plausible way of boosting IPOs. But to anyone who worries about the hyping of the aftermarket in IPOs, there is a clear-cut sacrifice of investor protection in the name of capital formation and job creation. How this all plays out depends on how well investors have learned from the scandals to bring a healthy skepticism to anything a broker with a conflict says. Unfortunately, this book is filled with reasons to doubt such acuity, and it's doubtful the capital formation objective would be met if investors did remain skeptical. Early academic assessment indicates—not surprisingly—that the optimism of analysts has increased since the change and accuracy has dropped, so that analyst behavior is reverting to patterns that existed before the global settlement.[22]

If we indeed get more IPOs, innovation, and job creation as a result, many will consider it an acceptable trade-off. We'll see. For all of the JOBS Act reforms, the regulation—and publicness pressures—that come from being a public company are still substantial, and it's far from clear that Congress has offered inducements sufficient to change the minds of entrepreneurs who prefer holding onto the private benefits of control or keeping their business models secret. In academia, there are many doubters that regulation was the main factor in the observed drop in the rate of IPOs.[23] So we might mainly have a deterioration of the information environment of IPOs that mostly would have occurred anyway, diluting the gains that were supposed to offset the threat to investors in the social calculus.

There is also a big question of precisely how many new US-based jobs IPO companies create. In the legislative hearings advocates promised 10 or 20 million new jobs from a freshened capital-raising environment, but that was pandering. Many larger IPOs are for tech companies competing in already thin domestic pools of science and engineering talent. And successful innovation can often kill jobs in other sectors of the economy (retail being a good example), with no reason to believe that labor migration to new opportunities will be seamless. Even innovation benefits are muddled—many studies show that the rate of innovation *drops* after a company makes its IPO, as the core talent goes seeking other opportunities after cashing in.[24] Those subtleties, however, get lost in the politics of economic anxiety. The JOBS Act IPO provisions were a gift to entrepreneurs, venture capitalists, and the securities industry, with ordinary citizens promised without substantial evidence that more jobs would be forthcoming in due course. Aftermarket investors never really had much of a say.

"PRIVATE" INVESTMENTS

Not all capital-raising has to be via a registered public offering. A company can escape these burdens by making an offering that is exempt from registration. A number of exemptions are available, but by far the most interesting and important for our purposes is for "nonpublic" offerings. In 2013, more money was raised privately in the United States ($1.6 trillion) than publicly ($1.3 trillion). We've already seen the allure of privateness to executives frustrated by SOX-style disclosure and governance regulation.

Given how big the legal divide is between public offerings and nonpublic ones, you would think that Congress would have clearly defined the distinction back in the

1930s. It didn't, which left the matter to the discretion of the courts and the newly created SEC. When it got hold of the question, the Supreme Court very unhelpfully said that a nonpublic offering was one made to those who don't need the protection of regulation, hinting that not needing help was a deeply subjective matter of sophistication and access to information via sheer bargaining power.[25]

Fending for Themselves

That made things hard for entrepreneurs. Big institutional investors can be very picky, likely to slam the door in most faces. But casting a net more widely, asking ordinary people to believe in the dream and invest their money, was largely off limits because of how the Supreme Court and the SEC read the law. This chilled new business formation, which is problematic if we believe that innovation occurs only when capital is reasonably accessible to the entrepreneurial class (a point the famous economist Joseph Schumpeter made some time ago). So began a decades-long political tug of war between the small business capital-raising community and investor protectionists, who saw unregistered offerings as an invitation to fraud.

Eventually, the main argument came down to whether, beyond the limited class of professional investors, we should declare as a matter of law that a certain level of income or wealth makes one able to fend for oneself.[26] There is a positive correlation between cognitive ability and income, and those who have earned their wealth have usually shown some level of economic sophistication. And those with wealth can certainly choose to hire expert advisers to protect their interests. There is a strong dose of antipaternalism at work here—if someone is well off enough, does that person really deserve taxpayer-funded protection when choosing to invest? These libertarian ideas gained force, and after the election of Ronald Reagan as president in 1980, finally got an embrace from a deregulation-minded SEC. In what was called Reg D, the SEC announced an innocent-sounding general rule: an offering could be exempt from registration if made to no more than thirty-five sophisticated purchasers, who must all be given a detailed disclosure document. But then, with drafting that only a lawyer could love, it said in a definitional rule that someone who is deemed an "accredited investor" will not be considered a purchaser, even if that person purchases the securities. In other words, there can be an *unlimited* number of accredited investors, who need *not* be sophisticated, and they get *no* disclosure. Accredited investor was defined to include, in addition to many different kinds of institutional investors, any person who makes more than $200,000 per year ($300,000 joint income if married) or has a net worth of more than $1 million.

While a striking revision, this was not entirely revolutionary—back in 1982, when Reg D was adopted, $200,000 in income or millionaire status in net worth was a lot of money. But once put into the regulation, these dollar amounts never changed, even with the high inflation of the later 1980s and the economic booms of the 1990s and early 2000s. They are still the same today. The eye-opener here is less the income test (most Americans still do not come close to making $200,000 a year), but net worth. As noted earlier, Americans today are charged with planning for their own retirements, with no pension and limited expectations as to Social Security. A nest egg of $1 million at retirement sounds like a lot (and is to most of us) but really doesn't make someone truly wealthy if that is all there is to live on into old age. The problem was worse when home equity could be included in this calculation, especially during the real estate boom years, but Congress changed that in 2010.

So the ability to make an unregulated private offering steadily expanded into the upper reaches of the middle class. Doctors, dentists, and lawyers became fair game (anecdotal evidence suggests that these high-status professionals are particularly attractive to clever salespeople because their outsize egos are so easy to manipulate). Seniors were unprotected as well, especially as they neared or passed retirement age with a lifetime accumulation of savings. Gradually more and more Americans became "able" to fend for themselves, according to Reg D.

While the possible victimization of senior investors goes well beyond private investments in exempt offerings, we should pause here to consider that issue in broader context. As people grow older, cognitive decline occurs for most, but many seniors resist acknowledging that and are hence overconfident in their investing abilities.[27] This is also a time of growing loneliness, anxiety, and fear, psychological forces, as we've seen, that may lead to excessive trust and willingness to take inappropriate risks. No one wants to outlive savings and become a burden on the family, or worse. Especially with today's painfully low interest rates on fixed-income investments, that fear can be very debilitating, and there is disturbing evidence of securities salespeople taking advantage of it. One of the largest-scale private offering frauds in recent years involved a company called Medical Capital that sold more than $2 billion in notes promising between 8.5% and 10.5% annually to more than twenty thousand retail investors. According to Jennifer Johnson, a law professor involved in the effort to recover funds for the victims, there were many elder investors in what amounted to an elaborate Ponzi scheme, including an eighty-five-year-old with dementia and a seventy-seven-year-old with Alzheimer's, whose children had asked the broker not to contact him.[28] This conduct occurred even though stockbrokers cannot lawfully recommend an investment that is not "suitable" for that customer.

Efforts to push for greater investor protection here have met with intense political opposition. Some indication of how much is at stake came when FINRA, the industry's self-regulator, tried to cap brokerage commissions for privately placed securities. The pushback was too intense, and it was withdrawn. When so much money goes to sales compensation, the conflicts of interest are pretty clear. Those who want freedom from regulation seem to insist that what happens in the dark, stays in the dark.

The JOBS Act

When Reg D was created, there was a restriction on the selling of private offerings in the form of what was called a ban on "general solicitations." This was an SEC-imposed requirement that prohibited advertising and other marketing efforts that might excite interest from unsophisticated investors (and you couldn't just put a label on the advertising saying it was for qualified investors only). The effect was that private-offering sales pitches could only be made *after* the investor was determined to be qualified (i.e., meeting the wealth or income standard). By and large, that required that a broker be involved to do the prequalification without whetting their appetites, making offerings slower and more costly (and lucrative for the brokers, who have fought ever since to preserve that particular revenue stream).

So we come, yet again, to the JOBS Act, Congress's effort to free up entrepreneurial capital-raising from the burdens of overregulation. Congress wanted to put private offerings on steroids, and thus did away with the ban on general solicitations when the private offering in question is sold only to persons reasonably verified to be accredited investors. Entrepreneurs can now make direct offerings on their websites, for example; brokers can do much more aggressive sales pitches without waiting for prequalification, as long as they can certify the purchaser's accredited status at the back end.[29] (Recall the psychological research showing that cheating is much more likely if speed bumps come after the fact rather than before.)

Whatever happens to sales tactics, the market for private offerings will continue to grow, and with it temptation. To some investor advocates, an obvious fix is to raise the wealth and income standards for accredited status—after all, it hasn't been adjusted since 1982. Perhaps, but the numbers were arbitrary then and don't really answer the question of how or why we declare people able to fend for themselves. Does it mean able to understand and bargain over the economics of any given investment (fewer people) or is it more the antipaternalistic sense that people should know when to walk away from what they don't or can't understand? If it's the latter, the current income and wealth standards might even be on the high side, at least for people with normal cognitive functioning. Others have suggested administering a test for investment sophistication. But how challenging would such a test need to be? If hard enough to test for real investment savvy, only a small percentage of the population would pass (and most probably wouldn't want to try). If too easy, it becomes a joke, and might even enable abuse. Research evidence suggests that victims of investment scams are characterized by somewhat *higher* investment knowledge than nonvictims, a result attributable to the perils of ego and overconfidence. A little knowledge can be a dangerous thing.

In all likelihood, the pattern here is one of segmentation, just as we observe in other sales-oriented settings. At the high end, reputable brokers and placement agents with relatively savvy clients promote what are usually good-quality deals, fairly priced for the level of risk. But down the hierarchy, investor sophistication drops and the brokers' incentives change. Salesmanship takes the place of reputational intermediation, and returns suffer.

No solution avoids ideology. A plausible argument has been made that, assuming enough clarity and risk compensation, private investments are a distinct asset class that belongs in a diversified portfolio, along with commodities, real estate, and the like.[30] There is a democratic case to be made for giving ordinary investors the same opportunity to make the attractive returns that alternative investments promise.[31] Fair enough, but we don't know for sure how profitable this world is—the data simply aren't there across the universe of these "dark" investments.[32] It's entirely possible that any supranormal returns are because of how sophisticated investors make and monitor their funding choices. Those who invest in private businesses for a living—venture capital firms, and even professional "angel" investors—do substantial due diligence and often bargain for protective rights before handing over their money to an entrepreneur. Absent independent due diligence and control rights, private investments look more like lottery tickets, which don't belong in most portfolios.

CROWDFUNDING: WISDOM OR MADNESS?

As we've just seen, external funding for start-up or early-stage entrepreneurs has been hard to come by, for a combination of economic and regulatory reasons. With rare exceptions, entrepreneurs depend on their own money to get started, sometimes borrowed via credit cards or home equity loans, and that of friends and family. An IPO isn't remotely an option until substantial success has already been achieved, and experienced venture capital and angel investors generally want to see something more than a dream.

Can the Internet help? You've probably heard of Kickstarter and other crowdfunding sites that allow people with an idea for a product, event, or some other venture to raise money from sympathetic funders, promising anything from tickets, T-shirts, or the item itself (when finally in production) in return. It doesn't take much imagination to see how an entrepreneur might want to try the same thing to fund the start-up of an entire business by offering some kind of financial return on the contribution if and when the venture succeeds. Until recently, that couldn't happen in the United States if what was promised fell under the definition of a security—it would almost certainly be an illegal public offering because it involved a general solicitation.

This is the JOBS Act's most publicized innovation: trying to bring the United States into the equity crowdfunding world. But this was also the most polarizing debate about the legislation, leading to a compromise at the behest of some of the more liberal members of the Senate that crowdfunding enthusiasts think may have snuffed out much of its promise. We'll come back a little later on to the disappointment with what was enacted (which the SEC has only recently implemented). For our purposes, it may be more interesting to think about crowdfunding in its pure form.[33]

Equity crowdfunding involves an online offer of an investment (stock, debt, or novel forms of participation) in an enterprise to a large number of people, without regard to their knowledge or sophistication The principal form of protection for potential investors comes from the "wisdom" of the crowd—the offering allows for open communication among potential investors, and can be structured so that no one invests unless a critical mass of investors commits to a certain level of investment after a chance for inquiry and discussion. In its pure form, there would be little or no mandatory disclosure, though lies and half-truths would be illegal.

Does that make you uncomfortable? The wisdom-of-crowds idea arises out of a well-respected body of work about information aggregation drawn from the study of settings like prediction markets (which have had a pretty good track record on matters like US presidential elections) and other structured group efforts. Intuitively, groups can cancel out the erroneous beliefs of outliers; if a deal can go forward only by attracting group consensus, the more median beliefs will be determinative. It's the power of averaging. One can see how and why this might work especially well with respect to ideas and products that are consumer-oriented—the act of crowdfunding merges into the premarketing of the idea, seeing how much customer appeal there really is and, at the same time, stimulating demand once the venture has a product to sell. Much of the success of crowdfunding thus far has been on matters of taste—arts projects, games, music, food.[34] It shows some promise for, among other things, reducing geographic barriers (helping rural entrepreneurs and urban ones far away from conventional start-up financing clusters) and overcoming the difficulties that women often have in competing for funding from male-dominated institutional sources of money.

Skeptics, on the other hand, point to a longer history of thinking about the "madness of crowds" as displayed, in the investment world, in bubbles, fads, rumors, and manias. Most start-ups fail, so there is already large risk (and you'd have to think that if this new company was a demonstrably good idea, it would have been funded through more conventional channels). Under the wrong circumstances, groups can herd in the direction of erroneous or extreme beliefs. Loud, confident voices get disproportionate attention. And, of course, as we saw in our discussion of spam and Ponzi schemes, social proof can be used manipulatively—seeing someone else do something doesn't mean that person knows what he or she is doing, but we are heavily affected by the behavior of others. Psychologists are not particularly fond of claims that crowds are wise.[35]

Crowdfunding enthusiasts don't depend simply on crowd self-protection, however. They presume that crowdfunding sites will see opportunities for profit if they can build a reputation for hosting honest and successful crowdfunding events, and thus police themselves. They may ask for some disclosure from those seeking funds, albeit sensitive to not imposing a level of disclosure costs that effectively dissuade entrepreneurs from using their services in the first place.

There is a surprisingly diverse ideology in the enthusiasm for crowdfunding. Some of it is just antipaternalistic, a distaste for costly societal limitations on the economic freedom (including the freedom to fail) of both entrepreneurs and investors. But there is a progressive element, too, among those who think most of the value in emerging companies goes to early-stage investors, effectively off limits to anyone who is not a wealthy investor or a friend, family member, or employee of the founders or principals. We just saw how that played out with respect to private investments. And the image of the entrepreneur with ambition and a dream has strong cultural resonance, especially among younger people at a time when there is great anxiety over the future of conventional high-paying careers.

That's a pretty potent political brew. To make the proposed deregulation more palatable as the JOBS Act was being composed, proponents added strict limitations on how much the entrepreneur can raise and how much an individual investor can buy. With that, they said, let there be spaces for entrepreneurial capital-raising that are very low cost and suited for speculative start-ups. Let the wisdom of crowds and the reputational incentives do their work, even if there is some risk in such reliance. Limit what entrepreneurs can gain and crowdfunding investors can lose. And then watch a thousand flowers (or start-ups) bloom. There will inevitably be some harm, as there is even in highly regulated markets, but much more good.

That was the pitch for crowdfunding reform in the United States. Both intellectually and politically, the soft spots in the romantic imagery of easy innovation and job creation were not hard to find, and worries easy to conjure up. In congressional testimony, Columbia's Jack Coffee memorably said that without effective restrictions on who could sell newly issued securities, "every barroom in America might come to be populated by a character, looking something like Danny DeVito, obnoxiously trying to sell securities to his fellow patrons."[36] Crowdfunding became the most controversial aspect of the JOBS Act proposals, and the bill's backers who very much wanted other reforms didn't want to endanger the chance of enactment by clinging to a libertarian ideal.

For better or worse, compromise ensued. There were limits on how much an entrepreneur could raise (no more than $1 million) and how much an investor could risk (a complicated formula depending on income and net worth—no more than the greater of $2,000 or 5% of her income or net worth, if they are under $100,000) each year. But Congress then piled on top significant disclosure requirements on companies seeking capital; disclosure and supervisory responsibilities for funding sites (called portals) regarding investor qualification, education, and protection; liability in a lawsuit for negligent misrepresentations; and significant authority to add even more to the regulatory obligations by both the SEC and FINRA.

We'll see how much business this much more heavily regulated crowdfunding model eventually attracts.[37] (Note a less burdensome alternative: crowdfunding limited to verifiably accredited investors, which essentially operates as Internet-based private offering. Some states have also established more liberal crowdfunding exemptions for solely in-state offerings.) Fearing that results may fall short of hopes, there is already an effort by enthusiasts in Congress to undo the compromise and reintroduce something more along the lines of pure-form crowdfunding.

As much as I fear opportunism in the way securities are peddled, I wonder here if the layering of obligations doesn't go a bit too far. One healthy thing about crowdfunding is its public nature, the Brandeisian sunlight, which deters the kinds of abuses that take advantage of the dark alleys of investing. What little evidence we have from elsewhere suggests that fraud is less of a risk than entrepreneurial overconfidence—projects begun in good faith but arriving late or not at all.[38] Still, is there some amount of money we should allow any investor to choose to put at risk, even if the risks are high? A thousand dollars per year? Two thousand? Assume that we channel these opportunities to certified, regulated portals (but let the portals set their own performance standards), keep a watch for fraud (easier to do when all the information is on the Internet), and by all means, prohibit arrangements to incentivize brokers and financial advisers to hype these as sound investments; then there is a good case for a less burdensome crowdfunding exemption than we got from the JOBS Act.

Two cautionary notes, however, haven't been as much discussed. One has to do, ironically, with the risk associated with the venture succeeding, not failing. Will the entrepreneur then act in investors' interests or grab what he or she can? If there is subsequent additional financing, will investors' equity be diluted beyond recognition? These are all agency cost problems, common to any form of business organization. Ample experience shows that when investors are small, dispersed, and uninformed, the traditional tools of corporate governance don't work very well. That is why venture capital and angel investing takes such a different form. You're exposed on the upside as well as the downside, and need protection that simple crowdfunding arrangements don't offer. One experienced angel investor, commenting on "the road to crowdfunding hell," stresses that crowd-based investing ignores nearly every lesson he learned about how to succeed.[39]

Maybe crowdfunding investors will turn out to be different, perhaps willing to take on some moral hazard risk on top of all the others in the name of supporting a worthwhile idea. Plus the Internet does offer tools for monitoring and shaming those who disappoint.[40] In Europe, where there is a bit more experience with equity crowdfunding, funding portals have experimented with hybrid ways of giving investors more confidence—for example, inviting reputable angel investors to make significant investments as anchors, subject to additional crowdfunding on the same terms. Indeed, one could foresee an alternative crowdfunding universe where the capital-raising itself is done by such intermediaries, based on a promise to invest in the best new ideas.

A related caution has to do with the kinds of businesses that can effectively crowdfund. The risk-return calculus works best in the retail and arts world, as a way of yoking the wisdom of crowds to shifting tastes. But the example everyone uses about crowdfunding is the sophisticated technological breakthrough, the next big thing. The problem here—palpable at the time of capital-raising and throughout the development process—is privacy. An inventor simply cannot reveal to a crowd much if anything about her idea until it gets a patent or copyright. (Venture capital and angel investing overcome this with confidentiality agreements.) Even a hint about how or why it will succeed invites others to steal the idea or threaten a costly infringement lawsuit if they think the idea is their own. That fear makes it impossible for the crowd to invest in innovative technology—or monitor—on any real wisdom at all, unless the entrepreneur already has a bankable reputation (in which case she probably doesn't need retail crowdfunding).

These particular issues aside, we might want to pay attention to the politics that led Congress to adopt such a muddy approach to a promising phenomenon. The general assumption is that the pure form of crowdfunding was done in by investor advocates, but they are not usually a particularly potent interest group politically. One has to wonder—here and elsewhere in the debates over deregulation—whether brokers who make so much money from highly intermediated capital-raising wanted nothing to do with a new-age phenomenon that promised to cut through the industry's stranglehold over entrepreneurial finance. Those are reasonable suspicions, though we have to be cautious here. How important sub-million-dollar transactions are to brokers is unclear; maybe that was mainly "friends and family" territory. On the other hand, if crowdfunding were to succeed without exhibiting severe investor protection problems, there would soon be strong pressure to raise the cap, so that the exemption would start siphoning off deals the brokers do covet. So maybe they did play a role. If so, however, they would have had numerous allies in the effort to quash. Establishment players—including elite lawyers—were critics, and venture capital and angel investor groups seemed nervous and hence ambivalent about this radical experiment in democratization of start-up financing. Nor did proponents handle themselves well, politically. There were loud voices, especially among portal innovators, confidently proclaiming their ability to be disrupters. The libertarianism was particularly jarring, no doubt sending a loud signal that this was a signature effort to start removing the government from the start-up capital markets entirely. That alone was enough to provoke reactance. If a killing it was, perhaps this was a little like *Murder on the Orient Express*, with the knife passed from many hands.

INVESTOR BEHAVIOR AND MUTUAL FUNDS

We now travel from entrepreneurial capital-raising to the opposite end of the investment spectrum. Mutual funds are the investment of choice for most investors; nearly half of all US households own mutual fund shares. Some investors are effectively forced to use mutual funds, as in employer-sponsored retirement accounts that offer a limited menu of options for where to put the tax-deferred savings.

The wisdom in mutual fund investing is easy to see. By becoming a shareholder in a portfolio that is professionally managed, the investor gets diversification—a position in enough different securities so that the risk associated with any given security in the portfolio is diminished. If the portfolio manager does well, the returns pass through to the investors. Plus, there is convenient liquidity (mutual fund shares are redeemable at net asset value), record-keeping, customer service, and so on.

Mutual funds are highly regulated, through a special statute first adopted in 1940 and amended many times since. The regulation is intensive, in terms of both the behavior of persons associated with the funds and full disclosure (if anything, there is probably overly stifling regulation here). As a result, we have a world much the opposite of what we were just examining—very high transparency and sunlight, monitored by the SEC and supported by a variety of services like Morningstar and Lipper Analytics, which allow investors access to an extraordinary array of comparative information and advice.

Wasted Money?

In such a competitive setting, investors should do well, and to an extent they do. Precisely because of the high degree of transparency, mutual fund investments are some of the most closely studied in all of financial economics, and what economists have discovered is somewhat puzzling.[41] For all the informational richness and robust competition, large numbers of ordinary investors make seemingly poor mutual fund investment choices, both in and out of retirement savings accounts.

There are two things at work here. One—to no one's surprise—is that investing through any intermediary, mutual fund or otherwise, is costly. Mutual funds pay their portfolio advisers (the firms that choose and management the funds' investments) a management fee that is a percentage of the assets. Since fund shareholders effectively own a piece of that portfolio, the fee is paid out of shareholders' pockets. When funds use stockbrokers to market their shares, investors usually pay a commission (load) that may be incurred at the time of the purchase, at the time of redemption or some combination. (Fund shares that are directly marketed tend to be no-load.) On top of this, there are so-called 12b-1 fees or their equivalent that also help cover marketing expenses. If you are confused by all of this, you're getting the point. How much you are paying for your mutual fund investments is hard to calculate on your own, partly because of the array of possibilities (which may be further adjusted by breakpoints, discounts, and the like), partly because the variables involved in the calculation include an ever-changing amount invested and, often, how long you've held the shares. What bothers economists is how much variation there is in average fees—some funds are very low cost, others relatively high (2% or more). Because these are charged each year, the compounded effect over a lifetime of paying too much on a portfolio is very significant.

All this would make some sense if high-cost funds predictably delivered more value than low-cost ones, but that doesn't seem to be the case (though an unfortunately large number of investors seem to think they do). And that's the second basic point. Precisely because so many professionals do research on the same investment possibilities to build portfolios for their clients, any informational edge they might discover will likely not last long. And the likelihood that if they've discovered something they're the only ones with the opportunity to exploit it is small. The notion of market efficiency, as we've seen, is that opportunities systematically to beat the market are largely illusory.

For now take as a given that *on average*, mutual funds do not outperform the market for assets in which they invest.[42] In any particular year, or even multiyear period, of course, there will be many funds that beat the market, and others that will lag. But this seems often to be more a function of luck than skill, and of the volatility associated with what they're investing in. There is some evidence of some persistent stock-picking and market-timing ability,[43] but to the extent that a handful people might be skillful enough to do what seems so hard, they are highly unlikely to be found for long in the mutual fund industry—in large part because of rules and regulations, they can make a lot more managing a hedge fund.

If market-beating is so unlikely, it makes no sense to pay higher-than-average fees to mutual fund promoters for which there is no rational expectation of future higher-than-average performance. That doesn't mean avoiding mutual funds, but rather finding low-cost ones that don't pay for the quixotic hope of supranormal returns but simply mimic the market. By and large these are index funds, or their functional exchange-traded equivalents, for which fees and expenses are relatively small (yet even here there are differences that are hard to explain rationally).

So the puzzle is why so many investors defy this logic, paying in the aggregate billions of dollars in search of superior returns. There is some evidence of simple naiveté—survey evidence shows a disturbing number of people who seem to believe that higher fees imply that the fund or adviser *must* be better. There can also be an overly narrow focus: most funds will do very well during strong stock markets, and if one just looks at absolute performance, even mediocre (and high cost) funds can look acceptable.

Much of this is psychological.[44] In any given period of time, some funds will beat their averages substantially and thus appear to have something of a "hot hand." Investor money tends to follow. As we have just seen, there is very little evidence of persistent skill rather than luck. Yet the human mind has a strong tendency to identify correlations and project onto them a causal narrative—a story about skill and talent that that means superior performance is bound to persist into the future. Overconfidence, yet again. And of courses other forces bolster the illusion. The financial media love to find and celebrate recently successful portfolio managers, giving them salience and apparent credibility. The inflow of money feeds on itself through word of mouth, offering "social proof" that this is an investment worth making right now.

Evidence abounds of widespread trend-chasing by mutual fund investors. By and large (albeit with enough random exceptions to confuse the message) these investors will not find the hoped-for gains. Even assuming skill, having more money to invest makes it somewhat harder for the fund to succeed. Assuming that the past performance was more luck than skill, the tendency is "reversion to mean"—performance that brings the long-run average closer to, well, average.

One famous study, entitled "Dumb Money," illustrates the tendency of large numbers of mutual fund investors to move money out of funds that start to lag and into those who are hot right now.[45] Yet this is exactly the opposite of investment wisdom—money is made by investing in what is not in favor now, not coming into a stocks or industries that are popular at the moment. And such sentiment-based investing crowds out focus on costs—the funds that most enthusiastically promote their past success are often the ones charging big fees. Laboratory experiments involving MBA students identified some of the biases that particularly affect mutual fund decision-making: positive illusions about one's own competencies and anchoring on the past with insufficient regard for the potential for change.[46] But their most striking finding was that participants not only overestimated future performance; they also overestimated how well they *had* performed, even though accurate information about performance was right there in front of them to see if they looked carefully. They evaluated their performance as at least being even with the available indices, even when they had in fact done much worse.

Nothing we've seen thus far necessarily places blame on the mutual fund industry for investors' illusions. Indeed, the SEC insists on the disclosure of past performance. This makes sense (who wants to be in a fund that was a bottom performer for the last few years, which might not have simply been bad luck?). But it also creates a focal point for trend-chasers. There is always a warning that past performance does not guarantee future success, but that's not the point. It's the odds of future success that are important, and the costs that come win, lose, or draw. A number of studies indicate that using disclosure to bring the relationship between cost and performance home to investors is a challenge, even when the choosers are well educated and financially well-off.[47]

There is a more disturbing insight, however. Many mutual funds are sold directly as no-load funds. Many others, however, are sold through what is called the broker channel—stockbrokers who recommend mutual funds to their customers and charge a commission based on these sales. We saw how complicated these commission and fee structures can be. Not surprisingly, compensating the broker adds to the up-front cost of the investment, eating into returns early on. This would be well worth it if brokers guided their customers toward the best available funds, countering the cognitive biases and other forces that might lead them to be dumb money.

But the academic evidence isn't so optimistic, because of the conflicts of interest. Harvard's Sendhil Mullainathan and associates did an extensive "audit study" looking at the actual advice given by a variety of financial advisers in the face of poor investment strategies by retail investors and found evidence that the advisers often not only fail to debias their clients but instead offer advice that "if anything may exaggerate existing biases or, in some cases, even make the clients worse off."[48] The brokers didn't stop the clients from chasing trends and sometimes even pushed clients away from index investing, toward actively managed (higher cost) funds that were shining at the moment. In synch with this was a finding that mutual funds purchased through the broker channel performed worse on average, taking into account both returns and expenses, than those purchased directly.[49] Another prominent study concludes that mutual funds perform comparably in the market to low-cost alternatives when directly sold, such that substantially all the evidence of mutual fund underperformance is from the broker channel.[50] Not needing as much evidence of good performance because of the salesmanship, fund managers don't invest as much in trying.

What we have here is market segmentation, similar to what we observe with credit cards and many other financial products. Smart investors who know how to minimize the costs of investing have little difficulty finding index funds and other efficient ways for building their portfolios. Such investors take advantage of the highly competitive structure of the mutual fund industry, and the industry makes relatively less off them as a result. They are cross-subsidized by less able investors, who pay too much for too little.

How troubling is this? Those skittish about too much governmental paternalism have plenty to work with—no one is actually lying to investors, and in any given time period active investing strategies by some funds and industry sectors will beat passive market indices. Everyone has a right to try to ask investors to go along for the ride. A more subtle point has to do with what researchers call "hand-holding" or being a "money doctor."[51] There may be value from the advisory relationship in terms of avoiding the even worse mistakes clients would make on their own—investing too little given future financial needs, leaving money in low-yielding bank accounts, overconcentrating their investments in their employers' stock, and so on. Brokers have to be compensated for their time and other services, and maybe this is just how it happens. Clients get some much wanted peace of mind, even if they're not being taken care of quite as well as they hope. On top of all this, money that flows to active portfolio management helps contribute to stock market efficiency (the intense competition among informed investors that helps keep stock prices in line), which index funds and other passive investment strategies do not. There is probably some social value to naïve investment strategies.

But there are billions of dollars at stake here, much of the money in much-needed retirement funds, and circumstantial evidence of opportunism by some brokers and promoters. Shouldn't we at least warn investors of the conflicts of interest? To some extent we do, though it may be buried in informational overload. Moreover, one of the most striking findings in the psychology literature, for our purposes, has to do with the effects of disclosing conflicts of interest. As noted in chapter 1, this can lead to more opportunism, not less. It's not a cure.

Retirement Accounts

In many cases, fear is at work in driving suboptimal investor behavior. Today, we live in a world where individual personal responsibility dominates: Fewer pensions, more self-directed retirement choices; a fraying and fragile social safety net. If we fail to invest well, we fall behind, threatening our own futures and raising the risk of being a burden on family or others. That's scary, and fear has quite a number of psychological consequences of interest to the world of investing (just watch the panic selling that occurs in a sudden market downturn). Sometimes fear and anxiety lead to paralysis—no choices at all. Often, it leads to increased risk-taking—people risk more to avoid a perceived loss than to chase a hoped-for gain (loss aversion). And it can also prompt more reliance on others who promise (really or just through imagination) to take these hard choices off our hands and thus remove the anticipation of regret for choosing badly.

All this has come to a political boil, yet unresolved. Both the SEC and the Department of Labor (for retirement accounts) are working on changes in the law to declare brokers "fiduciaries," with some legal obligation to steer clients away from high-cost options on funds and rollovers. Today, their obligation has been one of "suitability," but that goes more to risk tolerance, not costs. Because fee income is crucial to the business model of the industry, such a change would be disruptive—the not-empty threat is that brokers would simply stop serving smaller accounts if they don't generate enough revenue, leaving such persons in a worse place with no advice, at the mercy of bad judgment and salespeople from other industries selling poor substitutes. The industry would like as much of any new regulation as possible to be disclosure and consent-based, for obvious reasons. But we've seen what comes of that when investors aren't paying close-enough attention, or have other things on their minds.

Two economists once noted that it is hard to explain, via conventional rational expectations, why nearly a quarter of gross domestic product in the United States is spent on persuasion.[52] Salesmanship is central our cultural identity and (perhaps) economic growth, which is dangerous. Most of what we've covered in this chapter demonstrates how sales tactics often find the lucrative gray area of exploiting hope, fear, ego, and envy. Arguably, it's why we have such a robust consumer and financial economy.

Selling is a highly competitive field, and the conventional depiction is often of the sleazy stockbroker, slamming customers into unwanted purchases. While there are some sociopaths, the better argument accords with Trivers's idea: the best salespeople are those who already have sold themselves. To be sure, the degree to which firms in the industry encourage hard selling varies considerably. Some in good faith stress ethics, others not so much.

As we've seen, motivated inference is the widely studied mental phenomenon by which people so easily perceive that what they want is both right and reasonable. Most people want to see themselves as honest, and as we've seen, countless studies in behavioral ethics have shown that people cheat far less than they could even when the likelihood of detection is nil. But they also cheat much more than they should, so long as they can maintain the desired self-image. To manage this, the mind goes to work in a variety of ways to cast dirty deeds in the false light of good intentions, or at least to hide the ethical implications of a course of action, which some call ethical fading.[53] By most accounts (though this is still a matter of scientific argument)[54] these biases are unconscious, so that this is not just rationalization. Where competition is intense, a facility at self-deception—ethical plasticity—allows for more aggressive exploitation of the customer's biases and emotions without the baggage of doubt. To the adept and nimble go the spoils of being big producers. The securities business dangles lavish rewards for the best sellers—money, trips, and prizes—and uses aggressive quotas as a stick to motivate the laggards. In the literature on behavioral ethics, each of those is associated with a higher likelihood of cheating.

In selling investments, the self-serving inferences are not hard. A book about the training of insurance salespeople (from which this section's title is taken) shows how new recruits are taught to see life insurance as a moral good that the average person foolishly underspends on, threatening the financial security of their loved ones. In that light, even the most aggressive tactics seem benign.[55] Among stockbrokers, it becomes easy to see oneself as simply offering financial products to consider, with the client or customer a consenting adult with freedom and capacity to choose. Warnings can be communicated in writing, unlikely to actually be read (something the law often seems to bless by refusing to protect investors who have failed in their "duty to read"). Thoroughly repressed is how dependent and overwhelmed so many clients feel, having come to the financial advisor because they want and need help. But once trust is built, the relationship tends to be sticky even when the advice turns out to be poor.[56] We've seen the evidence that after disclosing a conflict of interest, many people feel more freedom to behave opportunistically. That's motivated reasoning at work. The heavier the pressure on salespeople—the quotas, goals, competitions, incentives—the heavier the cognitive grease needed to succeed. Other features of the work environment, including the stress, busyness, in-group identity, and visible trappings of wealth surrounding them, become further enabling. Securities firms can introduce their brokers to new product ideas in sales-training programs in a way that convinces them that the new offerings really are good—skepticism shoved aside by pointed reminders of the compensation that goes with pushing the product. They've been sold, making them all the more credible "money doctors."

We'll see more about this in the next chapter, where we look at the high-end world of investment banking. As just noted, the SEC was directed by Congress to consider a rule that would make retail stockbrokers fiduciaries as a matter of law, required to act with loyalty and care in their client's best interests. There is much to be said for that, but it will have to be very aggressively enforced to make much of a difference because of the ease with which brokers come to believe that that's what they are already doing. So long as there are such strong incentives to sell, the cognitive dissonance will be overwhelming, and likely resolved in favor of the profitable. In a dictionary of antonyms, look up "fiduciary" and you will find that its opposite is "salesperson." Of course, we see the same in many professional fields. Lawyers, doctors, and investment advisers have long been treated as fiduciaries. Each profession is under comparable stress precisely because so many of their key actors have taken on a profit-maximizing, rainmaking role in the face of intense competition. The cognitive short-cuts come easily to those who thrive, especially when there is low-intensity enforcement of the fiduciary duty or easy outs like a customer's duty to read the dense legalese that often counts for full disclosure.

Some lawyers think that attaching the label of fiduciary sends a powerful expressive message, that the law expects fidelity rather than profit-maximization. But that's a hard message to get people to take seriously, and not just because it's deflected by cognitive grease. We come back to the celebration of selling in American culture. Sociologists who study white-collar crime point out that con artists are almost always proud of their exploits, except for letting themselves get caught.[57] They won the interpersonal battles of wits, in a society that adores cleverness and success. Sales organizations often embrace team-building rituals to anoint winners (and subtly portray customers as prey), using war or sports imagery extensively. Against that, fiduciary labels can be ridiculed and lose all normative punch. A study of fraud by insurance brokers tells of an organization that tried to inculcate a rule that salespeople not "churn" old policies into new (with a big step up in commissions).[58] To enforce this they imposed a strict constraint on new policies within ninety days of the lapse of another. But sales quotas were not adjusted downward, and the salespeople quickly figured out how to separate lapses and new policies by ninety-one days. They convinced themselves that management could not really be serious about wanting things to change or they wouldn't have made it so easy to evade. So the dictate from above must have been window dressing. Looking back, one of the salesmen lamented that all good salespeople all have a little larceny in their hearts. Their identity is tied up in success, and so it takes a lot more than an easily evaded rule to put them off their game. Taking advantage of people's hopes and fears is part of the lore of championship salesmanship.

6

Lessons from the Financial Crisis

In an experimental study published in the journal *Nature*, some well-known Swiss researchers examined people's inclination to cheat, using as subjects employees at a large international bank. As is common in such experiments, there was no means of detection: subjects could cheat with only conscience or self-image as a check. In the control condition, they did not appear to cheat any more than others. But when their identities as bankers were primed—they were reminded of their professional roles—the rate of cheating rose significantly. This difference did not occur in other professions studied. Something about being a banker, it seems, prompted less ethical behavior, leading the researchers to conclude that the norms, not the people, were the problem.[1]

The bailout of much of Wall Street as part of the global financial crisis that began in 2007 is still fresh and painful in the minds of many, with a naive "never again" attitude still dominating contemporary political discourse even as the reforms put in place shortly thereafter are being dismantled or left uncompleted. Hundreds of books and thousands of articles deal extensively with the crisis and the regulatory dilemma of systemic risk, and it is much too big a topic to treat thoroughly here.[2] But it is irresistible to extend some of the ideas we've developed to the cataclysm, because as the Swiss study suggests, they fit so well.

Where do we even begin? The financial crisis and its regulatory causes and effects constitute a story of immense complexity. Technological evolution rapidly changed the nature of financial services, leading to a mutating mix of products, markets, and institutions that were massively large, politically and economically potent, and fully understood by no one. As any sociologist or social psychologist would point out, those conditions almost guarantee that widespread beliefs will emerge untethered to the truth, because we need some collective sense of stability and control, even if illusory. Thus the shock when it all came crashing down.

A SHORT HISTORY OF THE FINANCIAL CRISIS

Most descriptions of the crisis divide it into three phases. The first was the growth of financial products whose value was based on home mortgages. At one time, banking institutions made residential mortgage loans to keep on their books, but that had long since changed. Mortgages were now originated and sold off to intermediaries that would package them into bundles, interests of which were then sold off to investors (asset securitization). Institutional investors would thus be buying pieces of a diversified pool of mortgages, with the option to buy first-in-line priority to be paid (the safest, obviously) or further down the line, where returns depended on whether there was enough money coming in from the homeowners' mortgage payments to satisfy all the prior claims. That's more risky, and thus the expected return higher to justify the risk. But the expectation was that housing prices would continue to increase, limiting the risk of large-scale defaults in any of the tranches, especially the safer ones. Gradually, these mortgage-based financial products became more complex. Still, credit rating agencies like Moody's and Standard & Poors gave them investment-grade ratings, which investors seemed to trust. Gradually as well, the mortgages going into these pools (or in the case of derivatives, referenced for valuation purposes)[3] were increasingly "subprime," made to homeowners of limited means who may have been buying more house than they could afford, and thus had a higher prospect of default.

Three additional bits of "prehistory" may be helpful to understanding this first part of the story.[4] One is that the government was strongly encouraging all this in the name of broader homeownership, particularly via the implicit guarantee of mortgage-backed securities issued by Fannie Mae and Freddie Mac. Conservatives tend to see this meddling as a primary source of the crisis. Second was that the world was awash in dollars, many as the result of trade imbalances, which meant that entities holding dollars had a great appetite for safe, liquid investments that paid a bit more than the low-interest Treasury bills available during the early 2000s. Highly rated securitized debt fit this need well, which explains why there was such an extraordinary demand to be fed.

Third, and most importantly, this fast-growing market was not regulated with much regard for anything but *investor* risk, and that got a very light touch. Congress determined—infamously—that derivatives needed no direct regulation at all because they were traded in an institutional marketplace where people and organizations supposedly knew how to protect themselves and deal with risk sensibly. Securitization remained within the ambit of securities regulation, but because this was an institutional marketplace, there were relatively few obligations beyond don't commit fraud, and it was hardly policed at all. This contrasts with traditional banking regulation, which is about safety and soundness—avoiding too much risk. This subprime world had evolved outside of banking regulation—in the so-called shadow banking system, dominated by securities firms—and thus not directly subject to those prudential norms.[5] This was a quintessential example of regulatory arbitrage. Precisely because the shadow system was becoming so strong, banks demanded the ability to compete on an equal footing with the less-regulated securities firms, which meant that banking regulation became much softer and less effective, too. Regulators were being played off against each other.

Now back to the main story. This first phase ended in 2006–7 when what today seems so predictable happened: housing prices stopped going up, and in many parts of the country dropped. The rate of homeowner defaults thus went way up, which meant those securitized investments were worth much less (and certainly not safe). Where the products were built on borrowed money, the decline in value was amplified. (In the interest of simplification we won't go into how derivatives were structured or the prevalence of credit default swaps, by which some investors bought "insurance" against defaults and others sold that insurance by taking on that risk—suffice it to say that AIG, a central player in the crisis, found itself in the unenviable position of insurer of an immensely large portion of that credit risk.)

This crash alone would have been very painful for the economy, but not necessarily devastating. The second part of the story takes us to how the crisis metastasized. Many buyers of the mortgage-backed securities and derivatives (as well as many securitizers themselves) were financial institutions that had to maintain certain levels of equity capital to satisfy regulators. But as we saw, these standards had become relaxed, especially in the shadow market, and so it had become common for these firms to borrow a great deal of their working capital in the short–term debt markets. Other buyers were similarly exposed, even without capital adequacy rules, because they were borrowing on margin and thus faced margin calls if the value of the collateral dropped.

So when the value of the mortgage-backed debt and derivatives fell, a liquidity crisis set in. Institutions had to sell the debt for a variety of reasons (some regulatory), which meant a sudden supply in the face of insufficient demand. Prices dropped further, into a free fall, which then became contagious to other assets as well. As this happened, the sources of liquidity to the financial institutions disappeared in the face of massive uncertainty about the quality of those institutions' balance sheets. With this, the institutions were (or at least appeared to be) insolvent, unable to pay their debts to others. So the whole financial forest caught fire. And remember how many buyers of these products were outside the United States, making the conflagration a global one.

Thus the third phase, which is by now the most familiar part of the story. Governments (not just in the United States) had to decide whether to let the fire burn itself out or step in and, through various forms of financial support, rescue the big financial players who were at risk. There was a controversial rescue of Bear Stearns, then a failure to rescue Lehman Brothers. The Lehman decision was disastrous for confidence in the capital markets, and the government—in the last phases of the Bush administration and the first days of Obama—soon became committed to stabilization at whatever cost. Wall Street got its bailout; individual homeowners, and many others, were not so lucky.[6] The "great" recession, and a great deal of economic misery, set in.

The out-of-pocket costs were massive, though the government later recouped more bailout money than many people realize. The political costs were massive as well. There was a well-justified loss of faith in regulation, and a popular anger with government intervention. At the same time we learned that unregulated markets were dangerous, so there was no obvious solution. Congress passed the Dodd-Frank Act of 2010 without a coherent theory of how the crisis occurred or what would prevent the next one. And as the recession lingered, the overwhelming desire for prompt economic growth ran directly against the desire to make the financial system more risk averse, which (combined with heavy lobbying by financial firms) quickly weakened the new regulatory resolve.

It would take far too many pages (and not necessarily convincing ones) to assess whether we are better off now than before in terms of financial stability. Maybe. Since

2010, the SEC has found itself in an unfamiliar and uncomfortable role of regulating portions of the securities industry with a view toward preventing too much systemic risk. This is in coordination with other agencies with very different regulatory philosophies, and a new superregulator, the Financial Stability Oversight Council (FSOC), which is dominated by the banking regulators. This has been a political maelstrom for the SEC, as firms from the securities industry want it to take their side against the encroachment of costly bank-style prudential regulation, in favor of more market- and disclosure-driven strategies. Its lack of experience and knowledge puts it at a serious disadvantage in finding the path forward, given that we got into trouble by relying too heavily on such strategies in the past. The Commission's voice at the table has not been a confident one.

BLAME

This brief history was solely for the purpose of posing the question of who, if anyone, was to blame.[7] In the years leading to the crisis, financial services firms sold a great number of products that later turned out to be worth far less than expected, especially those with safe credit ratings. Some of these were "bespoke" transactions designed for particular customers; others were more standardized. Some had warranties about the nature or quality of the assets backing them, which in certain cases were grossly violated. Others made no such explicit promises.

The dominating legal question arising from the crisis is whether these transactions were deceitful. Many cases have been brought and settled, by the government and by purchasers of the instruments. Bank of America alone paid nearly $17 billion to resolve Justice Department claims. Other cases are still pending, and will be for some time.

The legal issues here are intricate, but the most interesting ones for our purposes come back to state of mind: did the sellers know but deliberately conceal the danger embedded in what they were peddling? By this point you should sense some of the difficult interpretive issues—whose knowledge, exactly, and what degree of danger? These are also relevant to a different kind of deceit that may have been practiced by the same financial institutions. Were they honest with their own investors in terms of the risks associated with their sales practices, and what was on their own balance sheets? To simplify all this (and address the question that the public most wants to know), *did the most senior officials at the big banks and securities firms know and conceal that what was being conveyed through their product pipelines was potentially toxic?* While many people think the answer to that is self-evident, there are at least four dramatically different narratives from those who have thoroughly analyzed the crisis. We'll go through them one at a time.

Banker Opportunism

The first answer, and probably the most common among journalists, politicians, and the general public, says that the answer is yes and it was all about greed. That's how many understood the well-publicized case the SEC brought and settled for $500 million against Goldman Sachs, claiming that Goldman structured and sold a derivative product to a German bank while concealing that, at the behest of a hedge fund that wanted to speculate on a housing price drop, it had loaded into the product mortgages that were particularly likely to default if there was a housing downturn.[8] Other claims that seem to fit with this greed story focus on the sale of mortgages or interests therein where there were inexcusable misrepresentations about creditworthiness or even the validity of the mortgages themselves. The credit-rating agencies—Moody's and Standard & Poors, in particular—play a villain's role in this story, supposedly giving high investment grades to products they knew were unsafe in breathless pursuit of lucrative fees.

To these storytellers, institutional buyers were the innocent victims. But that poses something of a puzzle, because most of these buyers were large, professionally managed, and quite sophisticated—presumably able to fend for themselves. At least by 2004 or 2005, if not before, there was a great deal of publicity about subprime mortgages ("liar loans" and the like) and creditworthiness issues, along with increasing discussion of the possibility of a housing bubble. Credit-rating agency objectivity was also highly publicized and doubted. So it seems odd that these otherwise sophisticated buyers would be so naive, failing to ask the tough questions or form their own opinions about risk. To put it more bluntly, is it plausible that the institutional sell-side could, top to bottom, know of the toxicity of such a risk while the institutional buy-side was so clueless?

Moral Hazard

That puzzle could be explained by a second and very different account, to which many economists are partial. Maybe the sophisticated buy-side appreciated the risk of toxicity pretty much as well as the sell side. But they were relatively indifferent to the risk because other people's money was involved: the individuals making the purchases for the institutions had short-term incentives to pump up their portfolios with higher-yield investments. If the risks went bad, those with interests in the portfolios they were managing (retirees, for example) would suffer. But the buy-side portfolio managers wouldn't necessarily be blamed, because these investments were commonplace and highly rated. Plus, the buyers might have predicted government bailouts to benefit creditors in the event of catastrophe, making them worry less about consequences of a market collapse.

In this moral hazard story, the institutional buyers were not deceived. (We'll put aside for now the subset of cases where buyers demanded explicit representations and warranties, which were given falsely.) But there still might be dishonesty to the extent that these buy-side agents concealed from their own investors, beneficiaries, or owners how much risk there was in their portfolios in return for pumped-up yields. The sell side would not escape responsibility, either for facilitating this or because as products were sitting ready to be sold, the risk was still their own. Many of the interests in the most complicated products turned out to be hard to sell and thus stayed on the investment banks' balance sheets. Given how dependent they were on borrowed money, that risk was considerable—especially to anyone contemplating the systemic consequences of a downturn in the housing markets.

There is much to be said for this moral hazard account,[9] and serious reason for concern about the interests of investors who put their money in managed accounts at banks, mutual funds, or pension funds. But at least as to fooling investors in the stock market by concealing the risk, we come to a similar puzzle. Given how well publicized these issues were, how could an efficient market so easily have been fooled? It's hardly likely that the stock market was clueless as to something that was common knowledge in the industry.

Cognitive Illusion

The first two accounts are essentially conspiracy theories, though not entirely implausible ones. Not the third. Suppose the sell-side bankers genuinely believed that the risk was less than it really was. That's not to say that there was no perceived risk; rather, the risk appeared remote enough to effectively disregard on a day-to-day basis. In other words, maybe being inside these institutions motivated managers and investors to underestimate the risk in these products, so that they were drinking the Kool-Aid and never fully appreciated the extent of the dangers. Psychological biases and cultural tropes generated a web of illusions. A number of well-known economists and psychologists have put forth behavioral explanations, whether for this particular crisis or financial crises generally—Gennaioli, Shleifer, and Vishny locate the source in the representativeness bias, Barberis in the same plus cognitive dissonance, Thakor in availability, Benabou in groupthink, Bracha and Weber in the illusions of control and confidence.[10] If these behavioral accounts are right, maybe there was no guilty state of mind at all at the highest levels of these institutions. This mimics our discussion of corporate fraud in chapter 2.

Beyond Comprehension

Finally, there is the "perfect storm" (or "black swan") account. In this telling, the probability of a serious financial crisis occurring *was* actually extremely small, small enough that it could rationally be ignored given all available information and the near-term profit opportunities available. Most people find this story hard to believe today, but that is judgment in hindsight. As we've seen, hindsight magnifies the perception that there was palpable risk at the time of prediction, simply because we know that the event did happen. At the time, the genuine best (unbiased) estimate was little or no risk of a financial meltdown.

The third and fourth explanations are hard to disentangle, because it is impossible to define with any precision the accurate perception of risk in the early to mid-2000s. They are also both frustrating because they read as excuses: the Wall Street types who got so rich by taking on so much firm-level risk didn't really think they were endangering all of us outside of acceptable bounds. Many people just don't want to hear them.

Combining the Explanations

So who's right? A clever study tests beliefs inside financial firms as of 2004–6 by looking at the personal real estate transactions of midlevel executives at firms heavily involved in securitizations.[11] They were situated precisely where one would think, under the fraud story, the awareness of risk was greatest. Indeed, like their firms, they *increased* their exposure to the real estate markets. That isn't conclusive proof (the study couldn't test whether these executives were hedging the risk in other portions of their personal portfolios, for example, nor did it focus on higher-ups in these firms) but does suggest caution before jumping breathlessly onto the complicity bandwagon. Higher up, Wall Street executives lost massively in terms of their own wealth, evidence that they did not appreciate the risk well enough to bail out before the troubles set in. One insider trading study found no evidence of unusual stock-selling activity by bank insiders in advance of the meltdown (in contrast to significant evidence that bank insiders later took advantage of knowledge that *bailouts* were coming their way).[12]

Of course, we can mix and match pieces of each of these stories. The period 2004–6 was a time of increasing conscious anxiety on Wall Street about the risks. What was entirely unclear, however, was the right strategic move—hold, fold, or run? For a wide variety of reasons that we're about to get into, that kind of ambiguity makes people and institutions more rigid and stuck in shared habits of cognition and behavior. Sociologist Donald MacKenzie observes that newly developed derivatives on asset-backed securities were being structured and valued—at a very fast pace—by separate groups in both banks and rating agencies without access to a growing base of technical knowledge in other divisions and groups, slowing down the learning process. The over-the-counter markets for complex securitizations and derivatives lacked many of the mechanisms of efficiency until very late, thus sending imperfect and misleading signals that nothing was amiss.[13] Indeed, it was the creation of a tradable index product in early 2007, allowing bets on downside predictions as well as the upside, that finally set off alarms by revealing so much market-wide anxiety that had theretofore been hidden. Only then did the herd start to turn.

It's possible that this hybrid account is entirely rational, so that the problem facing those in the market in 2004–7 was simply epistemological: too many unknowns, so that not enough information had been revealed to make the risk of meltdown truly palpable.[14] That would not be a matter of cognitive error. What this fails to explain, however, is why activity continued with so much apparent confidence, when an epistemological deficit should rationally prompt doubt instead.

Much attention from the financial crisis focused on the credit-rating agencies, which assigned high "investment-grade" ratings to the asset-backed bonds and derivative products that melted down to trigger the crisis. Most buyers couldn't have or wouldn't have bought without those ratings. The narratives of blame set forth earlier each have a special place for the rating agencies, an important gatekeeper for the debt markets. The common story of greed and corruption says that they deliberately ignored risk in unseemly pursuit of fees, which were paid by the issuers or securitizers, not investors—an obvious and long-recognized conflict of interest. To this we can add a more subtle point. Because many institutional buyers were legally restricted to investment-grade purchases, both issuers and investors had to use rating agencies to get deals done. As a result, the agencies had a guaranteed stream of business regardless of how insightful their ratings were, meaning that rating quality meant less. Marketplace discipline was largely gone.

But MacKenzie's sociological exploration of the selling of mortgage-backed securities looks closely at the rating agencies, and comes away unconvinced that there was much deliberate wrongdoing here either. It's also difficult to understand quite so much reliance on the rating agencies given that concerns about issuer-pays and ratings quality were well known at the time.[15] So maybe here, too, the palpable shortcomings in the ratings process were not entirely corrupt. That said, in 2015 Standard & Poors paid $1.375 billion to settle claims to the contrary made by the US Department of Justice and state authorities.

DANCE CONTEST

With a particularly evocative phrase that soon became one of the most-quoted references about the financial crisis, Citibank CEO Chuck Price said before the crisis hit, "When the music stops, in terms of liquidity, things will be complicated. But as long as the music is playing, you've got to get up and dance. We're still dancing."[16] This was not about securitization at all (the context of the interview was about the equally debt-fueled private equity market). But after the crisis erupted, Prince's quote was cited and deconstructed many times over as expressing how Wall Street sees financial risk.

The standard interpretation is about short-termism—make the money now, and worry about the long-term risks later (or not at all, because you may well be have moved on by that time). Myopia is undeniably important. The incentive compensation of Wall Street executives (indeed, lower-level personnel as well) was heavily based on annual performance, in the form of both bonuses based on profitability metrics and equity-based compensation that referenced the firm's stock price. Especially if long-term risk was hard to discern, it was in the firm's interests—and the executives' interests—to dance with as much shaking and rattling as possible as long as the music was still playing.

Dancing and Desire

That could be entirely rational, if somewhat greedy. But dancing evokes a form of emotional expression, not usually a logical one. And we've seen how one of the great growth areas in the study of financial decision-making—and financial risk-taking—draws from cognitive neuroscience. In congressional testimony shortly after the financial crisis started, Andrew Lo, an economics professor at MIT (who is also a hedge fund advisor), observed that "prolonged periods of economic growth and prosperity can induce a collective sense of euphoria and complacency among investors that is not unlike the drug-induced stupor of a cocaine addict."[17] While that might just be the foolish behavior of noise traders, Lo says not: professional traders dance, too. In other words, the visceral excitement of the dance makes it hard to slow down, much less stop.

Oxford neuroscientist (and former Wall Street trader) John M. Coates elaborates, noting how traders abandon caution and become increasingly aggressive and insensitive to risk. Coates originally became famous for his study of risk-taking by London traders over the course of trading days, measuring various hormonal influences that shift over the course of minutes and hours in response to changes in stimuli. Coates then extended these ideas over the longer term in an effort to explain the crisis, noting that financial risk-taking "is as much a biological activity, with as many medical consequences, as facing down a grizzly bear."[18] A mix of testosterone, adrenaline, and cortisol inside, and the punishment and reward systems on the outside, incite booms and busts.

While this account goes to individual brain function, there is, as both Lo and Coates acknowledge, a social contagion to these behaviors. Desire, confidence, and fear spread from one person to another. Inside financial firms, a contagion of enthusiasm (and diminution in the perception of risk) energizes others. Oxytocin, in particular, "serves a group-related purpose . . . to bind individuals to highly cooperative, higher-level units, often in the service of outcompeting other groups."[19] That energy operates as high-grade corporate grease, drawing others into the frenzy. The feeling is a good one, making everyone focus—quite adaptively, in the short term—on a mutually prosperous future. And in this upward spiral, those who are most drawn into the dancing become corporate exemplars. Their (self-fulfilling) predictions of more success turn out to be correct, and so they are anointed as smart. Their message is positive, and thus inspirational. And so they gain seniority and power. With that power and authority, they silence expressions of risk from people who might want to turn down the music. A risk manager who thinks things have gotten overheated and wants to prevent an aggressive trade is met with profanity-laced bluster and a demand for very precise proof that it will turn out bad. In a setting of high uncertainty, that is impossible to give, which means that the overworked, underresourced, and politically impotent Cassandra will have to back off. (And during 2005–6, the computer risk models were not generating cautionary proof because they were based on historical data that showed an ever-rising real estate market, because that had been the experience of the prior decade.) An interesting study suggests that banks whose senior executives better fit a heightened "power profile" were more aggressive in subprime loan activity than those with lower profiles.[20]

Competitive Arousal

That takes us from neuroscience to culture. In financial firms, there is much emphasis on team building and bonding, even as individuals realize they're in a

Darwinian competition within as well as outside their firms. A cultural anthropologist, Karen Ho, describes two key cultural tropes in investment banking. One is an obsession with "the market" as the ultimate arbiter of both success and value. The other is acting in the moment—the near term—because markets shift rapidly and unpredictably. There is a fatalism to all this, a desire not to think too hard about the long term because the market (like financial firms) is merciless to those who miss a move.[21]

Chuck Prince's dancing reference also evokes a strong sense of competitiveness—that if firms don't dance, they lose. If he was referring to the game of musical chairs, the resonant image is that the one who doesn't find the last chair quickly enough is out. This, too, has both cognitive and cultural consequences. As sports coaches endlessly stress, competitive demands require exceptional desire, focus, and intensity. Distractions are extremely dangerous. The more intense the competition, the more useful the mythical beliefs that rationalize aggressiveness—extreme confidence, in the moment.

Here, too, there is research in psychology that sheds light on these practices, as we saw in chapter 2. A common research finding is that when people are put in competition—take an auction, for example—there can arise a desire to win that comes to dominate even when winning becomes costly. A familiar example is a corporate acquisition, where the CEO of the acquiring company gets caught up in a bidding war and eventually overpays to win—an explanation for the often-observed failure of acquisitions to add as much to the bottom line as hoped, frequently becoming value-destroying. This is the phenomenon of "competitive arousal," exacerbated by rivalry, time pressures, and the presence of an audience prepared to judge the competition.[22] This stimulates the physiological arousal that crowds out the rational assessment of costs and benefits (this also connects to a loss frame, as executives come to think of the prize as theirs and are unwilling to lose it) and produces more unethical behavior.[23] Competition has its most intense psychological effect when the participants are familiar rivals, highly ranked and close to an identifiable standard of comparison. That's Wall Street, to be sure.

Recall also that testosterone is linked to power-seeking, social dominance, and a reduction in the fear response. It diminishes risk perception, as well. Coates points out that in the right situations—especially a boom market or a bubble—these tendencies are amply rewarded in probationary crucibles and contribute to the political power effects described earlier. There is lots of anecdotal evidence that Wall Street firms hire and promote by reference to precisely these traits, in which aggressive males are naturally favored. We'll come back to issues of gender diversity later in the chapter.

So that's the case for an illusions-based explanation: that there was a motivation-driven failure within financial services firms to appreciate the level of risk their activities were creating. That is not to say that no one in these firms was concerned. There will always be warnings and complaints, prescient in hindsight. But if those with power genuinely believe otherwise, the doubters are gradually silenced and marginalized, and evangelists for risk-taking celebrated and promoted.

Information Deficits

Motivation isn't necessarily the whole story, though. Quite apart from any psychological or cultural account for diminished risk perception, recall the familiar organizational pathologies that get in the way of accurate risk perception, especially at the top. Both information and responsibility are highly diffused among many people inside the firm, and their incentives are usually to accentuate their accomplishments and hide their failures when dealing with peers and superiors. Information can flow very poorly, especially as the size and scale of the firm becomes larger. As a result, much risk-based information in financial services firms can often be hidden in silos.[24] (This is something Donald MacKenzie also stresses in his sociological account of how complex derivatives were evaluated for risk.) And for a variety of legal and reputational reasons, higher-ups may not want to know—or at least be viewed by subordinates as not wanting to know—the truth. Killing the messenger is one of the enduring insights in all of organizational behavior. Put this together with the behavioral account and the case for diminished risk perception grows stronger. Internal controls systems are supposed to counter this tendency, but we have seen the problems. Given the inherent ambiguity and complexity of risk in financial firms, the truth is always contestable. Risk models are backward-looking and never clearly assimilate change. Too much risk aversion and the firm may fail in the marketplace. The incentives and power structure inside the organization favor the brave. The odds are stacked against the risk managers.

There is a fine line between uncertainty and illusion. An eye-opening study looks at the subject Chuck Prince really was talking about, the bubble in private equity financing that collapsed along with the onset of the financial crisis.[25] Researchers from MIT interviewed many participants in that market in 2005, and then again in 2010–11. Even before the catastrophe, many invoked the dance metaphor in explaining that there was a widespread perception that prices had gone much too high, yet most bankers were still doing deals. The uncertainty was not about risk but timing, and hence immense confusion about the right strategy. The illusions were not about valuation, but the result of misperceptions about what peers were doing and the state of marketplace liquidity, both of which were only dimly visible in the marketplace. Given these misperceptions, the common wisdom was that *not* dancing was too risky.

Pleasing Investors

There is one more reading of Prince's dancing quote to consider. Dancing is a form of performance art; people often dance to please an audience. Maybe Citi had to get up and dance because the crowd—investors and the stock markets—was demanding it.

One of the common themes coming out of the financial crisis was that securities firms and banks were pressured to seize short-term profit opportunities presented by securitization and heavy leveraging because they were themselves publicly traded companies and their stock prices would suffer—indeed be pummeled—if they didn't. A depressed stock price has all sorts of adverse consequences, not just to shareholders. To be sure, shareholders do become unhappy and may start calling for new management. But also, acquisitions using stock as currency become more expensive. And the value per share of stock-based executive compensation drops. If the firm's competitors are seizing the opportunities while it holds back, they gain the mirror-image advantages of a pumped-up stock price.

If the stock market was demanding that financial services firms compete aggressively in the world of securitization and derivatives, long-term consequences be damned, then the "dancing as performance" reading has punch and joins the broader debate about destructive short-termism. There is plenty of evidence about the market's potency at the time, showing that the banks where managers were most insulated from shareholder pressure took less risk than their less entrenched colleagues. Compare the relative stock prices in the mid-2000s of Countrywide (deeply into securitization), Citi (aggressive but not to the same degree because it was so diversified), and the one financial institution that seemed somewhat nervous about the potentially overheated market, J.P. Morgan.[26] Clearly, the stock prices of Countrywide and Citi did much better than Morgan, and Morgan felt immense pressure as a result. The hesitation was prescient given what soon happened, but very costly at the time. The market's wild applause and the deep fear that all performers have of disappointing the audience surely fed Chuck Prince's desire to dance.

GALLOWS?

After a slow start, the last few years have brought a fairly impressive list of sanctions against financial services *firms* for actions related to the financial crisis. The money collected from these financial institutions is well past $150 billion. We can argue over whether these fines and penalties have been too little (compared to the extraordinary level of firm profitability before the crisis and in the years since) or too much (given that these are effectively borne by the shareholders and sometimes were imposed on a firm simply because it acquired another that allegedly misbehaved before the acquisition). These amounts show seriousness on the part of enforcers, and may reflect the enforcers' impression of how distorted or corrupt the culture was at the time or now.

To many critics the more troubling question is why so few high-ranking financial executives have been targeted. As we've seen, some political explanation is usually given, currying favor with the "Wall Street elite" in a quest for future career opportunities or immediate campaign contributions. This is the contemporary—and more resentment-fueled—version of the longer-standing concern about leniency with executives that we touched on in chapter 2.

The desire is for prosecutions of CEOs and CFOs, not underlings, which immediately gets us to the information flow problem. High-ranking executives rarely get the whole truth, especially when the truth is exceptionally complex and contingent. Subordinates, as well as scores of accountants and lawyers, assure them that they are on top of things, so far as they know, which is very much what the executives want to believe. If the Kool-Aid story is right, the whole system of information flow and analysis can be tainted by a mix of organizational overconfidence and diminished risk perception. If the minimal rational risk story is right, little or nothing was tainted in the first place.

Prosecutors have to prove conscious complicity at the top executive level, and do so beyond a reasonable doubt. This is where the conflicting narratives matter so much. In an influential essay in the *New York Review of Books*, Judge Jed Rakoff—whom we met for his ruminations on the sentencing of insider traders—claimed that prosecutors could use charges like "conscious avoidance" or "deliberate indifference" to make their cases even if was some degree of ignorance.[27] But both claims assume a state of mind in which the executive is at least aware of a high risk of a terrible truth, and chooses to hide from it. Maybe, but it's far from inevitable. To be sure, a prosecutor could make such a charge and hope that a jury will be emotional enough or sufficiently influenced by hindsight to find liability anyway. But that takes a view of criminal prosecution that civil libertarians usually find troubling.

There is also the matter of precious prosecutorial resources.[28] With so much criminality to worry about within its jurisdiction, the Justice Department has to allocate carefully, which limits the number of executives (lawyered up, and with potentially good defenses) against whom action could be taken. That brings its own set of problems—claims of selective prosecution, as others inside the firm and at competitor firms remain unthreatened. Prosecutors will find it hard to deny that there was much more blame that this one actor deserves, especially if the prosecutors are already stretching on state of mind. And even if a conviction is obtained and sustained, the deterrence effect of that and a few other high-level executives is undermined as other executives see how many others are walking away free. We've already seen ample reasons why deterrence is muted in corporate settings; this might not change that very much.

Since the SEC has a lesser burden of proof (more likely than not, rather than beyond a reasonable doubt) it has more freedom to push aggressively within the bounds of administrative discretion. Though jail time is not possible in civil enforcement actions, the penalties for fraud can still be severe—civil penalties and bars from service as an officer or director of a public company, plus the reputational tarnish. But even here, you can see how an enforcer might in good faith come to believe that the legally culpable state of mind probably wasn't present at the highest levels.

To be clear, this doesn't mean that there was no intentional misrepresentation going on down below. As many of the big cases have stressed, there were representations and warranties made about asset quality that were simply untrue. But two points about this. First, this is the sort of information that would not likely be revealed high up in the organization. Second, it was easily rationalized. The problems with mortgage quality were highly publicized, and yet the thirst of institutional investors for these products was unquenchable. In the haste of putting together deal after deal, it wouldn't be hard to think that the buyers didn't really care that much about degradations in quality, and that the warranties were just so much boilerplate.

Given such diffusion of knowledge, responsibility, and rationalization, charging financial institutions rather than individuals avoids many uncomfortable complications. So that has been the route taken, frustrating though it is. Firms are much more willing to cut a deal when entity corporate liability is at stake, making it less likely that the fraud charge will be contested in a lengthy and messy trial. From the government's perspective, the settlement avoids airing an obviously sensitive issue: regulators themselves will be called to testify about why they, even though supposedly on top of things, never said that there was too much risk at the financial institution they were supervising.

There has been a great deal of discussion about some kind of alternative liability standard for top bankers or corporate executives generally, with which other countries are already trying.[29] This could be something like reckless endangerment, without needing proof of conscious awareness. But that still requires a sense of the risk as perceived, and becomes an uneasy standard when applied in hindsight, with jail time as the consequence. My sense is that some form of civil reckoning might be preferable in many cases: clawbacks or restitutionary recoveries of some or all of the extraordinary compensation and wealth that the executive got from running the financial train at full throttle.

Some of these ideas made their way into Dodd-Frank, including a direction to the SEC to establish a means of recapturing compensation from a wider range of executives after a discovery of wrongdoing on their watch. There are also to be special compensation rules for bankers, to scale back temptations to be too aggressive with depositor funds and deposit insurance.

Obviously, these are sensitive issues for business, and so the subject of intense lobbying. At heart, the problem is an acute form of publicness—financial institutions have considerable economic power, and the ability to cause massive negative externalities. Nonetheless, when it comes to who runs the institutions and how they are compensated, the world of finance claims the autonomy of private enterprise. In the background is the free-floating idea that financial innovation is too dear to the American economy to subject it to too much bureaucratic interference. As a country (and far more than most) we have acquiesced in that claim, with regulatory oversight that ebbs and flows but ultimately abides the private ownership/free enterprise paradigm.

We could reject that, of course, in favor of a declaration that systemically significant financial institutions (a label in Dodd-Frank) are public institutions. Senior executives could be subject to strict regulatory approval, threat of removal, and settling-up depending on how well they balanced their public and private goals, the first having primacy. (Claire Hill and Richard Painter have suggested a system of "covenant banking," wherein the most highly paid bankers would have limited but substantial risk exposure in terms of the bank's bad debts and legal settlements or fines, harking back to the partnership model that once prevailed in finance.) We could also have more intrusive regulation, making new financial products illegal unless licensed by regulators after a safety and efficacy analysis comparable to what the Food and Drug Administration does for pharmaceuticals—an idea that a number of legal scholars have proposed.[30]

But we don't, for reasons that are both economic and political. There has been a gradual loss of faith in the regulatory apparatus, so that the fear would be of inefficient regulatory decisions at best, highly politicized and corrupt ones at worst. We are back to our political ambivalence about publicness, and about finding the right balance between prudence and aggressiveness in an anxious society where growth and prosperity can't be taken for granted. In the meantime, don't expect to see many top financial executives behind bars.

THE CULTURE OF INVESTMENT BANKING

A few years ago, Matt Taibbi of *Rolling Stone* memorably invoked the image of the great vampire squid in a story about Goldman Sachs, suggesting that it was genetically endowed with the capacity to seize and suck the blood out of any unsuspecting prey that comes its way. More seriously, recall the study at the beginning of this chapter suggesting that the impulse to cheat is part of the bankers' self-identity. In recent survey evidence nearly half the respondents from the financial services industry say that they think their competitors have engaged in illegal or unethical conduct to gain an edge, and nearly a quarter say the same about their own colleagues.[31] (A study comparing dishonesty using a set of subjects from Wall Street as compared to political staffers in Washington found that the politicians were more honest.)[32] All this suggests that the economic, cognitive, and hormonal influences we've identified are not just individual, but cultural. High-end bankers, brokers, and advisors may have gatekeeper status, but their public-regarding role does not come naturally.

The problem of role conflict plagues Wall Street, in a setting far different from the early 1930s when the securities laws were passed. Consider how much has changed. Back then, the major firms were general partnerships, so that a misstep threatened each partner's investment in the firm, and not leveraged to any great extent. Their capital base was small and relatively precious. And they focused on classical investment-banking transactions—financing, mergers, and the like—bringing to bear knowledge and contacts that no one else possessed. Their customers were wealthy and sophisticated; they usually did business with the retail public only indirectly, through unaffiliated brokerage firms. They were no angels to be sure, but no vampire squids either.

Fast-forward to the 2000s and investment banks are part of global financial conglomerates, stirring classical investment banking into a mix with commercial banking, retail brokerage, insurance, commodities, derivatives, proprietary trading, mutual funds, hedge funds, and much else. They are publicly traded, with their own shareholders to please. And the markets in which they compete are heavily institutional, so there is immense interconnectedness in the financial system (a systemic risk factor that has not been addressed very well in the recent reforms) and presumptive sophistication on the part of most counterparties.

God's Work

In this new financial order, investment bankers needed a belief system that fit the opportunities and competitive demands of the moment without explicitly abandoning their roles as viewed through the regulatory lens. Reputation no longer had the pull it once did. Technology gave the buy side access to much more information, so that buyers were no longer as dependent on bankers for some special accumulation of knowledge.[33] As these reputational and informational advantages eroded, bankers had to find and seek legitimacy for other activities in which to exploit some kind of edge. There was more emphasis on the bank's own proprietary trading, and less input from deep knowledge than from quicker access to the mass of data and information that flows into the market each day. That connects to the growth of hedge funds and the insider trading problems explored in chapter 4, but the emergent trading culture had other effects as well.

In 2009, the CEO of Goldman Sachs, Lloyd Blankfein, described himself as a simple banker "doing God's work."[34] Maybe it was just facetious. But given that the world was well into financial crisis by then, that may not have been the most sensitive or thoughtful characterization, an illustration of investment banking's persistent public relations learning disability. Like Chuck Prince's dancing quote, this one also took on a life of its own. Funny or not, it was a glimpse into the cultural self-conception of investment bankers and an eye-opener when Goldman was later charged with deception by the SEC for a complex derivative product that it sold to a German bank.

We have already touched on this earlier in the chapter: the crucial edge was constant innovation in financial products, so that there was a new generation ready to market by the time the buy side learned the old products enough not to need much banker help. This was the new age of data analytics and financial engineering, albeit still with a strong dose of high-end salesmanship.

Remember our discussion of the idea that the banker's culture is of the moment, bowing to the innate legitimacy of the market mechanism, seeking unquestioning synchronicity with it. I doubt that too many bankers see these markets as entirely efficient—indeed, their smartest-guy-in-the-room attitude reflects the impression that other market actors are often not that sharp. Rather, the embrace of the market is more like that of the many disciples of Friedrich Hayek, who stress the essential freedom of persons and firms to be tested in the crucible of the marketplace. So the market moves toward efficiency via a process of trial and error in which rewards and punishments are apportioned for good and bad choices.

That's not God's work, but can seem so inside the system. Goldman's mantra was that it was a market-maker, and as such owed no special moral or ethical obligations to its customers. While that phrase is commonly understood as simple intermediation (and thus not a setting that is unusually profitable), the "maker" part is culturally loaded.[35] The constant innovation of financial products put it in the role of manufacturer of new crucibles in which willing participants could test their skills, knowledge, and mettle. That effort could be rewarded lavishly, without guilt.

There is a thick coating of grease here. Doing God's work is a classic form of moral rationalization, enabling corner-cutting and rule-bending. The counterparty is simply the willing participant in the game, the harsh rules of which they should fully understand.[36] The line between victimization and just desserts becomes very confused. Such cultures can come to denigrate outsiders, by projecting onto them an inflated disposition for selfishness and guile, justifying tit-for-tat responses. Self-serving rules of the game can be imagined as universally understood and accepted—sports and military metaphors and imagery are common to this end. As psychologists have shown, group dynamics can suppress empathy for those outside the group who pose a competitive threat, maybe even heighten pleasure in their suffering.[37] The danger point comes when a long enough time passes without the firm and its people being called out on their self-deception because during that time the culture feeds on itself and people rise up in the ranks who are its exemplars and cheerleaders, as well as zealous risk-takers.[38]

This Hayekian mindset is an ideology, not a truth. During good times, when pay-offs are bountiful, it becomes easy to embrace—aided by a good bit of political lobby-ing by Wall Street to ensure its continued acceptance. But when crises occur, the social Darwinism of "just making markets" becomes harder to swallow for all but those so dazzled by the myth that their identities (or legal prospects when threatened with a lawsuit) depend on it. We see a glimpse of this in the Goldman case, in the behavior of the key salesperson involved, Fabrice Tourre. His emails upon completing the deal were grossly self-congratulatory (he calls himself "Fabulous Fab"), suggesting a role far from mere table-setter inviting participants to a market transaction. Instead, he cel-ebrates his ability to persuade the German bank to throw in its ante with Goldman yet again. The act of salesmanship in high-end settings is about manipulating and manag-ing desires, usually after building some level of trust. That is why good salespeople like Tourre are paid so much.

The Lure of Innovation, Yet Again

A belief system that exalts innovation and financial engineering is a potent motiva-tor, an idea that extends well beyond investment banking. Recall the Enron story, where those inside the company developed an inflated sense that they were remak-ing the world of energy as a commodity, developing markets that would revolutionize the delivery of natural gas, electricity, water (and eventually broadband and a host of other essentials). But then again, Enron had already turned itself into something of an investment bank, and clearly drawing on many of the same images and ideas that were enabling investment banking to seem so smart, exciting, and special.

Investment banks are far worse candidates to play the gatekeeper role than they used to be, for reasons that should by now be amply clear. Reputation means less, and the culture is hardly one of probity and restraint. A fascinating study shows that Wall Street firms that received more negative publicity arising from the financial crisis were *more* likely to receive coveted public offering book-running assignments from their peers.[39] The implication is that displays of what the local culture of financial insiders values—not what the public values—determine status and stature.

This is not to say that imposing added liability on investment banks in settings like IPOs is wrong; to the contrary, turning up the heat proportionate to the bankers' role in the transaction in question makes a great deal of sense. If bankers are manufactur-ers and engineers, they should warrant their products. While the Dodd-Frank desire to "fiduciarize" securities firms to this point has been limited to retail settings, there is a new provision dealing with securitizations that tries to restrain the salesman role where conflicts of interest are lurking in the background. And many other provisions try to take some of the profit opportunity out of previously lucrative transactions—the best example here is the effort to force as many derivatives transactions as possible onto open clearinghouses, rather than leave them to the opaque world of bespoke customization that bankers effectively controlled.[40]

Once again, we can't delve deeply into the new regulatory world that tries to put the brakes on too much risk, systemic or otherwise.[41] It's still a work in progress, dependent on a great deal of regulatory discretion, and subject to significant rollback as the political winds blow in a different direction. The pushback we are experiencing is predictable enough—these new regulations interfere with transactions between sophisticated parties able to fend for themselves, and dampen the pace of financial innovation. These two related points deserve a word or two before we finish this section.

As to the first, we're back to the battle of ideologies. There is plenty of evidence that, in the run-up to the crisis, *some* institutional investors didn't fend for themselves very much at all, and acted in ways that make it hard to blame the bankers on the sell side entirely. We still lack a persuasive account for why the buy-side diligence was so lax. Maybe it was too great a willingness to trust the banks that came with fancy new financial products to offer, but if so, the buyers should have known better and asked more questions, refusing to buy what they couldn't understand. I'm reasonably persuaded that buy-side incentives to do due diligence are often lax, because the decision-makers are managing large pools of other people's money and those other people are not sensitive enough to risk to do anything about it. A small public employees' pension fund in Green Bay doesn't have high-powered incentives to perform, for a variety of political and economic reasons. And that makes it difficult to choose the right regulatory response. The natural conservative view is to make such failures painful enough that beneficiaries start demanding better service. But that is a lot of pain, and the market may not be quite so responsive (especially in the case of pension funds in which beneficiaries have little or no choice). And so it's not surprising to hear a call to force investment bankers to be more kind and gentle in their sales interactions, in the name of those vulnerable beneficiaries whose own agents may not be protecting them very well.

Bankers hate that idea, of course, and lobby hard to retard any such regulatory initiatives. The standard party line is the one we've seen already: making bankers too risk averse via legal threats or regulatory burdens discourages the financial innovation that has improved our markets in recent years, in which the United States remains a global leader. Part of this is simple economic geography. By the end of the last century, financial services (not just investment banking) produced twice the economic activity of our total gross domestic product just a couple of decades earlier. New York City in particular has long been heavily dependent on industry profitability for tax revenue and local wealth creation. So are certain professions, like law, in terms of the work the securities industry generates. No doubt there is a tipping point of intrusive regulation that causes this activity to move to other countries. London and Hong Kong compete for this business and would like to take as much of Wall Street's share as they can;

other cities are poised to compete as well. Those who lobby to deregulate can enlist those who want to be locally protectionist, even if the latter otherwise might prefer a stronger regulatory hand. Most New York Democrats cannot be anti–Wall Street, no matter how queasy they might feel about the risk-taking.

There have been many calls for more severe regulation of both banking and securities in the name of prudence and financial stability, all of which run essentially into the same set of arguments. We've seen some already, like the proposal to require advance regulatory approval of new financial products, after testing their safety and efficacy. More broadly, some would like to restore what once seemed a pillar of financial regulation—get securities firms out of the business of shadow banking so that they don't force banks into overly aggressive competitive behavior, and then make sure banks and their affiliates stick to the conventional business of banking. Banking would thus be channeled into a safe mode, with risk significantly curbed.[42] That would dismantle Wall Street as it currently exists, which is precisely the proponents' point. There could also be a breaking up of both banking and securities firms into smaller pieces so that we don't have the massive (far too big to fail) behemoths like Citi dominating the financial markets.

These have all been thoroughly debated, without closure. Some of the problems are conceptual (is there really enough of a difference between the domains of securities and banking to make separation work in a high-tech world?); some are economic (would breaking up banks really address systemic risk if those banks are so interconnected in their dealings that failures would rapidly spread from one to another anyway?); some are political (would regulators have the capacity and will to enforce the new rules?). And then there is the geographic point that radical reform in the United States would be limited in its success if other countries did not do the same, with riskier capital transactions simply moving offshore as Wall Street withers?

The responses to these questions share a common conundrum—what, really, is the value to society of financial innovation? Endless editorial writers have lamented how many of our brightest young people go to Wall Street, to private equity or hedge funds (or the law firms that service them), rather than pursuing more obviously valuable careers as doctors, scientists, and engineers. (Venture capital seems to get something of a pass here, because of its connection to hard-core technological innovation.) Financial innovation generates extraordinary private wealth out of what seems often to be just a slicing, dicing, reshuffling, and renaming of assets and liabilities. But it does good and important things, too,[43] and confidently separating the productive from the rent-seeking is hard.

The counterfactual of a world where more and better things get made is undeniably appealing. It's probably something of an illusion to assume that shrinking Wall Street would get us to an obviously better place rather than just redirecting energies toward more efficiently satisfying consumer desires that themselves are debatable (endlessly new and better versions of World of Warcraft?) and also potentially harmful to our collective future. It would take a more profound change in our culture to change the behavior of those now drawn to Wall Street and its suburbs, in pursuit of such status and wealth.

For much of this book, we've stressed how competitiveness and an appetite for risk is Janus-faced, offering both value and danger. We've also tied this, in part, to testosterone and other hormonal influences. None of this is to say that male domination is natural or inevitable in finance—there is too much history of misogyny and associated myth-making about what constitutes success for that. But it does pose as an obvious question: would we observe as much risk-taking and other excesses if male privilege and domination were weakened? If so, it might be good policy to hasten the demise of that privilege.

Since the onset of the global financial crisis, this has been a serious debate in regulatory circles. In a memorable quote deriving from the World Economic Conference at Davos in 2009, Neelie Kroes, an EU official, claimed that the crisis would not have happened as it did "if Lehman Brothers had been Lehman Sisters."[44] As the *Economist* then explained, "The 'Lehman Sisters' fancy assumes that women are less risk-taking, less obsessed with money and status, and generally less full of themselves than men." In Europe this is no mere academic or social debate. Quotas for a minimum number of women on European corporate boards of directors are becoming more common, and capital adequacy requirements for financial institutions there have been linked to diversity initiatives. While this has not (yet) become part of the regulatory agenda in the United States, the Lehman Sisters question is taken seriously here as well as part of the movement—not limited to gender, of course—to diversify corporate boards and executive suites in the name of both strategy and equity.[45]

There is a large amount of research on the correlations between gender diversity and corporate financial performance, much of it focusing on boards of directors. As with all such research, causation can point in different directions—do firms perform relatively well (or poorly) because they have more women in power, or are high-performing (or low-performing) firms more likely to seek out women? Not surprisingly, the data are inconclusive and allow for multiple interpretations on whether the presence of more women in power dampens the kind of overenthusiastic dancing that Chuck Prince described.

Some things seem clear enough in the experimental and survey evidence.[46] Women show less of an inclination to take big risks or enter into status- or compensation-based competitions. As investors, they seem to be more patient, conservative, and diversified, less likely to prompt a bubble.[47] They are more concerned with ethics and fairness, less likely to do battle simply because assigned to one team or another. These virtues resist some of the more troubling tendencies we've observed in the male-dominated financial world. John Coates, the financial neuroscientist whose work on the biology of risk-taking we looked at earlier, devotes much of the last chapter of his book to the need to feminize more of Wall Street.

Yet, as we've emphasized throughout, those who obtain power in business and finance aren't randomly drawn from the general population. Perhaps it starts early. In a study of elite MBA students at the University of Chicago, researchers found that women were significantly less likely to choose a career in investment banking or finance than men. They also found that such a choice was more likely for higher-testosterone students and those lower in risk aversion, regardless of gender. From that they infer that those women who enter, persist in, and succeed in the tournament rounds in that field may actually be *more* risk-preferring (certainly no less) than their male peers.[48] In a research paper doubting the Lehman Sisters hypothesis, the authors looked at a number of dimensions relating to gender in some three hundred US banks and bank holding companies and found that those with more female directors did not engage in fewer risky activities or have lower aggregate risk than other banks.[49] (They did, on the other hand, find some evidence that greater diversity paid off in firm performance and how the bank handled the crisis, an indicator that a greater level of conscientiousness by the female directors may have mattered even in the face of high risk-taking.)

The ability to test the Lehman Sisters theory is limited, of course, by the fact that there are currently so few high-ranking women in finance, especially in investment banking and on the trading floors. Hence the pool of potential directors is smaller than it should be, and women are a distinct minority on boards anyway. One can readily see why comparing performance between a financial institution with two women directors out of fourteen and a firm with three or four out of fourteen would not show much one way or the other. We can also ask how much boards of large financial institutions matter in driving performance, compared to other kinds of companies. These may be too complex for anyone not deeply embedded inside the business to comprehend, anyway.

A fair test of the Lehman Sisters theory, therefore, would require much greater female representation on boards and in senior management than we have the opportunity to observe—there simply are no compelling examples among larger financial institutions for useful comparison, much less the numbers necessary for good statistics. Outside the field of finance, where we would expect to see greater variations in both competitive intensity and gender stereotypes, the evidence is also suggestive of healthy differences. Companies with more women as senior executives seem to make fewer corporate acquisitions, consistent with a lower level of hubris.[50] Of particular interest for securities regulation, data from China produced a fairly strong finding that gender diversity mitigates both the severity and likelihood of securities fraud.[51]

So an inferential case, at least, can be made in favor of the Lehman Sisters hypothesis if we further assume a significant increase in female presence and power. But how do we get from here to there? There is slow progress in that direction, noted by the very gradual growth in the number of women directors and the appointment of female CEOs. But the percentages remain small at the board level, and there is much discussion in the literature about a "glass cliff" effect, the tendency to appoint a woman as CEO when the firm is troubled and that office thus a precarious assignment.[52] The appointment signals recognition of a problem and a mess to be cleaned. But if the role is a failure, as is not unlikely given the situation, the woman becomes the scapegoat, which hardly reinforces a positive message.

The European trend toward quotas is an accelerant for sustainable female presence and power, an embrace of the Lehman Sisters hypothesis in finance and beyond notwithstanding the equivocal data. The stock market reaction to this move so far has not been positive. The stock prices of Scandinavian companies forced to quickly add a substantial number of women to their boards reacted negatively.[53] Conversely, companies that were able to reorganize themselves so as to avoid the requirements were rewarded.

Why? Maybe this is just market efficiency at work. Given the relatively smaller pool of women with experience and records of business success from which to draw—and for which many companies were all of a sudden competing—there could have been a genuine belief that board quality had necessarily eroded. But the negative market reactions have not been limited to quota-induced additions in Europe. Evidence from the United States seems to indicate that even small, voluntary additions of women to corporate boards are met with a negative marketplace reaction, even though there is no corresponding evidence that near-term corporate performance will be adversely affected.[54]

Perhaps this has to do with the short term versus the long term, where we saw some market skepticism about policies insufficiently tied to the bottom line. There are some data to support the suspicion that in the long run, women pay more attention to other company stakeholders and less to shareholder wealth.[55] If markets want to see a high-intensity obsession with profits, that might make them nervous. The women may be an indication that the firm has been captured by the distracting forces of publicness. Or this could simply be stereotyping, an implicit gender bias that survives the mechanisms of market efficiency. The sought-after equality in the financial world is threatening, in opposition to a long-entrenched culture that sees business and finance as a male-dominated activity. A number of researchers who have noticed what appear to be unexplained negative stock price reactions to board or CEO appointments see mainly prejudice or resentment at work.[56] Supporting evidence comes from the mutual fund world, where we find funds managed by women lagging in how much money they attract vis-à-vis other funds with comparable or even lesser performance.[57]

Rational or not, the market's apparent suspicion of women gaining power impedes change. Quotas and similarly assertive measures are portrayed as quack governance or value-destroying, a form of political grandstanding. The negative stock price reactions are offered as proof. In the United States, an aversion to quotas has taken that kind of reform off the table, guaranteeing that progress will remain incremental. To date, the only regulatory strategy has been a lame effort by the SEC to require public companies to disclose how they address board-level diversity, which has produced more waffling than insight.[58] A fair test of the Lehman Sisters hypothesis will come someday, but not soon enough or without more struggle.

Conclusion

Chasing the Greased Pig

Our journey ends with an anomaly. There is a palpable distrust in Wall Street, corporations, and our financial markets, and if the foregoing chapters are persuasive, ample reason to doubt blandishments of honesty from the financially self-interested. Yet investing has historically delivered good returns, on average, and people's revealed preferences indicate a continuing strong demand for securities. Maybe that should be a caution to anyone who takes what we have learned as reason to dial up the regulatory intensity. Markets and intermediaries do work, if far from perfectly. Regulation that blatantly exposes reasons to mistrust corporations or Wall Street—sensible as that may be—risks deflating something that has powered economic growth for at least a century.

On the other hand, today's growth seems to be delivering less and less to ordinary Americans, and it is tempting to try to find something more fair and inclusive, and less risky. As we've seen repeatedly, confidence itself is a loaded idea, a form of self-deception that turns out to be a remarkable survival trait in a threatening world. Although this is not a history book, I would make the claim that for most of the second half of the last century, the culture (and democratization) of investing in the United States was built on a widespread societal perception of robust growth, a genuine economic optimism. Hope was the trope. Gradually, however, the grounds for optimism about never-ending growth faded; the hope became less realistic but more fervent, as so often happens under stress.[1] This led to shifts on Wall Street in how securities are sold. The messages, subtly, became more about separating winners and losers as opposed to sharing in a bountiful future. As economists point out, the shift from optimism to pessimism triggers more selfish "last period" activity; behavioralists would put an exclamation point on that prediction. I don't think it's coincidental that as this disillusion was gradually settling in, there was a greater appetite for risk (loss aversion) in our economy, fed by innovative forms of leveraging—securitization, derivatives, and high-velocity short-term lending. Politically and economically, these (along with an overstimulated housing market) were steroids for faltering economic strength, with the consequences that often come from dangerous drugs.[2] So the connection to the global financial crisis, and the postcrisis wonderings about whether signs of new growth are illusory and last-period anxiety still warranted.

And so our look in the last chapter at the SEC's role in the financial crisis illustrates many things that are useful to understanding the contemporary state of securities regulation, and a fitting way to end this book. The Commission watched the buildup of complexity in securitized products and derivatives with no sense of alarm, or even much interest. It was complicit in a deregulatory agenda with respect to over-the-counter derivatives (joining most of the banking agencies)—echoing the case that big institutions can fend for themselves—and clueless at best when, in 2005, it assumed responsibility for the capital adequacy of nonbank financial firms like Lehman Brothers and Goldman Sachs. The aggressiveness of its cleanup enforcement efforts is debatable, as we've seen. We can rewind time and spot many other apparent failings as well.

There are excuses, of course. The SEC's budget has never been generous or immune from the larger ideological struggles over spending imbalances and the size of the government. As a result, it has to pick its fights and react to what is concerning at the moment, without full control over priorities that are heavily influenced by the media and increasingly controlled by Congress. The 2000–2007 regulatory agenda was dominated by the popping of the tech stock bubble and the investment analyst scandals, financial misreporting (Enron and WorldCom), carrying out the controversial mandates of Sarbanes-Oxley, mutual fund market timing malfeasance, and the fallout from a long line of options-backdating cases that called into question Silicon Valley's compensation practices. In the background was increasing appreciation of the challenges of globalization, watching the world of finance thrive elsewhere and not wanting to put US firms at a competitive disadvantage. Republican appointees were in control, so that regulatory enthusiasm (or internal morale) was often not that high anyway, especially as the decade wore on. There was a constant threat of abolishing the SEC, merging it into some larger financial regulatory entity. Systemic safety and soundness were never part of its core legislative assignment anyway, and more specialized bank regulators weren't sounding alarms.

But let's step back from the excuses and turn the lenses of politics, economics, and human nature back on the SEC itself. Crafting good securities regulation is hard enough, even if we define the task simply in terms of finding the sweet spot between basic investor protection and capital formation. As we've seen, investor behavior falls short of ideal, leading to opportunities for rent-seeking and exploitation not fully countered by the forces of competition or market efficiency. Efforts to combat the opportunism gets us into politically contested territory because of the paternalism associated with protecting the gullible, because some of that opportunism promotes capital formation, and because Wall Street and the business community covet the wealth it generates. Efforts to deter the opportunism struggle as well—as our inquiries into human nature on the sell side show—because the expressive messages and legal threats that regulation sends are distorted by self-deception and cultural forces that rationalize what others might call opportunism into what those on the inside see as virtuous or at least valuable: innovative, intense, smart, competitive.

For most of the last century, the political battles about securities regulation were fought along this fault line. These were good fights for the SEC, if not always successful ones, and the Commission had powerful allies in Congress and the press that allowed it to hold its own and even grow the regulatory enterprise from time to time. The virtue of investor protection and some form of the precautionary principle (at least as to retail investors) were both taken for granted. Key to this relative success was an ally lurking in the background of the story we've been telling, but now deserving special mention: elite securities lawyers. Securities lawyers benefit from regulation of their clients, the more intricate (and malleable in the hands of an expert) the better. The nation's best law firms thrived on the resulting revenue, but lawyers could also find some nobility in the calling—partnering with the SEC to bring some integrity to business practices in the name of investor confidence and robust capital markets.

Today, as we have seen, the battle lines are different.[3] From the right there is a more strident antipaternalism, an obsession with capital formation, and doubt about the ability of regulators limit their reach. On the left we see the emergence of a publicness agenda wherein the hard-enough task of investor protection morphs into a much bigger set of concerns about stability, sustainability, equity, and the accountability of the economically and politically powerful. At the moment, the harshest critic of the SEC is Massachusetts senator Elizabeth Warren, a longtime student of financial regulation, strongly committed to those values. But they are far from the SEC's comfort zone, and challenge long-standing assumptions about its mission. The wear and tear is palpable inside the agency, which undermines morale. After all, bureaucracies are human institutions, subject to their own individual and cultural beliefs and biases.[4] Lack of confidence and an ill-defined mission always make things harder.

The special-interest politics are more challenging as well; allies (establishment lawyers, for example, who are under stresses of their own) have become far less dependable. That the financial services industry tops the list of campaign contributors to both political parties is familiar enough. The business connection to Republicans is a truism, but Democrats also depend on donors in Silicon Valley and hedge fund moguls. The industry knows to distribute its largesse to anyone with power, or who could come to power, regardless of party affiliation. Politicians know that keeping open a threat of regulation ensures that the contributions will keep coming, but there also has to be a return on the lobbyists' investments. A recent study of voting patterns on financial deregulation amply demonstrates the powerful effects of targeted spending on key candidates.[5]

Less familiar is how efficient the political market has become, in ways that are not just about money—what we might call an efficient political markets hypothesis. The SEC acts officially by a majority vote of five commissioners, all presidential appointees (with limited power of removal), of whom no more than three can be from the president's party. That bipartisan design was deliberate, one reason even Wall Street supported the creation of the SEC in 1934. But with the growing ideological divide in the United States, there is a greater perception in which the commissioners have to synch their actions and words to their own parties' agenda, staying on-message at all times. The financial media and private social media magnify all that happens on a real-time news cycle, instantly transmitting information and inference about who's helping the cause and who's hurting it. The inclination to compromise becomes smaller when so many principals are watching, a point amply demonstrated in the psychology literature. (Given our emphasis on the idea on both buy-side and sell-side financial behavior, it's interesting to note recent academic evidence that overconfidence drives divisive political attitudes as well.)[6] This has been less awkward for Republicans, because a probusiness deregulatory agenda has resonance throughout its base. It is harder for Democrats, who face more dissonant claims by its left-leaning progressive wing—for whom Occupy Wall Street has appeal—and its successful elites with deep connections to the financial markets, for whom hoarding wealth is not such a bad thing notwithstanding their abstract desire for a more just society.

There are also legal constraints. The SEC does not have plenary statutory authority to regulate risk in investment-related products; the disclosure philosophy is hardwired in what it is authorized to do. It shares the regulatory space with alien bureaucracies, an ecology that produces its own institutional strangulation.[7] And when the SEC wanders into controversial territory, it is increasingly likely to be sued by affected businesses for being arbitrary and insensitive to costs—the Commission went through a losing streak in the courts starting in 2005 after it pushed its authority to regulate, particularly on matters of corporate governance. With the perception of more intense congressional and judicial monitoring, regulatory autonomy diminished. Globalization amplifies the challenge, as other money centers and would-be money centers relish pointing out American regulatory zeal and invite institutions and transactions offshore.

So the SEC is resource constrained, legally constrained, and politically constrained. As a result, it is less able to act as it wants, especially when public frustration subsides after a scandal, almost inevitably leading to softening and pullback (Jack Coffee calls this the "regulatory sine-curve").[8] But is that all? Assessing administrative agency motivation is challenging at any level other than vague generalities. The conservative claim, plausibly enough, is that because bureaucracies face little in the way of performance incentives, they gradually become mindless and self-aggrandizing. They cater to public whims, and abet proponents of regulation whose real goal is to dampen competition and protect their own rents.

The progressive account is that financial regulators lose the will to challenge elite power, perhaps because the revolving door creates opportunities to graduate from regulator to elite lawyer or banker, perhaps because of a deeper sort of cultural bias that implicitly accepts the virtue of having a robust and successful financial sector while also believing in the need to regulate. Others have put forth this deep capture argument,[9] which is hard to test empirically. The SEC is a lawyer-dominated agency with a considerable outflow of talent to private practice or the industry. As we saw in chapter 2, the available evidence, at least in enforcement, is mixed: aggressiveness (within limits) seems to be rewarded, yet politically well-connected targets do better than those who aren't. Lawyers are professional elites, and the higher-ranking SEC officials often come with a record of success in the private sector, stay for a time, and then return. My impression is that they both come and go with professional pride, intending to make things better for the constituencies the Commission serves and, when finished, believe they've done some good even with the inevitable bureaucratic frustrations. That can be self-serving inference, however. Professional success—within a bureaucracy or across a longer career span—depends on some level of cognitive flexibility. It is good to know when to attack; better yet to know when to go along. Moderation, caution, and a healthy respect for the status quo can be useful survival traits, especially when too much change is upsetting to the powerful. Because of constant personal interactions between the staff and agents of those they regulate, there is a natural inclination to be cooperative, not unreasonably confrontational. Over time, I suspect, the SEC has internalized those traits, which are reinforced by the palpable resource impoverishment, the growing workload, and the constant barrage of external criticism stressed earlier. The result is a loss of passion. Being reminded of the mythical glory days in the SEC's history doesn't energize; it grates.

Work still gets done, of course. Most of those with economic and political power still find the SEC useful—exposed fraud is bad for politics and bad for business— and so want basic functionality. In recent years, the securities industry has used the Commission as a shield to counter efforts by banking regulators to take more control over their activities in the name of safety and soundness. The SEC has cooperated to an extent, acting protectively to maintain as much dominion as possible over money market funds and so-called systemically important financial institutions. The Commission retains *some* autonomy, especially if it remembers who its friends are, a circumstance that readily plays out along paths of lesser resistance like the resonant insider trading cases we saw in chapter 3. That dramaturgy still works (at least when the cases are successful), offering a welcome dose of positive feedback in a hypercritical world.

Otherwise, however, tolerance of the status quo becomes a matter of routine, which is surely a soft form of capture. As a result, the SEC is largely reactive and often a step slow, keeping its institutional mouth shut as profound changes occur in finance that raise serious policy issues for the public and investors. Do we have too much financial activity, for example? A good example, as we've seen, is high-frequency trading, which is extraordinarily costly in an arms race to capture tiny edges in the speed of trades. This pays off for the hedge funds and others engaged in the race, presumably, and enhances liquidity. But it's hard to believe that there is enough social value from all that spending. A similar point has been made about the constant innovation of complex securitized, leveraged, and derivative products that are sold to buyers who may not understand entirely how they work. Again, some of this will be valuable, but other innovations are mainly rent extraction.[10] And it's not been lost on critics that the costs are not simply financial—the intense competition for an edge, as we've noted, draws a disproportionate portion of the nation's smartest young people away from careers that might have a better social payoff.

That's an untouchable issue for the SEC. Naturally, it senses that its reason for being is the presence of large-scale financial activity in the United States; any reduction in the strength and power of Wall Street or large public corporations threatens its status, too. And being lawyer dominated, the Commission remains comfortable with complicated regulation—which enriches legal elites—as a matter of professional identity as well as revolving door opportunities. The Commission encourages big law and well as big finance.

So, too, is it comfortable with a nation of active investors. We've seen the enormous costs associated with active trading, especially individual securities and actively managed mutual funds, which are rarely justified in terms of above-average performance. Money doctors and hand-holders have a value, but we have to wonder whether there is a strong enough public voice about what sound long-term investing means. It doesn't come from the SEC, whose efforts on fees and costs have been far from bold. Arguably—and now getting into even deeper water—we should ask how prudent it is to encourage investors to depend so heavily on common stock in their portfolios. We have plenty of evidence of short-term bubbles and busts. The last century, to be sure, rewarded equity investing over time, and that experience is what we draw from in assessing the right balance of assets in our portfolios. As Henry Hu points out in an essay on faith and magic in investing, however, if history does not repeat, those allocations could be unwise.[11] True, if the future is filled with sustained economic troubles, most all assets will be adversely affected—there is nowhere to hide, really. But the celebration of an equity marketplace culture may someday seem less wise in hindsight than it does today.

Also alarming for the SEC is whether economic forces are leading to an eclipse of the public corporation, so that public equity gradually becomes less available as an investment opportunity. Smaller IPOs are disappearing, and the number of public companies traded on the stock exchanges has been cut by more than half in recent decades. We've seen the debate here as to whether overregulation is the culprit; even the perception that it is constrains the SEC and motivates deregulation, as amply evidenced by the JOBS Act. While distaste for regulation and its costs has an effect—the allure of being the CEO of a public company (as opposed to a private one) may be losing its appeal, to nonnarcissists at least—there is a very serious argument that the economy is headed away from conditions where public ownership was an efficient form of corporate finance. Arguably, public ownership worked for companies whose business models were relative transparent and hence subject to a reasonable level of external monitoring by shareholders—old-line companies in chemicals, steel, and auto manufacturing, or retail-oriented producers of consumer goods and services. But in an economy that values innovation and aggressiveness—creative disruption—transparency doesn't work well. Private equity-style financing, allowing more confidential forms of governance, may be better.[12] And as noted toward the end of chapter 5, the private markets are growing, inspired in part by deregulation, in part by disenchantment.

That is a direct threat to publicness, as well as to the SEC's comparative regulatory advantage. We've seen how public (not just investor) demands for transparency and accountability have become one of the most notable—and controversial—features of contemporary securities regulation. If appreciably more companies go dark and choose private financing and private markets open only to wealthier or sophisticated investors, that route shuts down. Indeed, that's precisely the point of many of the deregulatory strategies we're seeing.

But all this remains contested territory, wherein the SEC must tread carefully. The perception that ordinary investors are discriminated against in the new world of investing is politically troubling, especially if they sense that riches are being kept out of their reach. Letting them in, on the other hand, undercuts the prime justification for leaving that space less subject to regulation—we'll have to see how the awkward experiment with crowdfunding turns out. Yet even if the barriers to retail participation stay high, ordinary investors still indirectly participate in the private markets through pension funds and alternative investment vehicles. I suspect that it would take only one big private company scandal—in the right political environment—to call into question a regulatory regime that lets companies choose whether they want legal accountability or not. No doubt some of that response to scandal would be bad regulation, maybe even quackery. That is always the risk along the boundary between economic freedom and social legitimacy. There's a reasonable argument that the SEC is positioned to buffer against the push for too much regulation, when the winds blow in that direction.[13]

So we do come back to politics, rooted in human nature. Money in finance is powerful and corrosive. Public choice theory in economics and political science has for some time now said that regulatory outcomes depend on how well organized interests groups are in terms of being able to spend effectively. That's special-interest politics. But strict public choice has doubters in the academic community, who note that money means influence but that voters' revealed preferences are not so easily controlled, especially in key states where elections can be close. The academic field of behavioral public choice has emerged to understand how public sentiment interacts with special-interest pressure, both in Congress and in regulatory agencies. (Sentiment is by no means the same as wisdom, so that many researchers use this methodology to explain overregulation and other bad lawmaking.) As we've seen, the SEC plays to the public's feelings in order to get a little autonomy in an otherwise constrained political environment. In that, at least, progressive politicians are natural allies in shaping sentiment that favors regulation. The risk is that what the public and those allies want will be at odds with those of the SEC's core constituency and reason for being, wealth-seeking investors. We've seen throughout this book how difficult it is to walk that path. Postmodern securities regulation is characterized by a loss of faith in the old beliefs about how and why to regulate—what to do when politics, economics, and human nature all seem flawed and unreliable.

The economic conditions in the United States and the rest of the world over the next decades will no doubt drive political sentiment as it relates to securities regulation even more strongly. As noted earlier, we seem of two minds. There is a loss of trust in the world of finance, and a fear that more financial crises are looming. That would seem to play to regulators' advantage. But trust in regulation and politics is low, too, so that the dominant sentiment is frustration rather than demand. Moreover, the palpable anxiety about jobs and fair opportunity in the middle class gives an edge to whatever interest group can couple its preferred political strategy with a claim that better times will follow—again, the JOBS Act, as well as how the financial industry has pushed its deregulatory agenda. People will assume considerable risk to avoid feared losses, and be both shortsighted and emotional in the risk/return calculation. That's very exploitable.

Notwithstanding great public anxiety and frustration, we are not yet seeing the conditions from which one can confidently predict a new progressivism in America. For all the skepticism about contemporary political and economic institutions, political psychology research reveals what is probably an overoptimistic sense of personal opportunity for many, and a desire to be let free to pursue what chances emerge without strong communitarian obligations. Just-world thinking—that outcomes are usually deserved—still captures the views of a large segment of the population.[14] Entrepreneurship thus resonates, which is another exploitable sentiment. The stock market is still doing well, too. For all the doubts about trustworthiness, finance is still celebrated in America—a large clustering of society's big winners, about whom we remain fascinated and envious. The mix of hope and fear can feed a regressive attitude of winner take the prize, devil take the hindmost.

We began this concluding chapter by asking why the SEC seems tied to the status quo as changes occur that alter the financial and regulatory landscape around it. The answers are political, psychological, and cultural. So is there any reason to expect change?

It comes back to the anxiety about the future with which we began this conclusion. If our economy remains on a relatively even keel, with asset prices stable and only the occasional short busts and crises, it's hard to see how, and even more so if the recent period of deregulation is followed by a new era of growth, seemingly proving the conservatives right (whether or not it's an illusory correlation). If the pessimists are right, on the other hand, and we are heading for accelerating job loss in the face of technology and globalization and a shrinkage in wealth and job opportunities for the middle class, we could see publicness on steroids. Imagine if a boom in robotics and artificial intelligence destroyed many more jobs than it created, and we decided that crowdfunding and on-ramp IPOs funded that boom. At that point, investors themselves would no longer be a favored class. The age of democratic capitalism would be over.

But we're not there yet, and hopefully won't ever be. For now, simply appreciate how much the cause of investor protection is squeezed and diminished in between business' hunger for capital (and the securities industry that so profitably feeds it) and the popular demand for regulation that makes the private more public. In a world swayed by both sentiment and opportunism, finding the right balance is hard for even the most sincere regulator. But a voice for investors is important precisely because of the squeeze. Not today's muted, easily filtered voice, but one with the clarity and punch that Brandeis, Frankfurter, and Douglas wanted but never quite got. My sense is that the relative poverty of the SEC goes back much longer than the last decade, and reflects something more ingrained in the political process. It's also ironic, because the SEC is actually a moneymaker for the government, bringing in more in fees, fines, and disgorgement than it costs to run the agency—self-funding has always been an easy resource fix. But keeping the Commission habitually needy and underresourced accommodates both congressional control and special-interest influence. The agency lacks the luxury of deep surveillance into the financial world, and has to tread carefully before undertaking any major battles. The SEC is a proud old agency with enough myths and internal routines to deflect some self-doubt, but frustrated enough to accept its limitations. The task is to imagine the counterfactual ideal of securities regulation done with adequate resources, expert knowledge, independence, and a healthy sense of knowing when not to add burdens. Perhaps you see this, as I do, as the goal to work toward, even in the face of critics' warnings that such is a fairy-land search bound to end in disappointment.

And so we come back to something from the book's introduction. There you were asked to think about taking on the task of the nation's chief securities regulator. How much in the way of resources would you ask for to do the job right, and how would you know if you were succeeding or failing, or being used? Hopefully, by now you appreciate the challenge much better, even if the answers aren't easier to come by. That's what faces our regulators, and so stay in character. You've just been appointed chair of the SEC, and the president is about to call you to be sworn in and meet the press, to explain why you are the right person to overcome all those challenges and do right for investor protection, capital formation, and the public interest. Your job is to nourish investor confidence. As you're coming around the curtain, backstage to center stage, what are you thinking and what will you say and do?

I'll leave that to you. Show everyone that you've got the right map to a better place. The world's financial markets will be judging you. The pigs are lathered up and running fast. See if you can catch them.

Notes

Introduction

1. Engelberg and Parsons, "Worrying."
2. Huck, "Taking a Beating."
3. E.g., Coglianese, "Legitimacy and Corporate Governance," 160–62; Sale, "J.P. Morgan," 1632–37; and Langevoort, "Social Construction," 108.
4. For a comparative look at some of these same political, economic, and legal issues in Europe, see Moloney, *How to Protect*. On global regulatory challenges, see Brummer, *Soft Law*.

Chapter 1

1. The deservedly classic legal-historical study is Seligman, *Transformation of Wall Street*.
2. For a recent discussion, see Mahoney, *Wasting a Crisis*, 77–99.
3. Quoted in Kirilenko and Lo, "Moore's Law," 52.
4. Especially when we rely on our gut feelings. See Partnoy, "Don't Blink," 2–7.
5. For book-length overviews with extensive citations, see Statman, *What Investors Really Want*, and Baker and Ricciardi, *Investor Behavior*.
6. Kahneman, *Thinking*.
7. Ibid., 367–69.
8. Chang, Solomon, and Westerfield, "Looking."
9. Kuhnen and Knutson, "Influence of Affect," 47–48.
10. For a review, see Lerner et al., "Emotions and Decision Making."
11. Barber and Odean, "Trading Is Hazardous," 774–75.
12. See Hirshleifer and Teoh, "Thought and Behavior."
13. Hong, Kubik, and Stein, "Thy Neighbor's Portfolio," 2802–4.
14. Seybert and Bloomfield, "Contagion," 739–40.
15. On this debate, see Staw and Sutton, "Macro-organizational Psychology."
16. See Westbrook, *Out of Crisis*.
17. See Zingales, "Future of Securities Regulation," 392–94.
18. See Banner, "What Causes Securities Regulation."
19. Forsythe, Lundholm, and Reitz, "Cheap Talk," 482–84.
20. Tetlock, "Cognitive Biases," 294–95.
21. Quoted in Pritchard and Thompson, "New Deal Justices," 849.
22. Ben-Shahar and Schneider, *More Than You Wanted*.
23. Nor do financial literacy interventions work as we might hope. See Willis, "Financial Education Fallacy."

24. Applied Research & Consulting, "Fraud Susceptibility."
25. See Schwartz, "Regulating for Rationality," 1374–78.
26. See Loewenstein, Cain, and Sah, "Limits of Transparency."
27. See Statman and Scheid, "Buffet in Hindsight," 1–2.
28. See Huberman and Regev, "Contagious Speculation," 1387–89.
29. See Baker and Wurgler, "Investor Sentiment."
30. Cooper, Dimitrov, and Rau, "Rose.com," 2372–73.
31. Hirshleifer and Shumway, "Good Day Sunshine," 1010–11.
32. See Zuckerman, "Market Efficiency."
33. LaBlanc and Rachlinski, "Praise of Irrational Investors."
34. Black, "Noise," 533.
35. Jung et al., "Social Media."
36. E.g., Kelley and Tetlock, "How Wise Are Crowds," 1230–31.
37. Gilson and Kraakman, "Market Efficiency," 315.
38. See Kirilenko and Lo, "Moore's Law," and Fox, Glosten, and Rauterberg, "New Stock Market."
39. See Karppi and Crawford, "Social Media."
40. Barber and Odean, "Trading Is Hazardous," 774–75.
41. Greenwood and Scharfstein, "Growth of Finance," 17.
42. Weick, *Sense Making in Organizations*, 154.
43. Johnson and Fowler, "Evolution of Overconfidence," 320.
44. Sharot, "Optimism Bias."
45. Kennedy, Anderson, and Moore, "When Overconfidence Is Revealed," 267–68.
46. Hirshleifer, Low, and Teoh, "Overconfident CEOs," 1457–59.
47. Goel and Thakor, "Overconfidence," 2738–40.
48. Bentley and Bloomfield, "Drinking Kool-Aid."
49. Capps, Koonce, and Petroni, "Natural Optimism," 35–36
50. Miller, "Downside," 3.
51. For book-length surveys, see Ariely, *(Honest) Truth*, and Bazerman and Tenbrunsel, *Blind Spots*. On the current state of the research and open questions, see Feldman, "Behavioral Ethics."
52. Dana, Weber, and Kuang, "Moral Wiggle-Room," 68–70.
53. *SEC v. W.J. Howey Co.*, 328 U.S. 293 (1946).
54. There is no federal system of insurance regulation, which makes this question an especially loaded one.
55. On the challenges and opportunities for global financial regulation, including securities law cooperation, see Brummer, *Soft Law*.
56. For a good discussion, see Romano, "Empowering Investors."
57. See Park, "Rules, Principles," 157.
58. Seligman, *Transformation of Wall Street*, 205–10.
59. Romano, *Genius*.
60. Roe, "Delaware's Politics," 2492.
61. Fox, "Required Disclosure."

Chapter 2

1. Dyck, Morse, and Zingales, "How Pervasive?"

2. Sadka, "Economic Consequences," 440–44; and Sidak, "Failure of Good Intentions," 208–9.
3. Velikonja, "Cost of Securities Fraud"; and Langevoort, "Social Construction," 1836–37. On employees in particular, see Greenfield, "Unjustified Absence."
4. Povel, Singh, and Winton, "Booms, Busts," 1220–21.
5. Dyck, Morse, and Zingales, "How Pervasive?," 4.
6. Dichev et al., "The Misrepresentation of Earnings," 10.
7. For other data, see Cumming, Dannhauser, and Johan, "Financial Market Misconduct."
8. McGuire, Omer, and Sharp, "Impact of Religion," 646–48.
9. For an overview of the enforcement ecology, see Coffee, "Law and Markets."
10. Karpoff, Lee, and Martin, "Costs to Firms"; and Karpoff, Lee, and Martin, "Consequences to Managers."
11. Dechow et al., "Predicting Material Accounting Misstatements," 17–19.
12. See Langevoort, "Organized Illusions."
13. Libby and Rennekamp, "Self-Serving Attribution," 198–200.
14. Ahmed and Duellman, "Managerial Overconfidence," 2–4.
15. Free and Murphy, "Ties That Bind," 37–38.
16. Hoyt et al., "Leadership," 391–93.
17. Welsh and Ordonez, "Dark Side," 80–81.
18. Brown, "Advantageous Comparison," 849–51.
19. McLean and Elkind, *Smartest Guys*.
20. See Rick and Loewenstein, "Hypermotivation," 645–47.
21. Abdel-khalik, "Prospect Theory."
22. For a thoughtful history and extension of this risk-taker propensity into the world of corporate governance, see Skeel, *Icarus in the Boardroom*.
23. Ben-David, Graham, and Harvey, "Managerial Miscalibration," 1547–50. See also Libby and Rennekamp, "Self-Serving Attribution," 198–99.
24. Chen, Crossland, and Luo, "Making the Same Mistake."
25. Malmendier and Tate, "CEO Overconfidence," 21–23.
26. Chattergee and Hambrick, "Executive Personality," 203–5; and Rijsenbilt and Commandeur, "Narcissus," 414–16. On the legal implications, see Barnard, "Shirking," 655–63.
27. Wiesenfeld et al., "Fair Bosses."
28. Jia, Van Lent, and Zeng, "Masculinity," 53–55.
29. Davidson, Dey, and Smith, "Off the Job Behavior," 6–7.
30. Carney and Mason, "Testosterone," 668.
31. Bentley and Bloomfield, "Drinking Kool-Aid."
32. See Carney, "Powerful People."
33. Murphy, "Attitude," 243–44.
34. What Erik Gerding calls episodes of "compliance rot." Gerding, *Law, Bubbles*, 2, 10–11.
35. Nguyen, "Does Your Daughter?"
36. Hutton et al., "Political Values."
37. Kedia and Rajgopal, "SEC Preferences," 260–61; and Calluzzo et al., "Catch Me."
38. See Acharya, Myers, and Rajan, "Internal Governance of Firms," 690–92.
39. Kluver, Frazier, and Haidt, "Behavioral Ethics," 154.
40. Greve, Palmer, and Pozner, "Organizations Gone Wild."
41. Parsons, Sulaemon, and Titman, "Geography."

42. Bizjak, Lemmon, and Whitby, "Options Backdating," 4822–23.

43. Tyler, *Why People Obey.*

44. *Ernst & Ernst v. Hochfelder*, 425 U.S. 185 (1976).

45. Gulati, Rachlinski, and Langevoort, "Hindsight," 773–78.

46. See Ferrell and Ferrell, "Last Interview."

47. Hueston, "Enron."

48. Not surprisingly, the numbers are not entirely objective, either. See Velikonja, "Reporting Performance."

49. Correia, "Political Connections," 241–43.

50. Gadinis, "Enforcement," 680–82.

51. DeHaan et al., "Revolving Door."

52. Mayew and Venkatachalam, "Power of Voice," 2–5; and Druz, Wagner, and Zeckhauser, "Tips and Tells."

53. Rapp, "Intelligence Design."

54. Dimmock and Gerken, "Predicting Fraud," 154–57.

55. 485 U.S. 224 (1988).

56. Baker and Griffith, *Ensuring Corporate Misconduct*, 42–75.

57. Grundfest, "Predicting Fraud Damages," 308–9.

58. This subject has been the subject of extensive legal scholarship, my own included. For a good recent summary of the debate, with many citations, see Bratton and Wachter, "Political Economy."

59. *Halliburton Co. v. Erica P. John Fund Inc.*, 134 S. Ct. 2398 (2014).

60. See Fisch, "Confronting the Circularity Problem," 340–46.

61. *Blue Chip Stamps v. Manor Drug Stores*, 421 U.S. 723 (1975).

62. See Coffee, *Gatekeepers*, 215–16.

63. See Cox and Thomas, "Mapping."

64. *Morrison v. National Australia Bank*, 561 U.S. 247 (2010).

65. Bartlett, "Do Institutional Investors Value?" 187.

66. For doubts about added value, see Rose, "Multi-enforcer."

67. When the corporation is a defendant, scienter must come via attribution of knowledge. On the many problems associated with attribution, see DeMott, "When Is an Agent?"

68. Klausner and Hegland, "How Protective?," 2–4.

69. Arlen and Carney, "Vicarious Liability," 692–96.

70. Furchtgott and Partnoy, "Disclosure Strategies."

71. For a survey, see Cox and Thomas, "Mapping."

72. Donelson, Hopkins, and Yust, "Role of D&O Insurance."

73. Bratton and Wachter, "Political Economy," 70–71.

74. For a good set of suggestions for how corporate managers should engage with investors and the marketplace, see Lev, *Winning Investors Over*, 87–144.

75. Ayres, "Back to Basics."

76. Rogers et al., "Artful Paltering."

77. *Eisenstadt v. Centel Corp.*, 113 F.3d 738 (7th Cir. 1997).

78. See Hoffman, "Puffery," 1395–99.

79. *Asher v. Baxter Int'l Inc.*, 377 F.3d 727 (7th Cir. 2004).

Chapter 3

1. 904 F. Supp.2d 349 (S.D.N.Y. 2012).
2. 904 F. Supp.2d 354. The Gupta sentencing is analyzed in Haugh, "Sentencing the Why," 3144–47.
3. Langevoort, "Rereading Cady," 1320–22.
4. See, for example, Cox, "Insider Trading." There is a massive literature on the economics of insider trading, of which this is but a brief overview.
5. Bainbridge, "Regulating Insider Trading," 96–98.
6. Acharya and Johnson, "More Insiders," 501–2.
7. Pritchard, "Justice Powell."
8. *Chiarella v. United States*, 445 U.S. 222 (1980).
9. *United States v. Willis*, 737 F. Supp. 269 (S.D.N.Y. 1990).
10. *Carpenter v. United States*, 484 U.S. 19 (1987).
11. *United States v. O'Hagan*, 521 U.S. 642 (1997).
12. Nagy, "Insider Trading."
13. *SEC v. Cuban*, 620 F.3d 551 (5th Cir. 2010).
14. *SEC v. Rocklage*, 470 F.3d 1 (1st Cir. 2006).
15. *SEC v. Dorozhko*, 574 F.3d 42 (2d Cir. 2009).
16. *Dirks v. SEC*, 463 U.S. 646 (1983).
17. *SEC v. Switzer*, 590 F. Supp. 756 (W.D. Okla. 1984).
18. See "SEC Charges Stockbroker and Law Firm Managing Clerk in $5.6 Million Insider Trading Scheme," Press Release 2014-55, March 19, 2014 (*SEC v. Eydelman and Metro*).
19. For a good journalistic account, see Gasparino, *Circle of Friends*.
20. These returns may not be as dramatic as portrayed. See Ibbotson, Chen, and Zhu, "ABCs of Hedge Funds," 15–20.
21. *United States v. Rajaratnam*, 719 F.3d 139 (2d Cir. 2013) and *United States v. Gupta*, 747 F.3d 111 (2d Cir. 2014).
22. See Keefe, "Empire of Edge," for a journalistic account; *United States v. Martoma*, 2014 WL 4384143 (S.D.N.Y. 2014) for the legal proceedings. Martoma's case is on appeal as of the summer of 2015.
23. Keefe, "Empire of Edge."
24. *United States v. Newman*, 773 F.3d 438 (2d Cir. 2014).
25. *SEC v. Adler*, 137 F.3d 1325 (11th Cir. 1998).
26. Jagolinzer, "Rule 10b5-1," 225–26.
27. Keefe, "Empire of Edge."
28. See Mehta, Reeb, and Zhao, "Shadow Trading."
29. The information here is from Statman, "Martha Stewart's Lessons." For a legal discussion, see Schroeder, "Envy and Outsider Trading."
30. See Statman, "Cultures," 656–60.
31. On this issue, see Fried, "Insider Trading."
32. See Fisch, "Regulation FD."
33. For empirical evidence on this advantage, see Jackson and Mitts, "Speedy Traders"; and Rogers, Skinner, and Zechman, "Run EDGAR Run."
34. For empirical evidence, see Irvine, Lipson, and Puckett, "Tipping," 742–44; and Klein, Saunders, and Wong, "Hedge Funds."

35. See FINRA News Release, November 24, 2014 (settling supervision case against Citigroup).

36. Haddock and Macey, "Regulation on Demand."

37. One place where executives did care was with respect to insider trading that helped enable hostile tender offers designed to oust incumbents from power. Consistent with this, the SEC adopted a special tender offer insider trading rule (Rule 14e-3) to put a stop to this practice without reference to fiduciary duty or other limitations.

38. Henderson, "Changing Demand," 242–50. Also Bozanic et al., "Endogenization."

39. See Greene and Schmid, "Duty Free Insider Trading."

Chapter 4

1. Romano, "Quack Corporate Governance," 1522–26.

2. Coates and Srinivasan, "SOX after Ten Years."

3. Coffee, *Gatekeepers*, 1–10.

4. Lev, *Winning Investors Over*, 61–86.

5. Compare Romano, "Empowering Investors," with Fox, "Retaining Mandatory Disclosure," and Goshen and Parchomovsky, "Essential Role."

6. Miller and Skinner, "Evolving Disclosure Landscape," 222–24. On the project of optimal information production from a securities law perspective, see Dombalagian, *Chasing the Tape*.

7. More and more, innovative financial products are themselves bundles of many different economic rights—far different from ordinary stocks and bonds—requiring a disclosure model different from the conventional one of issuer self-depiction. Securitized debt is a good example. See Hu, "Too Complex to Depict?"

8. Kitch, "Theory and Practice," 764–74.

9. See Gordon, "Rise of Independent Directors"; and Kahan and Rock, "Embattled CEOs."

10. Including some evidence that these influences check managerial overconfidence. See Banerjee, Humphrey-Jenner, and Nanda, "Restraining Overconfident CEOs."

11. See Macey and Boot, "Monitoring." Westphal, "Collaboration in the Boardroom," points out that cohesion and social support are not all bad, because good advice depends on two-way trust.

12. Khanna, Kim, and Lu, "CEO Connectedness," 1204–5.

13. Bizjak, Lemmon, and Whitby, "Options Backdating," 4822–23.

14. Hermalin and Weisbach, "Endogenously Determined."

15. See Welsh and Ordonez, "Dark Side," 80–83.

16. Morse, Wang, and Wu, "Executive Gatekeepers."

17. See *AUSA Life Insurance Co. v. Ernst & Young*, 206 F.3d 202, 209 (2d Cir. 2000) ("We agree with the district court that E&Y did not perform the most efficacious accounting in this situation. . . .. The accountants lacked the backbone to stand up to the intransigent and intimidating" CEO).

18. This colloquy is discussed in Bazerman and Tenbrunsel, *Blind Spots*, 136–39.

19. Bazerman and Tenbrunsel, *Blind Spots*, 82–83.

20. Aghazadeh and Joe, "Expressions of Confidence."

21. Coates and Srinivasan, "SOX after Ten Years," 628–30.

22. Dyck, Morse, and Zingales, "Who Blows the Whistle?"

23. Rostain and Regan, *Confidence Games*.

24. Fleischer, "Options Backdating," 1052–57.

25. In post-SOX commentary, Bazerman and colleagues stressed their doubts about the sustainability of any reforms, given both psychology and politics. Moore et al., "Conflicts of Interest."

26. Coffee, *Gatekeepers*, 152–56.

27. See Langevoort, "Organized Illusions"; and Miller and Rosenfeld, "Intellectual Hazard," 812–20.

28. Alexander et al., "Economic Effects," 268–70.

29. Coffee, "Political Economy," finds this a predictable pullback resulting from lobbying pressure.

30. See Langevoort, "Behavioral Ethics."

31. Lo, "Gordon Gekko."

32. "J.P. Morgan's Algorithm Knows You're a Rogue Employee before You Do." *Bloomberg Business*, April 8, 2015.

33. Tenbrunsel and Messick, "Sanctioning Systems," 685–87.

34. Gneezy and Rustichini, "Fine Is a Price," 2–3.

35. Graham, "Economic Implications," 4–7.

36. Bargeron, Lehn, and Zutter, "Sarbanes-Oxley," 35–36. Establishing this indirect effect empirically is not easy, however, as Coates and Srinivisan, "SOX after Ten Years," point out.

37. Arlen, "Potentially Perverse Effects," 834–36.

38. Regulators and prosecutors both judge internal controls ex ante and insist on governance reforms ex post in disposing of cases involving corporate wrongdoing, which few commentators think they do particularly well. E.g., Cunningham, "Deferred Prosecutions," 2–6.

39. For example, Waytz, Dungan, and Young, "Whistleblower's Dilemma."

40. See Bazerman and Tenbrunsel, *Blind Spots*, 91–94.

41. Feldman and Lobel, "Incentives Matrix," 1153–56.

42. While the language in those emails is jarring, keep in mind that people on Wall Street do use language like that fairly liberally, often out of frustration. It's possible, I suspect, to have confidence in a stock but disparage it in a momentary scatological outburst simply because of some unexpected bad news.

43. Gu, Li, and Yang, "Monitors or Predators?," 138–39.

44. See Brown et al., "Black Box."

45. See Malmendier and Shanthikumar, "Two Tongues," 1288–89.

46. Agrawal and Chen, "Analyst Conflicts," 504–6.

47. *Lentell v. Merrill Lynch & Co.*, 396 F.3d 161, 172–78 (2d Cir. 2005).

48. Brown et al., "Black Box."

49. Ariely, *Honest Truth*, 46–51.

50. Risk of sanctioning is relevant to the behavioral effects of disclosing conflicts. Church and Kuang, "Costly Sanctions," 506–7.

51. Black, "Institutional Preconditions," 808.

52. Rodrigues and Stegmoller, "Placebo Ethics."

53. See Davidoff Solomon and Hill, "Limits of Disclosure," 623–26. For a strong criticism of the abuse of managerial power, see Bebchuk and Fried, *Pay without Performance*.

54. DeVaan and DiPrete, "Impression Management."

55. See Roe, "Short-Termism," 980–88.

56. Graham, Harvey, and Rajgopal, "Economic Implications," 66.
57. Stout, *The Shareholder Value Myth*.
58. Kraft, Vashishtha, and Venkatachalam, "Real Effects."
59. Gilson and Gordon, "Agency Costs," 866–68.
60. *Business Roundtable v. SEC*, 647 F.3d 1144 (D.C. Cir. 2011). This debate was less about hedge fund-style activism and more about whether big public pension funds—arguably with a political agenda—should have such rights. To date, the evidence that such funds act contrary to other shareholders' interests is weak.
61. Williams, "Social Responsibility."
62. Schwartz, "Conflict Minerals."
63. Guttentag, "Political Spending," 594–97.
64. *Citizens United v. Federal Election Commission*, 558 U.S. 310 (2010).
65. Coates and Lincoln, "Kennedy's Promise."
66. Ferrell, Liang, and Renneboog, "Socially Responsible Firms."
67. Hong and Liscovich, "Halo Effect." See also Lev, *Winning Investors Over*, 204–9.
68. Private groups like the Sustainability Accounting Standards Board have already developed frameworks for such disclosure.
69. See Langevoort and Thompson, "Publicness," 368–71.
70. Bernstein, "Innovation."
71. Zimmerman, "Role of Accounting."
72. Derrien, Kecskés, and Thesmar, "Investor Horizon," 1756–58.
73. Mergers between public companies are a primary driver of this result.
74. Pollman, "Information Issues."
75. Adam Pritchard, "Abolishing IPOs," observes that public offerings would be better, for those companies that so choose, if there is a period of "seasoning" in these deep private markets that allows for a clearer sense of the companies' long-term value.
76. On the SEC's likely reaction, see Gubler, "Public Choice," 776–93.

Chapter 5

1. See Lewis, "Lebed's Extracurricular Activities."
2. Frieder and Zittrain, "Spam Works," 745–47.
3. Nelson, Price, and Roundtree, "Stock Spam Recommendations," 1156–58.
4. Kumar, "Who Gambles?," 1890–92.
5. *SEC v. Roderic Bolling III*, SEC Litigation Release 19779, July 26, 2006.
6. See Frankel, *Ponzi Scheme Puzzle*.
7. See Fairfax, "Friends Like These," 64–67.
8. For example, *SEC v. Hasho*, 784 F. Supp. 1059 (S.D.N.Y. 1992).
9. Kindleberger, *Essays in History*, 37.
10. Heimer, "Friends," 528–30.
11. Seligman, *Transformation of Wall Street*.
12. Mahoney, "New Financial Deal," 66–71.
13. See Davidoff Solomon and Rose, "Disappearing Small IPO." As the authors point out, smaller IPOs are disappearing partly as a result.

14. The underwriters make money by buying from the company at a lower price than investors will pay, pocketing a lucrative spread, often around 7%. See Chen and Ritter, "Seven Percent Solution."

15. See Wilhelm, "Bookbuilding." On how technology has changed the informational role of bankers, see Wilhelm and Morrison, "Trust, Reputation and Law."

16. Da et al., "Attention," 1462–63.

17. For a review, see Ritter, "Equilibrium"; some of the legal issues are discussed in Hurt, "Moral Hazard."

18. Langevoort and Thompson, "Slow Death," 904–6.

19. For empirical evidence, see Cook, "Marketing"; Ljunqvist, Nanda, and Singh, "Hot Markets"; and Chemmanur and Yan, "Product Marketing."

20. See Chaplinsky, Hanley, and Moon, "JOBS Act."

21. FINRA News Release, December 11, 2014, available at https://www.finra.org/newsroom/2014/finra-fines-10-firms-total-435-million.

22. Dambra et al., "Analyst Quality."

23. See Gao, Ritter, and Zhu, "Where Have IPOs Gone?," 1664–70.

24. Bernstein, "Innovation." Of course, the likelihood of an IPO is the reward that motivates earlier levels of innovation. But there are alternative forms of exit, and there is an argument that technology is evolving in such a way that makes exit via a merger with a larger, more established company a competitively smarter move. Gao, Ritter, and Zhu, "Where Have IPOs Gone?," 1664–66.

25. *SEC v. Ralston Purina Co.*, 346 U.S. 119 (1953).

26. A separate question was whether there were offerings sufficiently small in the amount being raised to warrant exempt status or at least a lower regulatory burden. Eventually, the SEC created small offering exemptions as well as ones based on investor qualifications.

27. See Gamble et al., "Causes and Consequences."

28. See Johnson, "Fleecing Grandma," 1002–3.

29. The verification requirement has turned out to be troublesome here, which raises an interesting issue for investors to ponder—especially when hit with a private investment sales pitch. How can any seller *verify* that an investor has enough income or wealth to meet the test? It's not enough for the investor simply to check the box and promise that she's accredited. One common way has been to turn over tax returns, bank account statements, and other records. But would you turn over your private financial information to an entrepreneur (or his or her lawyer or some "finder") just to establish accredited investor status? Hopefully not. But how else can reasonable verification take place? It's early, but nervousness about this seems to have deterred some entrepreneurs from taking full advantage of the elimination of the ban, preferring instead to pay brokers for doing private deals the old way. This raises the suspicion that the political influence of brokers may have been behind a strict verification requirement.

30. See Alces, "Legal Diversification."

31. Rodrigues, "Dirty Little Secret," 3389–92.

32. Thompson and Langevoort, "Entrepreneurial Capital Raising," 1616–19.

33. See Agrawal, Catalini, and Goldfarb, "Simple Economics."

34. Mollick and Nanda, "Wisdom or Madness?"

35. Larrick, Mannes, and Soll, "Wisdom of Crowds."

36. Testimony before the Senate Committee on Banking, Housing and Urban Affairs, December 1, 2011.

37. For a political deconstruction, see Heminway, "How Congress Killed Crowdfunding."

38. See Mollick, "Dynamics of Crowdfunding," 2–4.

39. Isenberg, "Crowdfunding Hell."

40. See Schwartz, "Digital Shareholder."

41. French, "Active Investing," 1538–40.

42. See Malkiel, *A Random Walk*, for a discussion and citations.

43. Kacperszyk, Van Nieuwerburgh, and Veldkamp, "Fund Manager Skill," 70–72,

44. See Bailey, Kumar, and Ng, "Behavioral Biases," 2–5.

45. Frazzini and Lamont, "Dumb Money," 300–303.

46. Moore et al., "Positive Illusions," 76–78.

47. For discussions, see Fisch and Wilkinson-Ryan, "Costly Mistakes"; Beshears et al., "Simplified Disclosure"; and Palmiter and Taha, "Mutual Fund Performance."

48. Mullainathan, Nöth, and Schoar, "Market for Financial Advice."

49. Bergstresser et al., "Assessing the Costs," 4130–32.

50. Del Guercio and Reuter, "Mutual Fund Performance," 1674–76.

51. Gennaioli, Shleifer, and Vishny, "Money Doctors."

52. McCloskey and Klamer, "One Quarter of GDP," 191.

53. Tenbrunsel and Messick, "Ethical Fading."

54. Feldman, "Behavioral Ethics," 219–20.

55. Oakes, *Soul of the Salesman*, 12–13.

56. This is especially so in interpersonal settings (the money doctors). But even online relationships can be sticky. See Agnew et al., "Individual Judgment."

57. See Harrington, "Financial Fraud," 398.

58. MacLean and Benham, "Dangers of Decoupling," 1509.

Chapter 6

1. Cohn, Fehr, and Maréchal, "Business Culture and Dishonesty," 86.

2. For a good introduction with a legal bent, read Skeel, *New Financial Deal*.

3. Without getting deeply into the law or economics of derivatives, one advantage of a synthetic derivative is that there didn't need to be any real mortgages involved at all—just a contract whose value depended on a "referenced" set of mortgages. This step meant that mortgage-backed products could be sold in a volume far in excess of the actual quantity of outstanding residential mortgages.

4. Rajan, *Fault Lines*.

5. Whitehead, "Reforming," 92–97.

6. Taub, *Other People's Houses*.

7. For a more thorough review of allegations of investment banker misconduct, with explanations drawn in part from the kinds of human nature issues we've been exploring, see Hill and Painter, *Better Bankers, Better Banks*.

8. Levitin and Bratton, "Transactional Genealogy."

9. See Hill, "Subprime Investors."

10. And many others. E.g., Akerlof and Shiller, *Animal Spirits*; and Langevoort, "Chasing."

11. Cheng, Raina, and Xiong, "Wall Street," 2798–30.

12. Jagolinzer et al., "Information Content." With respect to the disposition of equity holdings generally by insiders, the evidence is mixed.

13. Gilson and Kraakman, "Market Efficiency," 340–44.

14. Robb, "Epistemology," 132–35. See also Friedman and Kraus, *Engineering the Financial Crisis*, 132–39.

15. Partnoy, "Siskel and Ebert," 620–23.

16. *Financial Times*, July 10, 2007, 1-1. See also Langevoort, "Chasing," 1224–34.

17. Lo, "Testimony," 12–13.

18. Coates, *Hour*.

19. Kluver, Frazier, and Haidt, "Behavioral Ethics," 155.

20. Llewellyn and Muller-Kahle, "CEO Power," 290–92.

21. Ho, "Disciplining Investment Bankers," 186–87.

22. Malhotra, "Desire to Win," 139–42.

23. Pierce et al., "From Glue to Gasoline," 2–3. In their book, Hill and Painter touch on other behavioral and cultural forces affecting bankers, including status-seeking, the priming of money consciousness, and intensity of work schedules. *Better Bankers, Better Banks*, 109–22.

24. Miller and Rosenfeld, "Intellectual Hazard," 816–24.

25. Turco and Zuckerman, "Think You Can Dance?," 82–85.

26. Bratton and Wachter, "Shareholder Empowerment," 720. The fascinating story of the hesitation of Morgan's CEO Jamie Dimon is well told in Gillian Tett's book, *Fool's Gold*.

27. Rakoff, "Financial Crisis."

28. Richman, "Corporate Headhunting," 905–10.

29. Henning, "New Crime," 60–70.

30. E.g., Omarova, "License to Deal."

31. Notre Dame and Labaton Sucharow, *The Street*. The study was sponsored by a law firm specializing in both plaintiffs' securities litigation and whistle-blower protection.

32. Ariely, *Honest Truth*, 243.

33. Wilhelm and Morrison, "Trust."

34. *Times of London Magazine*, August 11, 2009, 12.

35. Thompson, "Vampire Squid," 324–39.

36. Pierce et al., "From Glue to Gasoline," 2–3.

37. Cikara et al., "Their Pain," 111–12.

38. On ways of changing this, see Zingales, "Finance"; and Awrey, Blair, and Kershaw, "Between Law and Markets."

39. Roulet, "No Such Thing."

40. That is not to say that we yet know how to manage the risks. E.g., Yadav, "Problematic Case."

41. See Gerding, *Bubbles and Financial Regulation*, for an excellent survey of postcrisis regulatory theory and practice.

42. Levitin, "Safe Banking."

43. Zingales, "Finance."

44. These quotes and relevant background come from Adams and Ragunathan, "Lehman Sisters."

45. E.g., Branson, "Initiatives"; and Dhir, *Challenging Boardroom Homogeneity*, chap. 3.

46. For a survey of gender differences in economic activity supporting the hypothesis, see van Staveren, "Lehman Sisters Hypothesis," 1000–1008.

47. Eckel and Fullbrunn, "Thar SHE Blows," 905–7.

48. Sapienza, Zingales, and Maestripieri, "Gender Differences."

49. Adams and Ragunathan, "Lehman Sisters."

50. Huang and Kisgen, "Gender," 823–25.

51. Cumming, Leung, and Rui, "Gender Diversity."

52. See Bruckmüller and Branscombe, "Glass Cliff."

53. Ahern and Dittmar, "Changing of the Boards," 138–39.

54. Dobbin and Jung, "Diversity and Stock Performance," 809–12.

55. Matsa and Miller, "Female Style," 136–37.

56. Dobbin and Jung, "Diversity and Stock Performance," 811–12.

57. Atkinson, Baird, and Frye, "Female Mutual Fund Managers," 1–3.

58. Dhir, *Challenging Boardroom Homogeneity*, 173–211.

Conclusion

1. In the midst of all this came the Internet revolution, which did generate substantial productivity gains and investment returns (albeit with a bubble that popped at the turn of the century). We are still sorting out the wealth distribution consequences of this remarkable period of innovation, a task I leave to others. For a time, at least, this shifted public and investor attention back to at least the illusion of hope, if not some reality of it.

2. Rajan, *Fault Lines*, 2–6.

3. Paredes, "Hedge Funds," 1006–10, on the dangers of the regulatory precautionary principle and undue publicness.

4. See Choi and Pritchard, "Behavioral Economics," 2–5. On bureaucratic error and misjudgment in the financial crisis, see Friedman and Kraus, *Engineering the Financial Crisis*, 120–35.

5. Igan and Mishra, "Wall Street," 1063–65.

6. Ortoleva and Snowberg, "Overconfidence," 504–5.

7. Carpenter, "Institutional Strangulation."

8. Coffee, "Political Economy," 1029.

9. Kwak, "Cultural Capture," 80–93; see also Hockett, "Testimony," 25–33.

10. Zingales, "Finance," 1328–30.

11. Hu, "Faith and Magic," 837–38.

12. See Zimmerman, "21st Century Firms."

13. See Coates, "Private versus Public," 69–70.

14. Jost, Banaji, and Nosek, "System Justification Theory," 882–84.

Bibliography

Abdel-Khalik, A. Rashad. "Prospect Theory Predictions in the Field: Risk Seekers in Settings of Weak Accounting Controls." *Journal of Accounting Literature* 33, nos. 1–2 (2014): 58–64.

Acharya, Viral V., and Timothy C. Johnson. "More Insiders, More Insider Trading: Evidence from Private Equity Buyouts." *Journal of Financial Economics* 98, no. 3 (2010): 500–523.

Acharya, Viral V., Stewart C. Myers, and Raghuram G. Rajan. "The Internal Governance of Firms." *Journal of Finance* 66, no. 3 (2011): 689–720.

Adams, Renee B., and Vanitha Ragunathan. "Lehman Sisters." Financial Research Network Research Paper (2014), available at http://papers.ssrn.com/sol3/papers.cfm?abstract_id=2380036.

Aghazadeh, Sanaz, and Jennifer R. Joe. "How Management's Expressions of Confidence Influence Auditors' Skeptical Response to Management's Explanations." Working paper, June 26, 2015, available at http://papers.ssrn.com/sol3/papers.cfm?abstract_id=2623537.

Agnew, Julie R., Hazel Bateman, Christine Eckert, Fedor Iskhakov, Jordan Louviere, and Susan Thorp. "Individual Judgment and Trust Formation: An Experimental Investigation of Online Financial Advice." *Management Science*, forthcoming, 2015.

Agrawal, Anup, and Mark A. Chen. "Do Analyst Conflicts Matter? Evidence from Stock Recommendations." *Journal of Law and Economics* 51, no. 3 (2008): 503–37.

Agrawal, Arjay, Christian Catalini, and Avi Goldfarb. "Some Simple Economics of Crowdfunding." In *Innovation Policy and the Economy*, edited by Josh Lerner and Scott Stern, 14: 63–97. Chicago: University of Chicago Press, 2014.

Ahern, Kenneth R., and Amy K. Dittmar. "The Changing of the Boards: The Impact on Firm Valuation of Mandated Female Board Representation." *Quarterly Journal of Economics* 127, no. 1 (2012): 137–97.

Ahmed, Anwer S., and Scott Duellman. "Managerial Overconfidence and Accounting Conservatism." *Journal of Accounting Research* 51, no. 1 (2013): 1–30.

Akerlof, George A., and Rachel E. Kranton. "Identity and the Economics of Organizations." *Journal of Economic Perspectives* 19, no. 1 (2005): 9–32.

Akerlof, George A., and Robert J. Shiller. *Animal Spirits: How Human Psychology Drives the Economy and Why It Matters for Global Capitalism.* Princeton, NJ: Princeton University Press, 2009.

Alces, Kelli A. "Legal Diversification." *Columbia Law Review* 113 (November 2013): 1977–2038.

Alexander, Cindy R., Scott W. Bauguess, Gennaro Bernile, Yoon-Ho Alex Lee, and Jennifer Marietta-Westberg. "Economic Effects of SOX Section 404 Compliance: A Corporate Insider's Perspective." *Journal of Accounting and Economics* 56, nos. 2–3 (2013): 267–90.

Applied Research & Consulting LLC. "Financial Fraud and Fraud Susceptibility in the United States." *FINRA Investor Education Foundation Research Report*, September 2013.

Ariely, Dan. *The (Honest) Truth about Dishonesty: How We Lie to Everyone—Especially Ourselves.* New York: HarperCollins, 2012.

Arlen, Jennifer H. "The Potentially Perverse Effects of Corporate Criminal Liability." *Journal of Legal Studies* 23, no. 2 (1994): 833–67.

Arlen, Jennifer H., and William J. Carney. "Vicarious Liability for Fraud on Securities Markets: Theory and Evidence." *University of Illinois Law Review* 1992 (1992): 691–734.

Atkinson, Stanley M., Samantha Boyce Baird, and Melissa B. Frye. "Do Female Mutual Fund Managers Manage Differently?" *Journal of Financial Research* 26, no. 1 (2003): 1–18.

Awrey, Dan, William Blair, and David Kershaw. "Between Law and Markets: Is There a Role for Culture and Ethics in Financial Regulation?" *Delaware Journal of Corporate Law* 38 (2013): 191–245.

Ayres, Ian. "Back to Basics: Regulating How Corporations Speak to the Market." *Virginia Law Review* 77 (1991): 945–99.

Bailey, Warren, Alok Kumar, and David T. Ng. "Behavioral Biases of Mutual Fund Investors." *Journal of Financial Economics* 102, no. 1 (2011): 1–27.

Bainbridge, Stephen M. "Regulating Insider Trading in the Post-fiduciary Era: Equal Access or Property Rights?" In *Research Handbook on Insider Trading*, edited by Stephen M. Bainbridge, 80–98. Cheltenham, UK: Edward Elgar, 2013.

Baker, H. Kent, and Victor Ricciardi, eds. *Investor Behavior: The Psychology of Financial Planning and Investing.* Hoboken, NJ: John Wiley & Sons, 2014.

Baker, Malcolm, and Jeffrey Wurgler. "Investor Sentiment in the Stock Market." *Journal of Economic Perspectives* 21, no. 2 (2007): 129–51.

Baker, Tom, and Sean J. Griffith. *Ensuring Corporate Misconduct: How Liability Insurance Undermines Shareholder Litigation.* Chicago: University of Chicago Press, 2010.

Banerjee, Suman, Mark Humphrey-Jenner, and Vikram K. Nanda. "Restraining Overconfident CEOs through Improved Governance: Evidence from the Sarbanes-Oxley Act." *Review of Financial Studies* 28, no. 10 (2015): 2812–58.

Banner, Stuart. "What Causes Securities Regulation: 300 Years of Evidence." *Washington University Law Quarterly* 75, no. 2 (1997): 849–55.

Barber, Brad M., and Terrence Odean. "Trading Is Hazardous to Your Wealth: The Common Stock Investment Performance of Individual Investors." *Journal of Finance* 55, no. 2 (2000): 773–806.

Barberis, Nicholas C. "Psychology and the Financial Crisis of 2007–2008." In *Financial Innovation: Too Much or Too Little?* edited by Michael Haliassos, 15–28. Cambridge, MA: MIT Press, 2013.

Bargeron, Leonce L., Kenneth M. Lehn, and Chad J. Zutter. "Sarbanes-Oxley and Corporate Risk-Taking." *Journal of Accounting and Economics* 49, nos. 1–2 (2010): 34–52.

Barnard, Jayne W. "Shirking, Opportunism, Self-Delusion and More: The Agency Problem Lives On." *Wake Forest Law Review* 48 (2013): 745–70.

Bartlett, Robert P. "Do Institutional Investors Value the Rule 10b-5 Private Right of Action? Evidence from Trading Behavior following *Morrison v. National Australia Bank Ltd.*" *Journal of Legal Studies* 44, no. 1 (2015): 183–227.

Bartlett, Robert P. "Going Private but Staying Public: Reexamining the Effect of Sarbanes-Oxley on Firms' Going-Private Decisions." *University of Chicago Law Review* 76 (Winter 2009): 7–44.

Bazerman, Max H., and Ann E. Tenbrunsel. *Blind Spots: Why We Fail to Do What's Right and What to Do about It.* Princeton, NJ: Princeton University Press, 2011.

Bebchuk, Lucian, and Jesse Fried. *Pay without Performance: The Unfulfilled Promise of Executive Compensation.* Cambridge, MA: Harvard University Press, 2004.

Benabou, Roland J. "Groupthink: Collective Delusions in Organizations and Markets." *Review of Financial Studies* 80, no. 2 (2013): 429–62.

Ben-David, Itzhak, John R. Graham, and Campbell R. Harvey. "Managerial Miscalibration." *Quarterly Journal of Economics* 128, no. 4 (2013): 1547–84.

Ben-Shahar, Omri, and Carl E. Schneider. *More Than You Wanted to Know: The Failure of Mandated Disclosure.* Princeton, NJ: Princeton University Press, 2013.

Bentley, Jeremiah W., and Robert J. Bloomfield. "Drinking Your Own Kool-Aid: The Role of Beliefs, Belief-Reversion, and Meetings in Persuasion." Working paper, April 22, 2014, available at http://papers.ssrn.com/sol3/papers.cfm?abstract_id=2423131.

Bergstresser, Daniel, John M. R. Chalmers, and Peter Tufano. "Assessing the Costs and Benefits of Brokers in the Mutual Fund Industry." *Review of Financial Studies* 22, no. 10 (2009): 4129–56.

Bernstein, Shai. "Does Going Public Affect Innovation?" *Journal of Finance* 70, no. 4 (2015): 1365–403.

Beshears, John, James J. Choi, David Laibson, and Brigitte C. Madrian. "How Does Simplified Disclosure Affect Individuals' Mutual Fund Choices?" In *Explorations in the Economics of Aging,* edited by David A. Wise, 75–96. Chicago: University of Chicago Press, 2011.

Bizjak, John M., Michael L. Lemmon, and Ryan J. Whitby. "Options Backdating and Board Interlocks." *Review of Financial Studies* 22, no. 11 (2009): 4821–47.

Black, Bernard. "The Legal and Institutional Preconditions for Strong Securities Markets." *UCLA Law Review* 48 (2001): 781–855.

Black, Fischer. "Noise." *Journal of Finance* 41, no. 3 (1986): 529–43.

Bozanic, Zahn, Mark W. Dirsmith, and Steven J. Huddart. "The Social Construction of Regulation: The Endogenization of Insider Trading Laws." *Accounting, Organizations and Society* 37, no. 7 (2012): 461–81.

Bracha, Anat, and Elke U. Weber. "A Psychological Perspective of Financial Panic." Public Policy Discussion Paper No. 12-7, Federal Reserve Bank of Boston, September 2012, available at http://www.bostonfed.org/economic/ppdp/2012/ppdp1207.htm.

Bradley, Daniel J., Bradford D. Jordan, and Jay R. Ritter. "The Quiet Period Goes Out with a Bang." *Journal of Finance* 58, no. 1 (2003): 1–36.

Branson, Douglas. "Initiatives to Place Women on Corporate Boards of Directors: A Global Snapshot." *Journal of Corporation Law* 37 (Summer 2012): 793–814.

Bratton, William W., and Michael L. Wachter. "The Case against Shareholder Empowerment." *University of Pennsylvania Law Review* 158 (February 2010): 653–728.

Bratton, William W., and Michael L. Wachter. "The Political Economy of Fraud on the Market." *University of Pennsylvania Law Review* 159 (December 2011): 69–168.

Brown, Lawrence D., Andrew C. Call, Michael B. Clement, and Nathan Y. Sharp. "Inside the 'Black Box' of Sell-Side Financial Analysts." *Journal of Accounting Research* 53, no. 1 (2015): 1–47.

Brown, Tim. "Advantageous Comparison and Rationalization of Earnings Management." *Journal of Accounting Research* 52, no. 4 (2014): 849–76.

Bruckmüller, Susanne, and Nyla R. Branscombe. "How Women End Up on the 'Glass Cliff.'" *Harvard Business Review* 89, nos. 1–2 (2011): 26–28.

Brummer, Chris. *Soft Law and the Global Financial System: Rule Making in the 21st Century.* New York: Cambridge University Press, 2012.

Buell, Samuel W. "What Is Securities Fraud?" *Duke Law Journal* 61 (December 2011): 511–81.

Calluzzo, Paul, Wei Wang, and Serena Wu. "Catch Me If You Can: Financial Misconduct around Corporate Headquarters Relocations." Working paper, July 2015, available at http://papers.ssrn.com/sol3/papers.cfm?abstract_id=2627760.

Capps, Gregory P., Lisa Koonce, and Kathy R. Petroni. "Natural Optimism in Financial Reporting: A State of Mind." *Accounting Horizons* 29 (forthcoming 2015).

Carney, Dana, and Scott Berinato. "Powerful People Are Better Liars." *Harvard Business Review* 88 (May 2010): 32–33.

Carney, Dana R., and Malia F. Mason. "Decision Making and Testosterone: When the Ends Justify the Means." *Journal of Experimental Social Psychology* 46, no. 4 (2010): 668–71.

Carpenter, Daniel. "Institutional Strangulation: Bureaucratic Politics and Financial Reform in the Obama Administration." *Perspectives on Politics* 8, no. 3 (2010): 825–46.

Chang, Tom, David H. Solomon, and Mark M. Westerfield. "Looking for Someone to Blame: Delegation, Cognitive Dissonance and the Disposition Effect." *Journal of Finance* (forthcoming 2015).

Chaplinsky, Susan, Kathleen Weiss Hanley, and S. Katie Moon. "The JOBS Act and the Costs of Going Public." Working paper, August 14, 2014, available at http://papers.ssrn.com/sol3/papers.cfm?abstract_id=2492241.

Chatterjee, Arijit, and Donald C. Hambrick. "Executive Personality, Capability Cues, and Risk Taking: How Narcissistic CEOs React to their Successes and Stumbles." *Administrative Science Quarterly* 56, no. 2 (2011): 202–37.

Chemmanur, Thomas, and An Yan. "Product Market Advertising and New Equity Issues." *Journal of Financial Economics* 92 (2009): 40–65.

Chen, Guoli, Craig Crossland, and Shuqing Luo. "Making the Same Mistake All Over Again: CEO Overconfidence and Corporate Resistance to Corrective Feedback." *Strategic Management Journal* 36, no. 10 (2015): 1513–35.

Chen, Hsuan-Chi, and Jay R. Ritter. "The Seven Percent Solution." *Journal of Finance* 55, no. 3 (2000): 1105–31.

Cheng, Ing-Haw, Sahil Raina, and Wei Xiong. "Wall Street and the Housing Bubble." *American Economic Review* 104, no. 9 (2014): 2797–829.

Choi, Stephen J., and Adam C. Pritchard. "Behavioral Economics and the SEC." *Stanford Law Review* 56 (2003): 1–73.

Church, Bryan K., and Xi Kuang. "Conflicts of Interest, Disclosure, and (Costly) Sanctions: Experimental Evidence." *Journal of Legal Studies* 38, no. 2 (2009): 505–32.

Cikara, M., E. Bruneau, J. J. Van Bavel, and R. Saxe. "Their Pain Gives Us Pleasure: How Intergroup Dynamics Shape Empathic Failures and Counter-empathic Responses." *Journal of Experimental Social Psychology* 55 (November 2014): 110–25.

Coates, John C., IV. "Private versus Public Choice of Securities Regulation: A Political Cost-Benefit Analysis." *Virginia Journal of International Law* 41 (Spring 2001): 531–82.

Coates, John C., IV, and Taylor Lincoln. "Fulfilling Kennedy's Promise: Why the SEC Should Mandate Disclosure of Corporate Political Activity." Report by Harvard Law School and Public Citizen, September 2011, available at http://papers.ssrn.com/sol3/papers. cfm?abstract_id=1923804.

Coates, John C., IV, and Suraj Srinivasan. "SOX after Ten Years: A Multidisciplinary Review." *Accounting Horizons* 28, no. 3 (2014): 627–71.

Coates, John. *The Hour between Dog and Wolf: Risk Taking, Gut Feelings, and the Biology of Booms and Busts*. New York: Penguin, 2012.

Coffee, John C. *Gatekeepers: The Role of the Professions and Corporate Governance*. New York: Oxford University Press, 2006.

Coffee John C. "Law and Markets: The Impact of Enforcement." *University of Pennsylvania Law Review* 156 (2007): 229–309.

Coffee, John C. "The Political Economy of Dodd-Frank: Why Financial Reform Tends to Be Frustrated and Systemic Risk Perpetuated." *Cornell Law Review* 97 (July 2012): 1019–82.

Coglianese, Cary. "Legitimacy and Corporate Governance." *Delaware Journal of Corporate Law* 32 (2007): 159–67.

Cohn, Alain, Ernst Fehr, and Michel André Maréchal. "Business Culture and Dishonesty in the Banking Industry." *Nature* 516 (December 2014): 86–89.

Cook, Douglas O., Robert Kieschnick, and Robert A. Van Ness. "On the Marketing of IPOs." *Journal of Financial Economics* 82 (2006): 35–61.

Cooper, Michael J., Orlin Dimitrov, and P. Raghavendra Rau. "A Rose.com by Any Other Name." *Journal of Finance* 56, no. 6 (2001): 2371–88.

Cornell, Bradford, and Aswath Damodaran. "Tesla: Anatomy of a Run-up." *Journal of Portfolio Management* 41, no. 1 (2014): 139–51.

Correia, Maria M. "Political Connections and SEC Enforcement." *Journal of Accounting and Economics* 57, nos. 2–3 (2014): 241–62.

Cox, James D. "Insider Trading and Contracting: A Critical Response to the Chicago School." *Duke Law Journal* 1986 (1986): 628–59.

Cox, James D., and Randall S. Thomas. "Letting Billions Slip through Your Fingers: Empirical Evidence and Legal Implications of the Failure of Financial Institutions to Participate in Securities Class Action Settlements." *Stanford Law Review* 58 (2005): 411.

Cox, James D., and Randall S. Thomas. "Mapping the American Shareholder Litigation Experience: A Survey of Empirical Studies of the Enforcement of the U.S. Securities Law." *European Company and Financial Law Review* 6, nos. 2–3 (2009): 164–203.

Cumming, Douglas J., Robert Dannhauser, and Sophia Johan. "Financial Market Misconduct and Agency Conflicts: A Synthesis and Future Directions." *Journal of Corporate Finance* 34 (2015): 150–68.

Cumming, Douglas J., Tak Yan Leung, and Oliver M. Rui. "Gender Diversity and Securities Fraud." *Academy of Management Journal* 58, no. 5 (2015): 1459–75.

Cunningham, Lawrence A. "Deferred Prosecutions and Corporate Governance: An Integrated Approach to Investigation and Reform." *Florida Law Review* 66 (2014): 1–85.

Da, Zhi, Joseph Engelberg, and Pengjie Gao. "In Search of Attention." *Journal of Finance* 66 (2011): 1461–99.

Dambra, Michael, Laura Casares Field, Matthew Gustafson, and Kevin Pisciotta. "Analyst Research Quality and the JOBS Act: Effects of Increased Pre-IPO Communication." Working paper, April 27, 2015, available at http://papers.ssrn.com/sol3/papers. cfm?abstract_id=2530109.

Dana, Jason, Roberto A. Weber, and Jason X. Kuang. "Exploiting Moral Wiggle Room: Experiments Demonstrating the Illusory Preference for Fairness." *Economic Theory* 33 (2007): 67–80.

Darley, John M. "The Cognitive and Social Psychology of Contagious Organizational Corruption." *Brooklyn Law Review* 70 (Summer 2005): 1177–94.

Davidoff Solomon, Steven M., and Paul Rose. "The Disappearing Small IPO and the Lifecycle of the Small Firm." Working paper, July 2014, available at http://papers.ssrn.com/sol3/papers.cfm?abstract_id=2400488.

Davidoff Solomon, Steven M., and Claire A. Hill. "The Limits of Disclosure." *Seattle University Law Review* 36 (Winter 2013): 599–637.

Davidson, Robert, Aiyesha Dey, and Abbie Smith. "Executives' 'Off-the-Job' Behavior, Corporate Culture and Financial Reporting Risk." *Journal of Financial Economics* 117, no. 1 (2015): 5–28.

Dechow, Patricia M., Weili Ge, Chad R. Larson, and Richard G. Slaon. "Predicting Material Accounting Misstatements." *Contemporary Accounting Research* 28, no. 1 (2011): 17–82.

deHaan, Ed, Simi Kedia, Kevin Koh, and Shivaram Rajgopal. "The Revolving Door and the SEC's Enforcement Outcomes: Initial Evidence from Civil Litigation." *Journal of Accounting and Economics* 60 (2015): 65–93.

Del Guercio, Diane, and Jonathan Reuter. "Mutual Fund Performance and the Incentive to Generate Alpha." *Journal of Finance* 69, no. 4 (2014): 1673–704.

DeMott, Deborah. "When Is a Principal Charged with an Agent's Knowledge?" *Duke Journal of Comparative and International Law* 13 (2003): 291–320.

Derrien, François, Ambrus Kecskés, and David Thesmar. "Investor Horizon and Corporate Policies." *Journal of Financial and Quantitative Analysis* 48, no. 6 (2013): 1755–80.

deVaan, Mathijs, and Thomas DiPrete. "Impression Management and the Biasing of Executive Pay Benchmarks: A Dynamic Analysis." Working paper, October 23, 2014, available at http://papers.ssrn.com/sol3/papers.cfm?abstract_id=2514165.

Dhir, Aaron A. *Challenging Boardroom Homogeneity: Corporate Law, Governance and Diversity.* New York: Cambridge University Press, 2015.

Dichev, Illia D., John R. Graham, Campbell R. Harvey, and Shivaram Rajgopal. "The Misrepresentation of Earnings." *Financial Analyst Journal* (forthcoming 2015).

Dimmock, Stephen, and William Gerken. "Predicting Fraud by Investment Managers." *Journal of Financial Economics* 105 (2012): 153–73.

Dobbin, Frank, and Jiwook Jung. "Corporate Board Gender Diversity and Stock Performance: The Competence Gap or Institutional Investor Bias?" *North Carolina Law Review* 89 (2011): 809–38.

Dombalagian, Onnig H. *Chasing the Tape: Information Law and Policy in Capital Markets.* Cambridge MA: MIT Press, 2015.

Donelson, Dain C., Justin Hopkins, and Christoper G. Yust. "The Role of D&O Insurance in Securities Fraud Class Action Settlements." *Journal of Law and Economics* (forthcoming 2015).

Druz, Marina, Alexander F. Wagner, and Richard J. Zeckhauser. "Tips and Tells from Managers: How Analysts and the Market Read between the Lines of Conference Calls." CEPR Discussion Paper No. DP10364, January 2015, available at http://papers.ssrn.com/sol3/papers.cfm?abstract_id=2559285.

Dyck, Alexander, Adair Morse, and Luigi Zingales. "How Pervasive Is Corporate Fraud?" Rotman School of Management Working Paper No. 2222608, February 22, 2013, available at http://papers.ssrn.com/sol3/papers.cfm?abstract_id=2222608.

Dyck, Alexander, Adair Morse, and Luigi Zingales. "Who Blows the Whistle on Corporate Fraud?" *Journal of Finance* 65, no. 6 (2010): 2213–53.

Eckel, Catherine C., and Sascha C. Füllbrunn. "Thar SHE Blows? Gender, Competition and Bubbles in Experimental Asset Markets." *American Economic Review* 105, no. 2 (2015): 906–20.

Engelberg, Joseph, and Christopher A. Parsons. "Worrying about the Stock Market: Evidence from Hospital Admissions." *Journal of Finance* (forthcoming 2015).

Engelberg, Joseph, Caroline Sasseville, and Jared Williams. "Market Madness? The Case of Mad Money." *Management Science* 58, no. 2 (2011): 351–64.

Fairfax, Lisa M. "'With Friends Like These . . .': Toward a More Efficacious Response to Affinity-Based Securities and Investment Fraud." *Georgia Law Review* 36 (Fall 2001): 63–119.

Feldman, Yuval. "Behavioral Ethics Meets Behavioral Law and Economics." In *Oxford Handbook of Behavioral Economics and the Law*, edited by Eyal Zamir and Doron Teichman, 213–40. New York: Oxford University Press, 2014.

Feldman, Yuval, and Orly Lobel. "The Incentives Matrix: The Comparative Effectiveness of Rewards, Liabilities, Duties, and Protections for Reporting Illegality." *Texas Law Review* 88, no. 6 (2010): 1151–212.

Ferrell, Allen, Hao Liang, and Luc Renneboog. "Socially Responsible Firms." ECGI Finance Working Paper 432/2014, European Corporate Governance Institute, July 10, 2014, available at http://papers.ssrn.com/sol3/papers.cfm?abstract_id=2464561.

Ferrell, O. C., and Linda Ferrell. "The Responsibility and Accountability of CEOs: The Last Interview with Ken Lay." *Journal of Business Ethics* 100, no. 2 (2011): 209–19.

Fisch, Jill E. "Confronting the Circularity Problem in Private Securities Litigation." *Wisconsin Law Review* 2009 (2009): 333–50.

Fisch, Jill E. "Regulation FD: An Alternative Approach to Addressing Information Asymmetry." In *Research Handbook on Insider Trading*, edited by Stephen M. Bainbridge, 112–29. Cheltenham, UK: Edward Elgar, 2013.

Fisch, Jill E., and Tess Wilkinson-Ryan. "Why Do Retail Investors Make Costly Mistakes? An Experiment on Mutual Fund Choice." *University of Pennsylvania Law Review* 162 (February 2014): 605–47.

Fleischer, Victor. "Options Backdating, Tax Shelters, and Corporate Culture." *Virginia Tax Review* 26 (Spring 2007): 1031–64.

Forsythe, Robert, Russell Lundholm, and Thomas Reitz. "Cheap Talk, Fraud, and Adverse Selection in Financial Markets: Some Experimental Evidence." *Review of Financial Studies* 12, no. 3 (1999): 481–518.

Fox, Merritt B. "Required Disclosure and Corporate Governance." *Law and Contemporary Problems* 62, no. 3 (1999): 113–27.

Fox, Merritt B. "Retaining Mandatory Securities Disclosure: Why Issuer Choice Is Not Investor Empowerment." *Virginia Law Review* 85, no. 7 (1999): 1335–419.

Fox, Merritt B., Larry R, Glosten, and Gabriel V. Rauterberg. "The New Stock Market: Sense and Nonsense." *Duke Law Journal* (forthcoming 2015).

Frankel, Tamar. *The Ponzi Scheme Puzzle: A History and Analysis of Con Artists and Victims.* New York: Oxford University Press, 2012.

Frazzini, Andrea, and Owen A. Lamont. "Dumb Money: Mutual Fund Flows and the Cross-Section of Stock Returns." *Journal of Financial Economics* 88 (2008): 299–322.

Free, Clinton, and Pamela R. Murphy. "The Ties That Bind: The Decision to Co-offend in Fraud." *Contemporary Accounting Research* 32, no. 1 (2015): 18–54.

French, Kenneth R. "Presidential Address: The Costs of Active Investing." *Journal of Finance* 63, no. 4 (2008): 1537–73.

Fried, Jesse M. "Insider Trading via the Corporation." *University of Pennsylvania Law Review* 164, no. 4 (2014): 801–39.

Frieder, Laura L., and Jonathan Zittrain. "Spam Works: Evidence from Stock Touts and Corresponding Market Activity." *Hastings Communications and Entertainment Law Journal* 30 (Spring 2008): 479–520.

Friedman, Jeffrey, and Wladimir Kraus. *Engineering the Financial Crisis: Systematic Risk and the Failure of Regulation.* Philadelphia: University of Pennsylvania Press, 2011.

Furchtgott, Michael, and Frank Partnoy. "Disclosure Strategies and Shareholder Litigation Risk: Evidence from Earning Restatements." San Diego Legal Studies Paper No. 15-186, March 18, 2015, available at http://papers.ssrn.com/sol3/papers.cfm?abstract_id=2585267.

Gadinis, Stavros. "The SEC and the Financial Industry: Evidence from Enforcement against Broker-Dealers." *Business Lawyer* 67 (2012): 679–728.

Gamble, Keith Jacks, Patricia A. Boyle, Lei Yu, and David A, Bennett. "The Causes and Consequences of Financial Fraud among Older Americans." Center for Retirement Research at Boston College Working Paper, November 2014, available at http://crr.bc.edu/working-papers/the-causes-and-consequences-of-financial-fraud-among-older-americans/.

Gao, Xiaohui, Jay R. Ritter, and Zhongyan Zhu. "Where Have All the IPOs Gone?" *Journal of Financial and Quantitative Analysis* 48, no. 6 (2013): 1663–92.

Gasparino, Charles. *Circle of Friends: The Massive Federal Crackdown on Insider Trading—and Why the Market Always Works against the Little Guy.* New York: HarperCollins, 2013.

Gennaioli, Nicola, Andrei Shleifer, and Robert Vishny. "Money Doctors." *Journal of Finance* 70, no. 1 (2015): 91–114.

Gennaioli, Nicola, Andrei Shleifer, and Robert Vishny. "Neglected Risks: The Psychology of the Financial Crisis." *American Economic Review: Papers and Proceedings* 105, no. 5 (2015): 310–14.

Gerding, Erik F. *Law, Bubbles and Financial Regulation: The Economics of Legal Relationship.* New York: Routledge, 2013.

Gilson, Ronald J., and Jeffrey N. Gordon. "The Agency Costs of Agency Capitalism: Activist Investors and the Revaluation of Governance Rights." *Columbia Law Review* 113 (May 2013): 863–927.

Gilson, Ronald J., and Reinier Kraakman. "Market Efficiency after the Financial Crisis: It's Still a Matter of Information Costs." *Virginia Law Review* 100 (2014): 313–75.

Goel, Anand M., and Anjan V. Thakor. "Overconfidence, CEO Selection, and Corporate Governance." *Journal of Finance* 63, no. 6 (2008): 2737–84.

Gordon, Jeffrey N. "The Rise of Independent Directors in the United States, 1950–2005: Of Shareholder Value and Stock Market Prices." *Stanford Law Review* 59, no. 6 (2007): 1465–568.

Goshen, Zohar, and Gideon Parchomovsky. "The Essential Role of Securities Regulation." *Duke Law Journal* 55, no. 4 (2006): 711–82.

Gneezy, Uri, and Aldo Rustichini. "A Fine Is a Price." *Journal of Legal Studies* 29 (2000): 1–17.

Graham, John R., Campbell R. Harvey, and Shiva Rajgopal. "The Economic Implications of Corporate Financial Reporting." *Journal of Accounting and Economics* 40, nos. 1–3 (2005): 3–73.

Greene, Edward, and Olivia Schmid. "Duty-Free Insider Trading?" *Columbia Business Law Review* 2013 (2013): 369–428.

Greenfield, Kent. "The Unjustified Absence of Federal Fraud Protection in the Labor Market." *Yale Law Journal* 107 (1997): 715–89.

Greenwood, Robin, and David Scharfstein. "The Growth of Finance." *Journal of Economic Perspectives* 27, no. 2 (2013): 3–28.

Greve, Henrich, Donald A. Palmer, and Jo-Ellen Pozner. "Organizations Gone Wild: The Causes, Processes, and Consequences of Organizational Misconduct." *Academy of Management Annals* 4, no. 1 (2010): 53–107.

Grundfest, Joseph. "Damages and Reliance under Section 10(b) of the Exchange Act." *Business Lawyer* 69, no. 2 (2014): 307–92.

Gu, Zhaoyang, Zengquan Li, and Yong George Yang. "Monitors or Predators: The Influence of Institutional Investors on Sell-Side Analysts." *Accounting Review* 88, no. 1 (2013): 137–69.

Gubler, Zachary. "Public Choice Theory and the Private Securities Market." *North Carolina Law Review* 91 (2013): 745–810.

Guiso, Luigi, Paola Sapienza, and Luigi Zingales. "Trusting the Stock Market." *Journal of Finance* 63, no. 6 (2008): 2557–600.

Gulati, G. Mitu, Jeffrey J. Rachlinski, and Donald C. Langevoort. "Fraud by Hindsight." *Northwestern University Law Review* 98 (2004): 773–825.

Guttentag, Michael D. "On Requiring Public Companies to Disclose Political Spending." *Columbia Business Law Review* 2014, no. 3 (2014): 593–662.

Guttentag, Michael D. "Stumbling into Crime: Stochastic Process Models of Accounting Fraud." In *Research Handbook on the Economics of Criminal Law*, edited by Alon Harel and Keith N. Hylton, 204–30. Cheltenham, UK: Edward Elgar, 2012.

Haddock, David D., and Jonathan R. Macey. "Regulation on Demand: A Private Interest Model, with Application to Insider Trading Regulation." *Journal of Law and Economics* 30, no. 2 (1987): 311–52.

Haidt, Jonathan. "Moral Psychology and the Law: How Intuitions Drive Reasoning, Judgment, and the Search for Evidence." *Alabama Law Review* 64 (2013): 867–80.

Harrington, Brooke. "The Sociology of Financial Fraud." In *The Oxford Handbook of the Sociology of Finance*, edited by Karin Knorr Cetina and Alex Preda, 393–410. Oxford: Oxford University Press, 2012.

Haugh, Todd. "Sentencing the Why of White Collar Crime." *Fordham Law Review* 82 (May 2014): 3143–88.

Heimer, Rawley Z. "Friends Do Let Friends Buy Stocks Actively." *Journal of Economic Behavior and Organization* 107 (November 2014): 527–40.

Heminway, Joan M. "How Congress Killed Investment Crowdfunding: A Tale of Political Pressure, Hasty Decisions, and Inexpert Judgments That Begs for a Happy Ending." *Kentucky Law Journal* 102 (2013–14): 865–89.

Henderson, M. Todd. "The Changing Demand for Insider Trading Regulation." In *Research Handbook on Insider Trading*, edited by Stephen M. Bainbridge, 230–51. Northampton, MA: Edward Elgar, 2013.

Henning, Peter J. "A New Crime for Corporate Misconduct?" *Mississippi Law Journal* 84 (2014): 43–89.

Hermalin, Benjamin E., and Michael S. Weisbach. "Boards of Directors as an Endogenously Determined Institution: A Survey of the Economic Literature." *Economic Policy Review* (April 2003): 7–26.

Hill, Claire A. "Why Didn't Subprime Investors Demand a (Much Larger) Lemons Premium?" *Law and Contemporary Problems* 74 (Spring 2011): 47–62.

Hill, Claire, and Richard Painter. *Better Bankers, Better Banks*. Chicago: University of Chicago Press, 2015.

Hirshleifer, David A., Angie Low, and Siew Teoh. "Are Overconfident CEOs Better Innovators?" *Journal of Finance* 67 (2012): 1457–98.

Hirshleifer, David A., and Tyler Shumway. "Good Day Sunshine: Stock Returns and the Weather." *Journal of Finance* 58, no. 3 (2003): 1009–32.

Hirshleifer, David A., and Siew Hong Teoh. "Thought and Behavior Contagion in Capital Markets." In *Handbook of Financial Markets: Dynamics and Evolution*, edited by Thorsten Hens and Klaus Reiner Schenk-Hoppé, 1–46. Amsterdam: North-Holland, Elsevier, 2009.

Ho, Karen. "Disciplining Investment Bankers, Disciplining the Economy: Wall Street's Institutional Culture of Crisis and the Downsizing of 'Corporate America.'" *American Anthropologist* 111, no. 2 (2009): 177–89.

Hoberg, Gerard, and Craig M. Lewis. "Do Fraudulent Firms Produce Abnormal Disclosures?" Working paper, April 20, 2015, available at http://papers.ssrn.com/sol3/papers.cfm?abstract_id=2298302.

Hockett, Robert C. Testimony before the Subcommittee on Financial Institutions and Consumer Protection, Senate Committee on Banking, Housing and Urban Affairs, November 21, 2014.

Hoffman, David A. "The Best Puffery Article Ever." *Iowa Law Review* 91 (2006): 1395–448.

Hong, Harrison G., Jeffrey D. Kubik, and Jeremy C. Stein. "Thy Neighbor's Portfolio: Word-of-Mouth Effects in the Holdings and Trades of Money Managers." *Journal of Finance* 60 (2005): 2801–24.

Hong, Harrison G., and Inessa Liskovich. "Crime, Punishment and the Halo Effect of Corporate Social Responsibility." NBER Working Paper No. 21215, May 2015, available at http://papers.ssrn.com/sol3/papers.cfm?abstract_id=2492202.

Hoyt, Crystal L., Terry L. Price, and Alyson E. Emrick. "Leadership and the More-Important-Than-Average Effect: Overestimation of Group Goals and the Justification of Unethical Behavior." *Leadership* 6, no. 4 (2010): 391–407.

Hu, Henry T. C. "Faith and Magic: Investor Beliefs and Government Neutrality." *Texas Law Review* 78 (March 2000): 777–884.

Hu, Henry T. C. "Financial Innovation and Governance Mechanisms: The Evolution of Decoupling and Transparency." *Business Lawyer* 70, no. 2 (2015): 347–406.

Hu, Henry T. C. "Too Complex to Depict? Innovation, 'Pure Information,' and the SEC Disclosure Paradigm." *Texas Law Review* 90, no. 7 (2012): 1601–715.

Huang, Jiekun, and Darren J. Kisgen. "Gender and Corporate Finance: Are Male Executives Overconfident Relative to Female Executives?" *Journal of Financial Economics* 108, no. 3 (2013): 822–39.

Huberman, Gur, and Tomer Regev. "Contagious Speculation and the Cure for Cancer: A Non-event That Made Stock Prices Soar." *Journal of Finance* 56, no. 1 (2001): 387–96.

Huck, John R. "Taking a Beating on the Stock Market: Crime and Stock Returns." Working paper, February 28, 2015, available at http://papers.ssrn.com/sol3/papers.cfm?abstract_id=2448047.

Hueston, John C. "Behind the Scenes of the Enron Trial: Creating the Decisive Moments." *American Criminal Law Review* 44 (Spring 2007): 197–239.

Hurt, Christine. "Moral Hazard and the Initial Public Offering." *Cardozo Law Review* 26 (2005): 711–90.

Hutton, Irena, Danling Jiang, and Alok Kumar. "Political Values, Culture and Corporate Litigation." *Management Science* 61, no. 12 (2015): 2905–25.

Ibbotson, Roger G., Peng Chen, and Kevin X. Zhu. "The ABCs of Hedge Funds: Alphas, Betas and Costs." *Financial Analysts Journal* 67, no. 1 (2011): 15–25.

Ibrahim, Darian M. "Financing the Next Silicon Valley." *Washington University Law Review* 87, no. 4 (2010): 717–62.

Igan, Deniz, and Prachi Mishra. "Wall Street, Capitol Hill, and K Street: Political Influence and Financial Regulation." *Journal of Law and Economics* 57, no. 4 (2014): 1063–84.

Irvine, Paul J., Marc L. Lipson, and Andy Puckett. "Tipping." *Review of Financial Studies* 20, no. 3 (2007): 741–68.

Isenberg, Daniel. "The Road to Crowdfunding Hell." *Harvard Business Review*, April 23, 2012.

Jackson, Robert J., and Joshua Mitts. "How the SEC Helps Speedy Traders." Working Paper, November 6, 2014, available at http://papers.ssrn.com/sol3/papers.cfm?abstract_id=2520105.

Jagolinzer, Alan D. "SEC Rule 10b5-1 and Insiders' Strategic Trade." *Management Science* 55 (2009): 224–39.

Jagolinzer, Alan D., David F. Larcker, Gaizka Ormazabal, and Daniel J. Taylor. "The Information Content of Insider Trades around Government Intervention during the Financial Crisis." Working paper, August 14, 2014, available at http://papers.ssrn.com/sol3/papers.cfm?abstract_id=2480796.

Jia, Yuping, Laurence Van Lent, and Yachang Zeng. "Masculinity, Testosterone and Financial Misreporting." *Journal of Accounting Research* 52, no. 5 (2014): 1195–246.

Johnson, Dominic D. P., and James H. Fowler. "The Evolution of Overconfidence." *Nature* 477 (September 15, 2011): 317–20.

Johnson, Jennifer J. "Fleecing Grandma: A Regulatory Ponzi Scheme." *Lewis and Clark Law Review* 16 (2012): 993–1013.

Jost, John T., Mahzarin R. Banaji, and Brian A. Nosek. "A Decade of System Justification Theory: Accumulated Evidence of Conscious and Unconscious Bolstering of the Status Quo." *Political Psychology* 25, no. 6 (2004): 881–919.

Jung, Michael J., James P. Naughton, Ahmed Tahoun, and Clare Wang. "Corporate Use of Social Media." Working paper, June 1, 2015, available at http://papers.ssrn.com/sol3/papers.cfm?abstract_id=2588081.

Kacperczyk, Marcin, Stijn Van Nieuwerburgh, and Laura Veldkamp. "Time-Varying Fund Manager Skill." *Journal of Finance* 69, no. 4 (2014): 1455–84.

Kahan, Marcel, and Edward B. Rock. "Embattled CEOs." *Texas Law Review* 88 (April 2010): 987–1051.

Kahneman, Daniel. *Thinking, Fast and Slow.* New York: Farrar, Straus and Giroux, 2011.

Karpoff, Jonathan M., D. Scott Lee, and Gerald S. Martin. "The Consequences to Managers for Financial Misrepresentation." *Journal of Financial Economics* 88 (2008): 193–215.

Karpoff, Jonathan M., D. Scott Lee, and Gerald S. Martin. "The Costs to Firms of Cooking the Books." *Journal of Financial and Quantitative Analysis* 43, no. 3 (2008): 581–611.

Karppi, Tero, and Kate Crawford. "Social Media, Financial Algorithms and the Hack Crash." *Theory, Culture and Society* (forthcoming 2015).

Kedia, Simi, and Shiva Rajgopal. "Do the SEC's Enforcement Preferences Affect Corporate Misconduct?" *Journal of Accounting and Economics* 51, no. 3 (2012): 259–78.

Kedia, Simi, and Thomas Phillipon. "The Economics of Fraudulent Accounting." *Review of Financial Studies* 22, no. 6 (2009): 2169–99.

Keefe, Patrick R. "The Empire of Edge: How a Doctor, a Trader, and the Billionaire Steven A. Cohen Got Entangled in a Vast Financial Scandal." *New Yorker*, October 13, 2014.

Kelley, Eric K., and Paul C. Tetlock. "How Wise Are Crowds? Insights from Retail Orders and Stock Returns." *Journal of Finance* 68, no. 3 (2013): 1229–65.

Kennedy, Jessica A., Cameron Anderson, and Don A. Moore. "When Overconfidence Is Revealed to Others: Testing the Status-Enhancement Theory of Overconfidence." *Organizational Behavior and Human Decision Processes* 122, no. 2 (2013): 266–79.

Khanna, Vikramaditya, E. Han Kim, and Yao Lu. "CEO Connectedness and Corporate Fraud." *Journal of Finance* 70, no. 3 (2015): 1203–52.

Kindleberger, Charles P. *Essays in History: Financial, Economic, Personal*. Ann Arbor: University of Michigan Press, 1999.

Kirilenko, Andrei A., and Andrew W. Lo. "Moore's Law versus Murphy's Law: Algorithmic Trading and Its Discontents." *Journal of Economic Perspectives* 27, no. 2 (2013): 51–72.

Kitch, Edmund W. "The Theory and Practice of Securities Disclosure." *Brooklyn Law Review* 61 (Fall 1995): 763–887.

Klausner, Michael, and Jason Hegland. "How Protective Is D&O Insurance in Securities Class Actions?" *Plus Journal* 23, no. 2 (2010): 1–4.

Klausner, Michael, Jason Hegland, and Matthew Goforth. "How Protective Is D&O Insurance in Securities Class Actions? An Update." *Plus Journal* 26, no. 5 (2013): 1–4.

Klein, April, Anthony Saunders, and Yu Ting Forester Wong. "Do Hedge Funds Trade on Private Information? Evidence from Changes in Analysts' Stock Recommendations." Working paper, April 7, 2014, available at http://papers.ssrn.com/sol3/papers.cfm?abstract_id=2421801.

Kluver, Jesse, Rebecca Frazier, and Jonathan Haidt. "Behavioral Ethics for Homo Economicus, Homo Heuristicus, and Homo Duplex." *Organizational Behavior and Human Decision Processes* 123, no. 2 (2014): 150–58.

Kraft, Arthur G., Rahul Vashishtha, and Mohan Venkatachalam. "Real Effects of Frequent Financial Reporting." Working paper, July 31, 2015, available at http://papers.ssrn.com/sol3/papers.cfm?abstract_id=2456765.

Kuhnen, Camilia M., and Brian Knutson. "The Influence of Affect on Beliefs, Preferences and Financial Decisions." *Journal of Financial and Quantitative Analysis* 46, no. 3 (2011): 605–26.

Kumar, Alok. "Who Gambles in the Stock Market?" *Journal of Finance* 64, no. 4 (2009): 1889–933.

Kwak, James. "Cultural Capture and the Financial Crisis." In *Preventing Regulatory Capture: Special Interest Influence and How to Limit It*, edited by Daniel Carpenter and David A. Moss, 71–98. New York: Cambridge University Press, 2014.

La Blanc, Gregory, and Jeffrey J. Rachlinski. "In Praise of Irrational Investors." In *The Law and Economics of Irrational Behavior*, edited by Francesco Parisi and Vernon L. Smith, 542–88. Stanford, CA: Stanford University Press, 2005.

Langevoort, Donald C. "Behavioral Ethics, Behavioral Compliance." In *Research Handbook on Corporate Illegality and Financial Wrongdoing*, edited by Jennifer Arlen. Cheltenham, UK: Edwin Elgar, forthcoming.

Langevoort, Donald C. "Chasing the Greased Pig Down Wall Street: A Gatekeeper's Guide to the Psychology, Culture, and Ethics of Financial Risk Taking." *Cornell Law Review* 96 (July 2011): 1209–46.

Langevoort, Donald C. "Organized Illusions: A Behavioral Theory of Why Corporations Mislead Stock Market Investors (and Cause Other Social Harms)." *University of Pennsylvania Law Review* 146 (November 1997): 101–72.

Langevoort, Donald C. "Rereading *Cady, Roberts*: The Ideology and Practice of Insider Trading Regulation." *Columbia Law Review* 99, no. 5 (1999): 1319–43.

Langevoort, Donald C. "The Social Construction of Sarbanes-Oxley." *Michigan Law Review* 105 (June 2007): 1817–55.

Langevoort, Donald C. and Robert B. Thompson. "IPOs and the Slow Death of Section 5." *Kentucky Law Journal* 102 (2013–14): 891–923.

Langevoort, Donald C., and Robert B. Thompson. "'Publicness' in Contemporary Securities Regulation after the JOBS Act." *Georgetown Law Journal* 101 (January 2013): 337–86.

Larrick, Richard P., Albert E. Mannes, and Jack B. Soll. "The Social Psychology of the Wisdom of Crowds." In *Social Judgment and Decision Making*, edited by Joachim I. Krueger, 227–43. New York: Psychology Press, 2012.

Leff, Arthur A. *Swindling and Selling: The Story of Legal and Illegal Congames*. New York: Free Press, 1976.

Lerner, Jennifer S., Ye Li, Piercarlo Valdesolo, and Karim S. Kassam. "Emotions and Decision Making." *Annual Review of Psychology* 66 (2015): 799–823.

Lev, Baruch. *Winning Investors Over*. Boston: Harvard Business Review Press, 2012.

Levitin, Adam J. "Safe Banking." *University of Chicago Law Review* 83, no. 1 (forthcoming 2016).

Levitin, Adam J., and William W. Bratton. "A Transactional Genealogy of Scandal: From Michael Milken to Enron to Goldman Sachs." *Southern California Law Review* 86 (May 2013): 783–868.

Lewellyn, Krista B., and Maureen I. Muller-Kahle. "CEO Power and Risk Taking: Evidence from the Subprime Lending Industry." *Corporate Governance: An International Review* 20, no. 3 (2012): 289–307.

Lewis, Michael. *Flash Boys: A Wall Street Revolt*. New York: Norton, 2014.

Lewis, Michael. "Jonathan Lebed's Extracurricular Activities." *New York Times Magazine*, February 25, 2001, 26. Available at http://www.nytimes.com/2001/02/25/magazine/jonathan-lebed-s-extracurricular-activities.html.

Lewis, Michael, and David Einhorn. "The End of the Financial World as We Know It." *New York Times*, January 3, 2009.

Libby, Robert, and Kristina Rennekamp. "Self-Serving Attribution Bias, Overconfidence and the Issuance of Management Forecasts." *Journal of Accounting Research* 50, no. 1 (2012): 197–231.

Ljungqvist, Alexander, Vikram Nanda, and Rajdeep Singh. "Hot Markets, Investor Sentiment and IPO Pricing." *Journal of Business* 79, no. 4 (2006): 1667–702.

Lo, Andrew W. "Reconciling Efficient Markets with Behavioral Finance: The Adaptive Markets Hypothesis." *Journal of Investment Consulting* 7, no. 2 (2005): 21–44.

Lo, Andrew W. "The Gordon Gekko Effect: The Role of Culture in the Financial Industry." NBER Working Paper No. 21267, June 2015, available at http://papers.ssrn.com/sol3/papers.cfm?abstract_id=2618655.

Loewenstein, George, Daylian M. Cain, and Sunita Sah. "The Limits of Transparency: Pitfalls and Potential of Disclosing Conflicts of Interest." *American Economic Review* 101, no. 3 (2011): 423–28.

Macey, Jonathan, and Arnoud Boot. "Monitoring, Corporate Performance: The Role of Objectivity, Proximity and Adaptability in Corporate Governance." *Cornell Law Review* 89, no. 2 (2004): 356–93.

MacKenzie, Donald. "The Credit Crisis as a Problem in the Sociology of Knowledge." *American Journal of Sociology* 116, no. 6 (2011): 1778–841.

MacLean, Tammy L., and Michael Behnam. "The Dangers of Decoupling: The Relationship between Compliance Programs, Legitimacy Perceptions, and Institutionalized Misconduct." *Academy of Management Journal* 53, no. 6 (2010): 1499–520.

Mahoney, Paul G. *Wasting a Crisis: Why Securities Regulation Fails.* Chicago: University of Chicago Press, 2015.

Malhotra, Deepak. "The Desire to Win: The Effects of Competitive Arousal on Motivation and Behavior." *Organizational Behavior and Human Decision Processes* 111, no. 2 (2010): 139–46.

Malkiel, Burton G. *A Random Walk Down Wall Street: The Time-Tested Strategy for Successful Investing.* 11th ed. New York: Norton, 2015.

Malmendier, Ulrike, and Devin Shanthikumar. "Are Small Investors Naïve about Incentives?" *Journal of Financial Economics* 85, no. 2 (2007): 457–89.

Malmendier, Ulrike, and Devin Shanthikumar. "Do Security Analysts Speak in Two Tongues?" *Review of Financial Studies* 27, no. 5 (2014): 1287–322.

Malmendier, Ulrike, and Geoffrey Tate. "Who Makes Acquisitions? CEO Overconfidence and the Market's Reaction." *Journal of Financial Economics* 89, no. 1 (2008): 20–43.

Manne, Henry G. *Insider Trading and the Stock Market.* New York: Free Press, 1966.

Matsa, David A., and Amalia R. Miller. "A Female Style in Corporate Leadership? Evidence from Quotas." *American Economic Journal: Applied Economics* 5, no. 3 (2013): 136–69.

Mayew, William J., and Mohan Venkatachalam. "The Power of Voice: Managerial Affective States and Future Firm Performance." *Journal of Finance* 67, no. 1 (2012): 1–43.

McCloskey, David, and Arjo Klamer. "One Quarter of GDP Is Persuasion." *American Economic Review* 85, no. 2 (1995): 191–95.

McGuire, Sean, Thomas Omer, and Nathan Sharp. "The Impact of Religion on Financial Reporting Irregularities." *Accounting Review* 87 (2012): 645–73.

McLean, Bethany, and Peter Elkind. *The Smartest Guys in the Room: The Amazing Rise and Scandalous Fall of Enron.* New York: Penguin, 2004.

Mehta, Mihir N., David M. Reeb, and Wanli Zhao. "Shadow Trading: Do Insiders Exploit Private Information about Stakeholders?" Working paper, March 5, 2015, available at http://papers.ssrn.com/sol3/papers.cfm?abstract_id=2575221.

Miller, Danny. "A Downside to the Entrepreneurial Personality?" *Entrepreneurship Theory and Practice* 39, no. 1 (2015): 1–8.

Miller, Geoffrey P., and Gerald Rosenfeld. "Intellectual Hazard: How Conceptual Biases in Complex Organizations Contributed to the Crisis of 2008." *Harvard Journal of Law and Public Policy* 33 (Spring 2010): 807–40.

Miller, Gregory S., and Douglas J. Skinner. "The Evolving Disclosure Landscape: How Changes in Technology, the Media and Capital Markets Are Affecting Disclosure." *Journal of Accounting Research* 53, no. 2 (2015): 221–39.

Mollick, Ethan R. "The Dynamics of Crowdfunding: An Exploratory Study." *Journal of Business Venturing* 29, no. 1 (2014): 1–16.

Mollick, Ethan R., and Ramana Nanda. "Wisdom or Madness? Comparing Crowds with Expert Evaluation in Funding the Arts." *Management Science* (forthcoming 2015).

Moloney, Niamh. *How to Protect Investors: Lessons from the EC and the UK.* Cambridge: Cambridge University Press, 2010.

Moore, Don A., Terri R. Kurtzburg, Craig R. Fox, and Max H. Bazerman. "Positive Illusions and Forecasting Errors in Mutual Fund Investment Decisions." *Organizational Behavior and Human Decision Processes* 79, no. 2 (1999): 75–114.

Moore, Don A., Philip E. Tetlock, Lloyd Tanlu, and Max H. Bazerman. "Conflicts of Interest and the Case of Auditor Independence: Moral Seduction and Strategic Issue Cycling." *Academy of Management Review* 31, no. 1 (2006): 10–29.

Morse, Adair, Wei Wang, and Serena Wu. "Executive Gatekeepers: The Paradox of Lawyers in Firms." Working paper, February 2015, available at http://papers.ssrn.com/sol3/papers.cfm?abstract_id=2446611.

Mullainathan, Sendhil, Marcus Nöth, and Antoinette Schoar. "The Market for Financial Advice: An Audit Study." NBER Working Paper No. 17929, March 2012, available at http://www.nber.org/papers/w17929.

Murphy, Pamela R. "Attitude, Machiavellianism and the Rationalization of Misreporting." *Accounting, Organizations and Society* 37, no. 4 (2012): 242–59.

Nagy, Donna M. "Insider Trading and the Gradual Demise of Fiduciary Principles." *Iowa Law Review* 94 (2009): 1315–79.

Nelson, Karen K., Richard A. Price, and Brian R. Roundtree. "Are Individual Investors Influenced by the Optimism and Credibility of Stock Spam Recommendations?" *Journal of Business Finance and Accounting* 40, nos. 9–10 (2013): 1155–83.

Nguyen, Vinh. "Does Your Daughter Make You a Better CEO?" Working paper, May 25, 2015, available at http://papers.ssrn.com/sol3/papers.cfm?abstract_id=2625046.

Notre Dame, University of, and Labaton Sucharow LLP. *The Street, the Bull and the Crisis: A Survey of the US & UK Financial Services Industry.* May 2015.

Oakes, Guy. *The Soul of the Salesman: The Moral Ethos of Personal Sales.* New York: Prometheus Books, 1990.

Omarova, Saule T. "License to Deal: Mandatory Approval of Complex Financial Products." *Washington University Law Review* 90 (2012): 63–140.

Ortoleva, Pietro, and Erik Snowberg. "Overconfidence in Political Behavior." *American Economic Review* 105, no. 2 (2015): 504–35.

Palmiter, Alan R., and Ahmed E. Taha. "Mutual Fund Performance Advertising: Inherently and Materially Misleading?" *Georgia Law Review* 46 (Winter 2012): 289–353.

Paredes, Troy A. "On the Decision to Regulate Hedge Funds: The SEC's Regulatory Philosophy, Style, and Mission." *University of Illinois Law Review* 2006 (2006): 975–1035.

Park, James. "Rules, Principles and Competition to Enforce the Securities Laws." *California Law Review* 100, no. 1 (2012): 115–81.

Parsons, Christopher A., Johan Sulaemon, and Sheridan Titman. "The Geography of Financial Misconduct." Working paper, May 15, 2015, available at http://papers.ssrn.com/sol3/papers.cfm?abstract_id=2412970.

Partnoy, Frank. "Don't Blink: Snap Decisions and Securities Regulation." *Brooklyn Law Review* 77 (Fall 2011): 151–79.

Partnoy, Frank. "The Siskel and Ebert of Financial Markets? Two Thumbs Down for Credit Rating Agencies." *Washington University Law Quarterly* 77 (Fall 1999): 619–712.

Pierce, Jason R., Gavin J. Kilduff, Adam D. Galinsky, and Niro Sivanathan. "From Glue to Gasoline: How Competition Turns Perspective Takers Unethical." *Psychological Science* 24, no. 10 (2013): 1–9.

Pollman, Elizabeth. "Information Issues on Wall Street 2.0." *University of Pennsylvania Law Review* 161 (2012): 179–241.

Povel, Paul, Rajdeep Singh, and Andrew Winton. "Booms, Busts and Fraud." *Review of Financial Studies* 20, no. 4 (2007): 1219–54.

Pritchard, Adam C. "Justice Lewis F. Powell, Jr. and the Counterrevolution in the Federal Securities Laws." *Duke Law Journal* 52, no. 5 (2003): 841–949.

Pritchard, Adam C. "Revisiting 'Truth in Securities' Revisited: Abolishing IPOs and Harnessing Private Markets in the Public Good." *Seattle University Law Review* 36 (2013): 999–1026.

Pritchard, Adam C., and Robert B. Thompson. "Securities Law and the New Deal Justices." *Virginia Law Review* 95 (2009): 841–925.

Raghavan, Anita. *The Billionaire's Apprentice: The Rise of the Indian-American Elite and the Fall of the Galleon Hedge Fund.* New York: Business Plus, 2013.

Rajan, Raghuram G. *Fault Lines: How Hidden Fractures Still Threaten the World Economy.* Princeton, NJ: Princeton University Press, 2010.

Rakoff, Jed S. "The Financial Crisis: Why Have No High-Level Executives Been Prosecuted?" *New York Review of Books,* January 9, 2014.

Rapp, Geoffrey C. "Intelligence Design: An Analysis of the SEC's New Office of Market Intelligence and Its Goal of Using Big Data to Improve Securities Enforcement." *University of Cincinnati Law Review* 82 (2013): 415–37.

Richman, Daniel C. "Corporate Headhunting." *Harvard Law and Policy Review* 8 (Summer 2014): 265–80.

Rick, Scott, and George Loewenstein. "Hypermotivation." *Journal of Marketing Research* 45, no. 6 (2008): 645–48.

Rijsenbilt, Antoinette, and Harry Commandeur. "Narcissus Enters the Courtroom: CEO Narcissism and Fraud." *Journal of Business Ethics* 117, no. 2 (2013): 413–29.

Riles, Annelise. "Market Collaboration: Finance, Culture, and Ethnography after Neoliberalism." *American Anthropologist* 115, no. 4 (2013): 555–69.

Ritter, Jay R. "Equilibrium in the Initial Public Offering Market." *Annual Review of Financial Economics* 3 (2011): 347–74.

Robb, Richard. "Epistemology and the Financial Crisis." *Critical Review* 25, no. 2 (2013): 131–61.

Rodrigues, Usha. "Securities Law's Dirty Little Secret." *Fordham Law Review* 81 (May 2013): 3389–437.

Rodrigues, Usha, and Michael Stegmoller. "Placebo Ethics: A Study in Securities Disclosure Arbitrage." *Virginia Law Review* 96 (2010): 1–57.

Roe, Mark J. "Corporate Short-Termism: In the Boardroom and in the Courtroom." *Business Lawyer* 68, no. 4 (2013): 977–1006.

Roe, Mark J. "Delaware's Politics." *Harvard Law Review* 118 (2005): 2491–543.

Rogers, Jonathan L., Douglas J. Skinner, and Sarah L. C. Zechman. "Run EDGAR Run: SEC Dissemination in a High-Frequency World." Research Paper, January 15, 2015, available at http://papers.ssrn.com/sol3/papers.cfm?abstract_id=2513350.

Rogers, Todd, Richard J. Zeckhauser, Francesca Gino, Maurice E. Schweitzer, and Michael I. Norton. "Artful Paltering: The Risks and Rewards of Using Truthful Statements to Mislead Others." HKS Working Paper, September 18, 2014, available at http://papers.ssrn.com/sol3/papers.cfm?abstract_id=2528625.

Romano, Roberta. "Empowering Investors: A Market Approach to Securities Regulation." *Yale Law Journal* 107, no. 5 (1998): 2359–430.

Romano, Roberta. *The Genius of American Corporate Law*. Washington, DC: AEI Press, 1993.

Romano, Roberta. "The Sarbanes Oxley Act and the Making of Quack Corporate Governance." *Yale Law Journal* 114, no. 7 (2005): 1521–611.

Rose, Amanda M. "The Multi-enforcer Approach to Securities Fraud Deterrence: A Critical Analysis." *University of Pennsylvania Law Review* 158 (June 2010): 2173–231.

Rostain, Tanina, and Milton C. Regan. *Confidence Games: Lawyers, Accountants and the Tax Shelter Industry*. Cambridge, MA: MIT Press, 2014.

Roulet, Thomas. "There Is No Such Thing as Bad Publicity: Social Disapproval of Investment Banks as a Signal of Proximity to a Field-Level Logic." Annual Conference on Professional Service Firms, Brooking Institute, August 8, 2014, http://www.sbs.ox.ac.uk/ideas-impact/psfstudies/thomas-roulet-there-no-such-thing-bad-publicity.

Sadka, Gil. "The Economic Consequences of Accounting Fraud in Product Markets: Theory and a Case from the U.S. Telecommunications Industry (WorldCom)." *American Law and Economics Review* 8, no. 3 (2006): 439–75.

Sale, Hillary A. "J.P. Morgan: An Anatomy of Corporate Publicness." *Brooklyn Law Review* 79 (Summer 2014): 1629–55.

Sapienza, Paola, Luigi Zingales, and Dario Maestripieri. "Gender Differences in Financial Risk Aversion and Career Choices Are Influenced by Testosterone." *Proceedings of the National Academy of Sciences* 106, no. 36 (2009): 15268–73.

Schrand, Catherine M., and Sarah L. C. Zechman. "Executive Overconfidence and the Slippery Slope to Financial Misreporting." *Journal of Accounting and Economics* 51, nos. 1–2 (2012): 311–29.

Schroeder, Jeanne. "Envy and Outsider Trading: The Case of Martha Stewart." *Cardozo Law Review* 26 (2005): 2023–79.

Schwartz, Alan. "Regulating for Rationality." *Stanford Law Review* 67 (2014): 1373–409.

Schwartz, Andrew. "The Digital Shareholder." *Minnesota Law Review* 100 (forthcoming 2015).

Schwartz, Jeff. "The Conflict Minerals Experiment." *Harvard Business Law Review* 6 (forthcoming 2015).

Seligman, Joel. *The Transformation of Wall Street: A History of the Securities and Exchange Commission and Modern Corporate Finance*. 3rd ed. New York: Aspen Publishers, 2003.

Seybert, Nicholas, and Robert Bloomfield. "Contagion of Wishful Thinking in Markets." *Management Science* 55, no. 5 (2008): 738–51.

Sharot, Tali. "The Optimism Bias." *Current Biology* 21, no. 23 (2011): R941–45.

Shiller, Robert. *Irrational Exuberance*. 3rd ed. Princeton, NJ: Princeton University Press, 2015.

Sidak, J. Gregory. "The Failure of Good Intentions: The WorldCom Fraud and the Collapse of American Telecommunications Regulation after Deregulation." *Yale Journal on Regulation* 20, no. 2 (2003): 207–67.

Skeel, David A. *Icarus in the Boardroom*. New York: Oxford University Press, 2004.

Skeel, David A. *The New Financial Deal: Understanding the Dodd-Frank Act and Its (Unintended) Consequences*. Hoboken NJ: John Wiley & Sons, 2011.

Statman, Meir. "The Cultures of Insider Trading." *Journal of Business Ethics* 89 (2009): 51–58.

Statman, Meir. "Local Ethics in a Global World." *Financial Analysts Journal* 63, no. 3 (2007): 32–41.

Statman, Meir. "Martha Stewart's Lessons in Behavioral Finance." *Journal of Investment Consulting* 7, no. 2 (2005): 52–60.

Statman, Meir. *What Investors Really Want: Discover What Drives Investor Behavior and Make Smarter Financial Decisions*. New York: McGraw Hill, 2010.

Statman, Meir, and Jonathan Scheid. "Buffett in Hindsight and Foresight." *Financial Analysts Journal*, July–August 2002, 1–8.

Staw, Barry M., and Robert I. Sutton. "Macroorganizational Psychology." In *Social Psychology in Organizations: Advances in Theory and Research*, edited by Keith Murnighan, 350–84. Englewood Cliffs, NJ: Prentice Hall, 1993.

Stout, Lynn. *The Shareholder Value Myth: How Putting Shareholders First Harms Investors, Corporations, and the Public*. San Francisco: Berrett-Keohler Publications, 2012.

Taub, Jennifer. *Other People's Houses: How Decades of Bailouts, Captive Regulators, and Toxic Bankers Made Home Mortgages a Thrilling Business*. New Haven: Yale University Press, 2014.

Tenbrunsel, Ann E., and David M. Messick. "Ethical Fading: The Role of Self-Deception in Unethical Behavior." *Social Justice Research* 17, no. 2 (2004): 223–36.

Tenbrunsel, Ann E., and David M. Messick. "Sanctioning Systems, Decision Frames, and Cooperation." *Administrative Science Quarterly* 44, no. 4 (1999): 684–707.

Tetlock, Philip E. "Cognitive Biases and Organizational Correctives: Do Both Disease and Cure Depend on the Politics of the Beholder?" *Administrative Law Quarterly* 45, no. 2 (2000): 293–328.

Tett, Gillian. *Fool's Gold: How Unrestrained Greed Corrupted a Dream, Shattered Global Markets and Unleashed a Catastrophe*. London: Abacus, 2010.

Thakor, Anjan. "Lending Booms, Smart Bankers and Financial Crises." *American Economic Review* 105, no. 5 (2015): 305–9.

Thompson, Robert B. "Market Makers and Vampire Squid: Regulating Securities Markets after the Financial Meltdown." *Washington University Law Review* 89 (2011): 323–76.

Thompson, Robert B., and Donald C. Langevoort. "Redrawing the Public-Private Boundaries in Entrepreneurial Capital Raising." *Cornell Law Review* 98 (September 2013): 1573–628.

Trivers, Robert. *Deceit and Self-Deception: Fooling Yourself the Better to Fool Others*. New York: Penguin, 2011.

Turco, Catherine J., and Ezra W. Zuckerman. "So You Think You Can Dance? Lessons from the U.S Private Equity Bubble." *Sociological Science* 1 (March 2014): 81–101.

Tyler, Tom R. *Why People Obey the Law*. Princeton, NJ: Princeton University Press, 2006.

van Staveren, Irene. "The Lehman Sisters Hypothesis." *Cambridge Journal of Economics* 38 (2014): 995–1014.

Velikonja, Urska. "The Cost of Securities Fraud." *William & Mary Law Review* 54 (2013): 1887–957.

Velikonja, Urska. "Reporting Agency Performance: Behind the SEC's Enforcement Statistics." *Cornell Law Review* 101 (forthcoming 2016).

Waytz, Adam, James Dungan, and Liane Young. "The Whistleblower's Dilemma and the Fairness-Loyalty Tradeoff." *Journal of Experimental Social Psychology* 49, no. 6 (2013): 1027–33.

Weick, Karl E. *Sense Making in Organizations.* Thousand Oaks, CA: Sage, 1995.

Welsh, David T., and Lisa D. Ordóñez. "The Dark Side of Consecutive High Performance Goals: Linking Goal Setting, Depletion and Unethical Behavior." *Organizational Behavior and Human Decision Processes* 123, no. 2 (2014): 79–89.

Westbrook, David A. *Out of Crisis: Rethinking Our Financial Markets.* Boulder, CO: Paradigm Publishers, 2009.

Westphal, James D. "Collaboration in the Boardroom: Behavioral and Performance Consequences of CEO-Board Social Ties." *Academy of Management Journal* 42, no. 1 (1999): 7–24.

Whitehead, Charles K. "Reforming Financial Regulation." *Boston University Law Review* 90 (February 2010): 1–50.

Wiesenfeld, Batia M., Naomi B. Rothman, Sara L. Wheeler-Smith, and Adam D. Galinsky. "Why Fair Bosses Fall Behind." *Harvard Business Review*, July–August 2011, available at https://hbr.org/2011/07/why-fair-bosses-fall-behind.

Wilhelm, William J., Jr. "Bookbuilding, Auctions, and the Future of the IPO Process." *Journal of Applied Corporate Finance* 17, no. 1 (2005): 55–66.

Wilhelm, William J., Jr., and Alan D. Morrison. "Trust, Reputation, and Law: The Evolution of Commitment in Investment Banking." *Journal of Legal Analysis* 7, no. 1 (2015): 1–58.

Williams, Cynthia. "The Securities and Exchange Commission and Corporate Social Responsibility." *Harvard Law Review* 112 (1999): 1197–256.

Willis, Lauren E. "The Financial Education Fallacy." *American Economic Review* 101, no. 3 (2011): 429–34.

Yadav, Yesha. "The Problematic Case of Clearinghouses in Complex Markets." *Georgetown Law Journal* 101 (January 2013): 387–444.

Zimmerman, Jerold L. "The Role of Accounting in the 21st Century Firm." *Accounting and Business Research* 45, no. 4 (2015): 485–509.

Zingales, Luigi. "Does Finance Benefit Society?" *Journal of Finance* 70, no. 4 (2015): 1327–63.

Zingales, Luigi. "The Future of Securities Regulation." *Journal of Accounting Research* 47, no. 2 (2009): 391–425.

Zuckerman, Ezra. "Market Efficiency: A Sociological Perspective." In *The Oxford Handbook of the Sociology of Finance*, edited by Karin K. Cetina and Alex Preda, 223–49. New York: Oxford University Press, 2012.

Index

140; imperfect information problem facing, 9–10; insider trading regulations and, 86; IPO deregulation and, 122–23; lobbying of, 93, 166; Pecora legislative hearings (1930s) and, 7; private equity markets and, 124–26, 129–30; public listing requirements for companies and, 111; regulatory competition and, 29, 31; regulatory requirements removed by, 2; Securities and Exchange Commission and, 8, 92, 161–62; social responsibility goals and, 109; whistle-blowers and, 99–100

consumer confidence surveys, 83

Cornell, Brad, 23

corporate fraud: awareness conundrum in, 43–44; boom markets and, 34, 39–40; class action lawsuits regarding, 48–52; cognitive distortions as factor in, 35–37; company employees as victims of, 51–52; corporate culture and, 40–42; costs of, 34, 52; credibility impacted by, 34; deterrence of, 53–56; disclosure as means of combating, 33; distorted perceptions and, 38–40, 143; efficient markets distorted by, 53; enforcement against, 42–48; executive compensation and, 35; extent of, 34; gender diversity and, 158; insurance against, 51–52, 54–55; investment diversification as means of ameliorating, 51–52; litigation and, 42–45; loss aversion and, 37–38; motivations for, 5, 34–40, 54, 60; negative externalities from, 33; obstacles to achieving, 34–35; optimism as factor in, 35–36; overconfidence as factor in, 35–36, 40; penalties for, 34, 100; puffery and, 58–61; slippery slope dynamic and, 36–38; stock price obsession as factor in, 41; testosterone and, 39–40

Countrywide, 149

covenant banking, 151

credibility: "boiler rooms" and, 118; corporate fraud's impact on, 34; crowdfunding and, 128; financial media's role in conferring, 133;

management and, 100; overconfidence's impact on, 60; Ponzi schemes and, 117; poor economic performance's impact on, 36; puffery and, 58–59; shareholder activism and, 108; stock analysts and, 83; stock prices impacted by, 58; whistle-blowers and, 99

credit-rating agencies, 139, 142, 144–45

crowdfunding: Congress and, 129–30; credibility and, 128; deregulated nature of, 2, 166; disclosure and, 127–29; JOBS Act and, 127–29; moral hazard and, 130; potential threat to democratic capitalism from, 167; salesmanship and, 5; Securities and Exchange Commission (SEC) and, 127, 129; wisdom-of-crowds philosophy and, 127–29

Cuban, Mark, 62, 68–69

Damodaran, Aswath, 23

Darley, John, 36

day trading, 13, 25, 84

deception. See also corporate fraud; self-deception: adaptive properties of, 27–28, 39; auditors and, 93–94; capital formation and, 41; deliberate nature of, 36–37; disclosure as a means to prevent, 88; in disclosure statements, 47; evolutionary basis for, 27; Financial Crisis and, 141; insider trading cases and, 63–64, 69–70, 81; investment banking and, 138, 152–53; justifications offered for, 36–37; legal burdens of proof regarding, 115; motivations for, 54, 60; optimism and, 44; overconfidence and, 44; power's facilitation of, 39; regulators impacted by, 33; remedies for, 51; Rule 10b-5 requirements regarding, 70; self-deception as predecessor to, 87

Delaware, 30–31, 113

Dell, 76

Democratic Party, 162

Department of Labor, 135

derivatives: Financial Crisis and, 13, 24, 74, 140, 142, 144, 149; regulation of, 29, 139, 161; short selling and, 74;

short-termism and, 149; synthetic derivatives and, 178n3; valuation of, 144

deterrence: class action lawsuits and, 48, 53–56; cognitive distortion's interference with, 44; as goal of enforcement, 44–46; probability of detection as factor in, 44–46; prosecution of high-level executives and, 150; Sarbanes-Oxley Act and, 88; size of penalty as factor in, 44, 55

Dirks, Raymond, 71, 85

disclosure. *See also* sunlight: accounting firm scandals (2000s) and increasing pressure for,95; auditors and, 104; boards of directors and, 92, 104; boundaries of responsibilities regarding, 64, 90; of conflicts of interest, 135; corrective forms of, 55; costs associated with, 14; crowdfunding and, 127–29; deception in mandated forms of, 47; difficulty measuring impact of, 55; discourse of, 56–61; executive pay and, 104–5; fair disclosure doctrine, 82–83, 101–2; full disclosure and, 19, 56, 88–89, 131, 137; half-truth doctrine and, 57; informational asymmetry and, 103–4; insider trading cases and, 80, 82–84; institutional capital's demand for, 112; investor protection through, 5, 19–20; investors' ignoring of, 3; judges' and juries' unfamiliarity with standards of, 43; limitations and failures of, 20, 24, 101–2; Management's Discussion and Analysis ("MD&A") and, 90; market incentives for, 89; as means of combating fraud, 33; mutual funds and, 131, 133–34; opportunism and, 104, 135; private equity transactions and, 124; protective disclosure and, 56; public companies' periodic requirements regarding, 56, 59; "reasonably likely" standard and, 56; Sarbanes-Oxley Act (SOX) and, 87–88, 91, 123; SEC regulations regarding, 31–32, 59, 82–83, 89–90, 100, 104–5, 108, 113, 119, 124, 133, 163; securities analysts and, 103; Securities Exchange

Act's requirements regarding, 87; shareholder activism and, 108; short-termism and, 106; small investors envisioned as beneficiaries of, 13–14; social media's impact on, 89; social responsibility goals and, 18, 108–10; "tips and tells" in, 47; whistle-blowers and, 99

District of Columbia Circuit Court of Appeals, 108

Dodd-Frank Act: clawback provisions in, 151; executive pay provisions and, 105; fiduciary responsibilities for securities firms in, 154–55; Financial Crisis as impetus for, 140; whistle-blower regulations in, 99–100

Douglas, William O., 19–20, 167

"Dumb Money" study, 133

Easterbrook, Frank, 61

economic sociology discipline, 12–13, 22

EDGAR (SEC disclosure website), 83–84

efficient markets: academic orthodoxy regarding, 3, 21–22; adaptive market hypothesis and, 23–24; arbitrage and, 22; bias addressed by, 20–21; corporate fraud as a distortion of, 53; cost of competing in, 83; disclosure requirements and, 89; inability to "beat the market" in, 74; informational efficiency *versus* fundamental efficiency and, 23; information costs and, 23; insider trading and, 63–64; investment banking culture and, 153; investor protection and, 24; legal cases citing, 58; limitations in the theory of, 21–24; long-term considerations and, 106–7; opportunism disciplined by, 30; puffery and, 58; regulation and, 24

Einhorn, David, 1–2

Elan, 75

emotional judgment in investing, 11

endowment effect, 11

enforcement: admissions of guilt and, 45–46; "broken windows" philosophy and, 45–46; deterrence as a goal in, 44–46; "false positives" problem in, 48; frequency of detection as factor in, 45–46; "revolving door" problem regarding, 46; size of penalties and, 45; technology's role in, 47–48

Enron: accounting scandal at, 93–94, 161; awareness conundrum and, 44; board of directors at, 91; business model at, 37; corporate behavior impacted by scandal at, 34; corporate culture at, 41, 154; employees' stock holdings in, 51; inflated revenues at, 37; insiders at, 37; litigation against, 43–44; regulation regime impacted by, 33–34, 87, 94, 96; stock price for, 37, 41; victims of fraud at, 48

equity crowdfunding. *See* crowdfunding

Equity Funding financial fraud case (1970s), 71

European Union, 86

executive pay, 104–5. *See also* compensation

Facebook, 111

fair disclosure doctrine, 82–83, 101–2

Fama, Eugene, 23

Fannie Mae, 139

Ferrell, Allen, 110

Feynman, Richard, 10

Financial Crisis: American economic optimism dented by, 160; bailouts and, 138, 140; "black swans" and, 143–44; blame for, 141, 144–45, 149–50, 155; cognitive illusions and, 143; competitive arousal and, 147; credit-rating agencies and, 142, 144–45; deception and, 141; default insurance and, 140; derivatives and, 13, 24, 74, 140, 142, 144, 149; informational deficits and, 148, 150; insider trading and, 144; investment banks' role in, 153; lack of legal prosecutions of Wall Street leaders after, 45, 149–52; liquidity crisis and, 140; moral hazard and, 142–43; opportunism in, 141–42; overconfidence and, 149–50; public employee pension funds as victims in, 13–14; regulatory changes following, 29, 73, 138, 140, 151, 154–56;

regulatory competition as a cause of, 30; regulatory failures and, 18, 24, 138–40, 151; restitution for, 151; risk perception and, 143–44; sanctions against financial service firms following, 149; Securities and Exchange Commission and, 8; short selling and, 74; short-termism and, 148–49; subprime mortgage lending and mortgage-backed securities in, 1, 138–40, 142, 144–45, 149–50; trade imbalances and, 139

Financial Industry Regulatory Agency (FINRA), 79, 84, 122, 125, 129

Financial Stability Oversight Council (FSOC), 141

First Amendment, 103, 109, 121

Fischel, Dan, 53

Flash Boys (Lewis), 24

"flash crash" (2010), 24

Food and Drug Administration, 57, 79, 151

Foreign Corrupt Practices Act, 96

framing, 11

Frankfurter, Felix, 7, 19, 120, 167

fraud. *See* corporate fraud

fraud-on-the-market class actions. *See* class actions

Freddie Mac, 139

full disclosure: customers' responsibilities regarding, 137; mutual funds and, 131; Securities Act of 1933 and, 19; shortcomings in, 56; U.S. decision to not embrace, 88–90

Galleon Capital, 73

Gennaioli, Nicola, 143

Gilman, Sidney, 75, 81

Gilson, Ron, 24

Ginsburg, Ruth Bader, 68

Giuliani, Rudy, 46

global arbitrage, 29

Global Financial Crisis. *See* Financial Crisis

Goldman Sachs: Buffett and, 62; corporate culture at, 154; Facebook IPO and, 111; Financial Crisis and, 62, 141–42, 153–54, 161; Gupta insider trading case and, 63; SEC case against, 141–42, 153–54; as "vampire squid," 152